EPISODES IN A LIFE

EPISODES IN A LIFE

Kit Salter

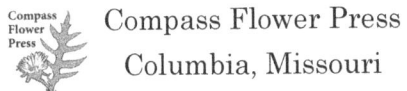
Compass Flower Press
Columbia, Missouri

© 2022 Christopher L. Salter

All rights reserved. No part of this book may be reproduced or transmitted in any form or by any means without permission from the author or publisher.

Published by

Compass Flower Press
Columbia, Missouri

ISBN 978-1-951960-38-4 Hardback
ISBN 978-1-951960-39-1 Trade Paperback

Contents

Acknowledgments ix
Introduction xi
Mother's Sense of Immortality xv

CHAPTER ONE:
The Founding Family 1

Mother and the Tucson Caper 1
Home Non-Schooling — Part I 5
Home Non-Schooling — Part II 9
Joel's Gibson and the New Shoes 13
Mother in Berea, Kentucky 15
Ripon, Wisconsin 17
On Becoming Thirty 18
Pat and the Tenner 19
1610 Adams Street 21
The Salterstone Ring 22
Difficult Times with Joel 23
The Salters of Rice Lake 25
Dockie's $3000 figure 27
Fishing with Dockie 30
Mothers and Sons 31
Jurgen's Anatomy Lesson 36

Jurgen's New Shoes 37
Fritzie's Mandate 39
Kate and the Key Alarm 41
The MS *Mongolia* 42
Jurgen and Jean's Career Change 44

CHAPTER TWO:
The Building of a New Family 49
A New Look 49
Tandem Fools 51
Truimph at the Karmann Ghia Exit 54
"And I suppose you're divorced
  and have two children." 55
Someone Like This 57
First Dates 58
Cottage Living 61
Only the Best of Intentions 65
"Clotheslines" 67
Racing to Walnut Creek 72
Sidestepping 73
Changing Lanes 75
Prodding Makes Perfect 76
Cathedral of Our Lady of the Angels 78
Conversations that Count 82
Rediscovered Art of Childhood 85
Changing Social Contracts 86
Published at Nineteen 88

CHAPTER THREE:
Travel and the Forces of Mobility and Change 91

Adam at 6 A.M. 91
Dimple and Flame 93
Guerrillas in Cuba 95
The Street as Learning Center 97
Crossing to the Hemingway Marina
  in Havana, Cuba 100
"Harvested" on the Havana Malacon 102
Evidence of Kit's Youthful Daring! 105
Serendepity in London 110
Mother and the Yellowstone Connection 112
Hemingway's Cuba 115
Road Movies 117
Mountaineering Mount Yu Shan 118
Themes for Writing on the Road 122

CHAPTER FOUR:
China 127

Bearing Witness 127
The Unscheduled Village Visit 129
Replacing Mao 134
The Great Brick Trek 138
English Lessons on the Pacific 141
The Peace Hotel Dinner Band 143
The Swimming Lesson 145

Alone—in Chongqing (Chungking) 150
The Bicycle as a Field Aid 155
The Great Wall 156
The Proposition 159
Shanghai 160
China Airways 161
A Harvest Ago 162
Stop the Bus! 164
Tom in Tunghai 166

CHAPTER FIVE:
Hitchhiking, Freights, and Speculation 169
My Road to Hitchhiking 169
Blessed at Pell Creek 174
Stick Shift 175
Signs of Lost Opportunity 177
From Here to Eternity 179
Asking for Directions 183
The Perfect Ride 185
The Trip to "Mountiful" or,
   Climbing Mount Oberlin 192
Steak and Rail 194
Minot, North Dakota 205
The Dixon, California Railroad Yard 211

CHAPTER SIX:
Teaching—The Essence of My Life 215

Tossing the Rock 215
Stuart Allen and Raven Press 216
The Spirit of East Saint Louis 218
Differing Sixth Grade Perspectives 222
The Bar is the Place 223
Simplify... Simplify... 224
Destroyed by the Deadline 225
Lessons in Cultural Classroom Geography 229
Rolling down the Coyote Hills
  and the Saint Louis Arch 231
The Pass/No Pass Student Encounter 233
An Unusual Road Measurement Approach 236
The Toothbrush Caper 238
Fall Field Gig 239

CHAPTER SEVEN:
Professional Geography 243

"Just Do It!" 244
Double Adventure in Acapulco Bay 245
Nearly Mugged in Philly 250
Skid Row Garden in L.A. 252
"This is no Goddamn Experiment!" 253
The Lawn Issue 254

The von Hoffman Press Coincidence 256
The Water Lecture 258
Lurking in L.A. 261
The Logging Road Scare 263
"What about Miss Jones?" 265
Amazement at Change 267
The Other Side of Discovery and the Art Caper 269
Serendipity and an East Asian Editorship 271

This book is dedicated to all the drivers
who picked me up on the road, and to all the students
who said, "Yeah—let's go!" when they heard their
Geography prof say, "Let's go figure out the local scene."

Acknowledgments

This book has grown from the simple process of narrative taking shape in the spontaneous expansion of a story line. There never was an overall book plan, but there was a wish to explain how these stories came to be. Along the way, the lively minds of family and friends stimulated everything from story lines to plot twists to narrative surprises through shared conversations. This interaction provided hours of guidance and perspective—and I thank all for that creative time and imagination.

Thanks to my parents, siblings, children, wife, nieces and other extended family for the roles you have played in my life. Most especially, to Cathy and our children Hayden and Heidi.

Thanks as well to my editor and publisher Yolanda Ciolli without whom this book would not have come to light. And to the artists whose graphics grace these pages—Suzanne Dunaway, Heidi Salter and Helen Marshall.

And to the many many others who have intersected and influenced my writing life over the years.

Introduction

In an effort to get off the dime and begin the final phase of these years of engagement, observation, note taking, and evaluation, I asked a set of friends about the merit of me writing some sort of life story. These quotes come from their varied and crisp responses.

"What pulpit are you in?" My full name is Christopher Lord Salter. I love talking to an audience that is anchored in front of my lectern. I take great pleasure in promoting belief in something I feel strongly about. And, because St. Christopher is the Patron Saint of Travelers, my life pattern makes me feel very much akin to my given name. Lord is a family name, but it would do well on a parish door. Salter is a homonym with psalter which means both an "instrument played by twanging" and the Book of Psalms in the Bible. All of these terms ring true in my mind.

Early in my teaching career, people would sometimes ask, with a clever glint in their creative eye, "Well, Kit—is it 'Publish or Parish?'" taking pride in their play on the more common phrase in Academia, "Publish or Perish." In my own life I have looked at the two nouns and decided that there was enough proselytizing in teaching about cultural landscapes and the humanized environment to be able to have the classroom be close enough to the parish world to satisfy my needs for a flock.

"Publish or Parish?" In my second year at UCLA (1969)

I was asked to a friend's wedding. I was also asked to give a narrative toast at the event. I had a fun time putting together a few thoughts and gave a quasi-improv toast, telling what I believed was a thoughtful story about the goodness of this person (it was *not* a roast toast). Upon conclusion of the ceremony, Professor Norman Thrower of the UCLA Department of Geography came to me and said, "Well, Salter, I can see for you that it may be a decision between 'publish or parish', he said, careful to spell out *p-a-r-i-s-h*. Since I was new at UCLA and I had heard so much about "Publish or Perish," the allusion to a life in the cloth if I could not publish caught my attention.

So, in terms of 'pulpit,' I am comfortable in my forty plus years in college and university classrooms to feel as though I have my niche well defined, and at eighty plus it seems a tricky time to change careers.

"Who is my audience?" That's a fine question. Having been told by my father, Dockie, early in our marginal father-son relationship that "He who hesitates listens," I learned early on to speak up when I had a thought, or when I saw an opening to join in the banter with my four siblings—all from eleven to sixteen years older than me. The search for an audience was secondary to a search for an observation or a question that seemed vital to understanding the moving conversational scene before me.

As I think of my hoped-for audience for *Epispdes of a Life,* I turn to the themes that have run thorough my consciousness for my eight decades plus of hanging in through thick and thin in my first decades. From Oberlin College graduation on, the audiences of my life include my students at Tunghai University in Taiwan, UCLA and the University of Missouri—

with a year at University of Oregon and a summer teaching at University of California, Berkeley—and years of pro bono teaching in the MU Osher School of Lifelong Learning. The profiles of those audiences were profoundly distinct, but they always captured my attention as I walked to the front of a classroom of sometimes 200 students, sometimes a seminar table of a dozen.

"Get rid of the dull stuff." This sounds so simple. But, in fact, all of us have been involved in conversation, storytelling, or even questioning others—only to find by reading their faces you know you are failing in getting or keeping their attention. The dull stuff in a lecture presentation, or the background information in prepping for a narrative of an historic or a personal event can be vital to understanding the full purpose of you speaking at all. Probably it is essential to fall back on the idea that "Dullness is in the eyes of the beholder." As the writer or the speaker or the lover imparts intelligence, it's always uncertain how the news is regarded or absorbed. The dull stuff is a moving target when trying to get rid it. The reader, of course, may just skip a paragraph or even a chapter—but know that the writer has reviewed those facts and *still* feels those words are not dull stuff, but necessary information to effectively make the larger point.

"If you ask, 'Why write?' maybe you shouldn't be writing." This is the keystone of this introduction. I have known a good number of writers, and a number of very good writers. I have lived with one writer for more than forty-three years. I have read and heard writers talk about writing in many voices. However, I turn to one of my very favorite authors in the context of this paragraph's opening comment.

"If I asked myself at the beginning of every column I write 'Who will read this? Who will be glad they've read it? Whose life will be changed by my words?' I'd never write a paragraph again. But, if I ask myself about the images and the implications of what I'm describing, then I can go item by item through my draft and get some satisfaction. The lonely thing about most writing is that you never really know how many lives you're touching with the written word—but, it beats putting these hours into doing crossword puzzles or making slogans from cut up license plates."

"You've got enough pens to write ten books—stop procrastinating and get writing!" I am drawn again to the childhood fable of the tortoise and the hare. The hare is busy all the while, going this way and that, looking fast and clever—but in fact, he is ultimately overtaken in quest of the finish line by the tortoise that just moves on and on and on toward the goal. No flash, but completion and, in this fable, victory. A guest at our first home in Missouri (Breakfast Creek where we lived sixteen years) told us after a visit, "You've got a writing table and pens and paper in every room in your house except the bathrooms." We did *not* then put small tables, pens, and paper in those rooms (although we did put magazines in baskets there) but that information serves in my response to this exhortation to get on with it as suggested by the top line in this paragraph.

However, I do have to admit that there is something nearly frightening on the number of free pens I have gathered up and distributed through all rooms, all desks, all possible places that someone might need to jot down a note or begin a novel. There is power in the pen and it even translates to a cheap pen you're offered at the bank or insurance office.

While I was telling myself that *I am enough* I found that very reminder the base line for my turning to a blank page and beginning to transcribe what I see as illuminating episodes in my unimaginably long life. I feel powerfully fortunate to still be alive after forty-nine years with insulin-dependent diabetes and a checkered upbringing as the fifth child in five and born to a mother of forty-two and a perpetually disinterested father. This chronicle of moving through these years from fascinating K-12 schooling in many different schools, good schooling at Oberlin, a demanding and stimulating graduate education at California, Berkeley—and long teaching stints at UCLA and Missouri—and then adding the amazing experiences in working for and with the National Geographic Society all have delivered me to my "extra life" begun in 2002 at retirement, graced with a modest check and decades of life with Cathy (Chloe), a grand and creative woman.

This mix of happenstance and careful planning has given me a strong sense of seeing this as a story worth telling—even if it is only for a justification for all of the pens, notebooks and journals I have piled up around my studios in several states.

By now, you may be asking, "What is an episode?" Here is a leading example. It involved almost all of the family. It was a spontaneous event and seemed to ring true for all present. It has a theme lead line, a date of occurrence, and it stands alone as a singular episode of life recollected by the author.

Mother's Sense of Immortality

In 1973, after our father's funeral, all five of the Salter children were chatting together at one time. We were at Mother's Pleasant St. home in Oberlin, Ohio.

Mother suddenly spoke up, asking, "Where do you want to be buried?"

The room fell silent. "What?" said several.

Mother repeated, "Where do you all want to be buried? Where do you all want to have your graves?" Mother asked this in the most wonderfully matter-of-fact way.

"Why are you asking this, Mother?" quizzed Pat.

Mother turned to her and said in a tone that was intended to make all of us feel stupid for not knowing the answer, "Because they will ask me. I will need to know, so tell me now so I can be ready to tell them of your wishes."

This delicious quality of timelessness and Mother's sense of ongoing command was often manifest, but this dialogue is a truly classic example of her feelings of immortality.

Chapter One:

THE FOUNDING FAMILY

KATHARINE SHEPHERD HAYDEN SALTER—MOTHER (1896-1988). Mother was the family member most constant in my life until I left Madison, Wisconsin for Oberlin in 1956. When I search in my mind and papers for lore of what had made life so interesting for me, I come to Mother's observation once as I changed schools again, "We have lived in twenty-two different addresses since you were born, Kit. It's surprising that you can get a school to enroll you with such a mixed-up record."

Let me set the stage with an episode that had real moment in my young life.

MOTHER AND THE TUCSON CAPER

When I was about five, our family was living in Palo Alto, California while Dockie (our name for my father, Dr. Jack Salter) had a teaching assignment at Stanford. I remember only two things about that California scene.

First was the ambient smell of citrus, oranges especially. The sweet fragrance of blossoms, oranges on the trees, even the taste of fresh orange juice still wells up when I think of that scene.

The other thing I remember was that we lived by a large concrete-walled storm channel. It was almost always dry but after a powerful rain a torrent of water would appear from nowhere and roar through the ten-foot deep channel. Watching it cascade by filled with storm runoff was always accompanied by the mute fascination one feels when dangerously close to barely controlled water flow. It was confined by the concrete walls, but it looked so mean in the channel that it seemed to have the potential for every scary thing. Mother was always on guard with me, telling me again and again not to get close to that channel—especially during times of rain when it was filled with branches, street trash, or even looser pieces of clothing and shoes. Although I do not recall our house or apartment, that storm channel is etched on my memory.

But the Tucson caper had nothing to do with either oranges or storm channels. While in Palo Alto, I climbed under a bed in search for something and breathed in a lot of dust. At about the same time, I got into a stash of chocolates and I ate way, way beyond the capacity of a five-year-old's stomach. As a result of too much dust in my system and all that chocolate, my asthma—which had been a factor in my very early life— took a serious turn for the worst.

I was taken to the Stanford University Hospital and, after an examination and being hospitalized there, a doctor apparently informed Mother that I was in danger of expiring from the severity of the congestion in my system from this dangerous combo of two things I was apparently allergic to— dust and chocolate. I do not know how long I was there, but Mother took charge of things after this doctor's assessment. This is what led to what I think of as the 'the Tucson caper.'

It is important to know that prior to our move to Palo Alto

and Stanford, Mother had been working off and on with activist Margaret Sanger on the promotion of aspects of birth control and family planning. Mother had not worked with her since 1937, but she had told her in 1943 about my onset of potentially terminal asthma. Mrs. Sanger suggested that Mother bring me to Tucson where thousands of people had regained health from serious asthma. She offered Mother a vacant adobe hut to live in if we came to the miraculous climate of Arizona.

Mother immediately agreed to the plan. The lore of the caper as I have heard it, is that she checked the Greyhound schedule for a bus to Tucson, Arizona. Then, with tickets and schedule in her purse, she came into the hospital late in the evening to visit her sickly child. When the coast was clear she gathered me up swaddled in hospital blankets and slipped out of the ward and hospital. She went directly to the Greyhound Bus Terminal and we soon boarded the bus to Tucson.

Once there, Mrs. Sanger made good on her promise and made an adobe hut available to us. When we were settled in my sister Jean came out to Arizona to help out. She was nineteen years old, and lived with us for several months. Within six months I had gained some twelve pounds and began a period of life almost completely free of asthma.

We all loved the Tucson adobe, both for the stunning desert environment of Tucson, and for the stark simplicity of the mud hut and its outdoor plumbing. It was an utterly new life for me, for Mother, and for sister Jean. After Jean had made space in the adobe for herself, Mother had to leave for the Cleveland Clinic for some medical needs of her own. This allowed Jean and me the fun of becoming desert rats and buddies as we lived on the far outskirts of Tucson. After a little time, she got a job working during the days stringing wires in B-29 bomber planes in a massive Tucson aircraft assembly plant.

I had the fun of hours on my own in exploration of my new desert world. The whole openness of the adobe hut and surrounding desert is a powerful recollection even now. It was there that Mother and I fell in love with the magazine *Arizona Highways,* for the evening twilights and nighttime skies made impressions on us that never left—and the magazine was brilliant in building stories around such settings.

There is an irony here, too. Cathy's father, Colonel William Earle Riggs, was a B-29 pilot for two years in the Pacific Theatre—perhaps flying planes that sister Jean had helped assemble. Like so many episodes of my life, my sources for details on when and why we left Tucson cannot be answered. I do, however, have a handsome scar on my left wrist that I got in climbing up the walls of our adobe hut early on and got a deep cut from a nail sticking out of a piece of construction wood just on the edge of the roof. Even now at eighty-three plus, I can see that inch-long scar as a reminder of the hidden costs of exploration in our frequently changing settings as I was growing up.

♦

The repeated chore of figuring out new school situations is one that I remember for many places. The episode below is from my efforts to enroll in sixth grade in a consolidated school in Lexington, Kentucky in 1950.

HOME NON-SCHOOLING – PART I

The summer before sixth grade, Mother and I moved from Madison to Lexington, Kentucky. She and my elder sister Kate found a place outside the city of Lexington on the Fayetteville Road. It was a farm home just recently abandoned. The farmer who had bought the farmland that had been a family farm got the house tossed in as the people moved to the city. He lived across the highway and agreed to rent the empty home to Mother and me (and any other siblings on the scene) for forty-five dollars a month.

We arrived in Kentucky in late summer. When it came time to go to school that August, J.R. Hicks, the owner of the home we were living in—and our neighbor across the highway—gave me a ride into town. He dropped me off at the largest school I had ever seen in my entire life. It was a complex universe of new brick buildings, each looking more foreboding than the rest. Farmer Hicks gave me a strong clasp on my shoulder as I got out. He wished me Good Luck on finding my way into sixth grade.

I went into what seemed to be the main doorway of the main building and saw a lady I thought was probably a teacher and asked, "Where do new kids go for sixth grade?"

Episodes in a Life

"Go to your teacher's room" she replied, clearly on her way somewhere.

"I don't have a teacher. I'm a new student."

She paused, then said, "Oh…okay, go to the office. It is down the hall there by the sign that says OFFICE."

I went to the office and asked a lady at the counter who I should see about getting a teacher.

She said, "Who have you been assigned to?"

"No one. We just moved to Kentucky."

"Where do you live? Why did you come to this school?"

"J.R. dropped me off here. He is a farmer and said this was probably the school I would go to."

"Where are your parents?"

"My father's in the Philippines. My mother is at the farmhouse we are living in."

"Why isn't she here with you?"

"We don't have a car. And even if we did, she wouldn't be here. She doesn't know how to drive."

By this time the lady was either interested in this case, or she was bothered by it. I cannot recall which. She went on.

"Well, why don't you come back to my desk. I will need some identification and you will need some money for book deposit. What grade are you going into?"

"I just finished fifth grade in Madison, Wisconsin last May. I guess sixth grade would be the best." I felt a little smug coming from Badgerland education to farmland schooling. I went on. "I don't have any identification, but I know my birthday and stuff like that. I even know my mother's maiden name. And I don't have any money."

This rush of information seemed to make things a little more tense.

The lady appeared almost irritated, but it was the first day of school and I figured she was probably very busy. She replied efficiently. "Of course, you know your birthday. What I need is something that shows where you were born..."

I started to interrupt to tell her about my birthplace and she stopped me before I even got to Greenport. "No, don't tell me...you were going to say that you know where you were born. I am sure you do know that but what you do not know is the kind of information necessary to get you into this school. You need to have papers and money."

"I have some paper at home, but I didn't bring it with me. I guess that was stupid. And we don't have any money. We are mostly living from our garden." Then I added, "I thought grade school was supposed to be free. Is Kentucky different?"

The lady was now getting into the spirit of this encounter. There were other people—kids and parents—at the counter and she nodded to some other office people to cover for her. She wanted to get this curious case squared away.

"Young man, by papers I mean identification. We can maybe let that go until your mother can come in. And by money, I mean ten dollars to pay for book rental. It is not even really a rental fee. It is to help cover the replacement of the books if you lose them."

"I won't lose them. Everyone in my family is reading all the time. All we do is read, except for my mother. Mostly she types. But anyway, I will take care of the books. And in any case, we do not have ten dollars." I could see she was eager to resolve this, so I added. "J.R. said that I could do some work on the farm and earn some money so if you can wait a while, I can maybe bring the money in later." I paused just for a second then said, "I don't know how Mom will get here. J.R.'s wife took her shopping once but that was on the weekend when she was off work. Are you or anyone here on Saturday?"

By this time, there were a few heads leaning toward the desk of this lady. Energized by the notice our strange conversation was getting from her office mates, she took new ground.

"Okay...here's what we'll do. I will add the note: 'Student will pay later.' That will take care of the money for now. For the ID, we will say that Mother has it, but she is not available today. That means we can go to the next step." She paused, looking at the stack of papers on her desk. "I will assign you a teacher. I will put you in sixth grade and we'll see how you do. I've a feeling you'll do just fine, but who is to know?" She then looked up with a nice grin.

"You will go to Building 36 and see Mrs. Wilkie. She is a good teacher and she is probably the best one for you to get started with. She will explain the system and rules here. How does that seem?" The lady looked pleased as she edged the pages into a folder and looked across her desk at me, beaming with the glow of completion!

"Building 36? Mrs. Wilkie? Okay. Thanks a lot. I will start saving money so that I can get the ten dollars, but you don't need to worry. I won't lose the books."

I left the office, walked down the hall toward the doorway into a brick universe of consolidated school buildings. I stepped out into the intense sunlight of a Kentucky August morning.

I spent the next twenty minutes looking for Building 36 in this collection of unwelcoming brick structures. I did not find it. I was also feeling bad about not having the ten dollars, and about not having the right identification, and not having a parent.... "0 for Three" was how I saw it by this time, so when I did not find Building 36, I walked back to the set of railroad tracks that neighbor Hicks had mentioned as we crossed them an hour earlier. He told me those tracks run right behind his farmhouse. He had said that if I could not find a school bus ride home, I should walk these tracks. In four or five miles, they would take me right to the back of his place. I could then go through his land, carefully run across the Fayetteville Road, and be home.

I did just that. I did not go to school for that entire semester. Mr. Hicks was true to his word and gave me some jobs to do around the farmstead. I explained to him that I was a little ahead of the class at that big school so I was taking some time to earn some dollars for the household and would go to school later. He seemed okay with that. I hustled my little buns off working for a dollar or two a day. I seem to recall that I was probably the major cash income source for Mom that entire fall.

HOME NON-SCHOOLING – PART II

In the months that followed this effort to find and get into school, I was given chores that related to farm clean up, sheep and lamb tending, some garden work, some tobacco crop work, firewood collection, shed cleaning, and other stuff that took about four to five hours a day. I loved it. I felt clever because I was not in Building 36. I felt excited by the different nature of the life I was experiencing compared to all the places I had lived before. And I loved the farm world. The biggest drama of this non-school term related to one of the jobs I was given when it began to get colder late in fall.

There were four older black men who lived nearby. Mr. Hicks hired them each fall and winter to work in a small shed attached to the tobacco barn. Their job was to pull stakes that had tobacco hanging on them and bring them into this small shed (probably about 8 x 20 feet in size) to prepare the tobacco crop for local sale. The shed had a small wood burning stove, a wall of windows, and a high table for sorting and grading tobacco. I was given the chore of bringing the tobacco sticks from the adjacent barn. The tobacco leaves had been drying on the sticks for some months.

At first, I thought that J.R. didn't want to have the men always have to go and get more tobacco. But I soon realized that his goal was actually to always have dry leaves at the ready so that a steady grading and sorting process could be attained and maintained. In retrospect I see the goal was efficient activity, but my sixth-grade self, thought it was just to help the men have an easier job. The continual delivery of sticks of dry tobacco leaves seemed to keep us all in steady motion.

In any case, I loved the work, the rich earthy tobacco smell, and the conversations I overheard. After one long afternoon I finished my work in the tobacco shed and went back to our house and into the kitchen. We had a wood burning cooking stove there. It was also the major heat source for the first floor of the old farmhouse. The kitchen was the most popular room in the nearly empty structure. I recall this particular conversation with Mother and have grinned at it in retrospect for years.

Mother greeted me as I came in. "Well, what was work like today, Kit?" She was in a more reflective mood than was common. I welcomed any questions about my unprecedented special semester of home non-schooling.

"Oh, it was neat. I got to learn some more stuff about tobacco and the kind of tobacco needed for cigars and stuff. I learn a lot with those men in that shed." Mother may have shown a little more interest in that line than I recall, but in any case, the conversation went along a little further.

"What sort of things do you learn? Tell me some of the ideas you get or the stories you hear." I seem to recall a higher level of interest as she posed this question.

"Well, a lot of what I learn is about how they grade tobacco. I had no idea that there were so many things that made a tobacco leaf valuable or maybe not so good. I learn about dryness and color and things like that." I had gone further than I usually went with conversations with Mother about my farm hand activities. She was usually the one defining and limiting any narratives we exchanged.

"But you said stories, too. What sorts of stories do you hear?" I think she had stopped peeling potatoes now.

"Well, I can't remember too many. But I do know that I get confused because I don't know some of their words."

"Like what? How can you not know the words of tobacco sorters?"

"I don't know, for example, what 'pussy' is. These guys talk all the time about it and they even say they have little picture books, but they don't want to show them to me yet. They say I've not worked long enough to see the books. They say they're like comic books."

Mother, I recall, said "Pussy? They talk about *pussy?*"

"Yeah...that seems to be their favorite topic. I feel too stupid to ask them what it is so if you know, tell me so I'm not missing so much in their stories. Okay?"

The look of alarm on my mother's face told me that I had gone too far in talking about my day. In fact, it was this particular conversation that effectively ended my tobacco shed career.

But, very soon after this revelation, a truant officer came

to the doorway of our recently abandoned, but now cozy, farmhouse and knocked on the door. Mother answered and the man asked. "Is there a Christopher Lord Salter who lives here?"

Mother acted as though she was not certain she wanted to give out the facts on this case too quickly. She said, "Perhaps. Why do you want to know?"

The man looked behind her at me, standing just back and off to her side. He gave us both a kindhearted grin—as though he had been in similar conversations before. Looking at me he asked, "Would you be young Christopher?" With just a short pause the county official continued with his query but addressing Mother. "I have been told that he came to school in August and had quite a conversation with Mrs. Lincoln and then went out to find Mrs. Wilkie. He seems never to have located Building 36 or Mrs. Wilkie."

I saw this as time for me to speak to the events of that recent August summer day. "Yes, that's right. I had a nice talk with a lady but when I got into the big blacktop schoolyard and tried to find Building 36, I began to feel bad about not having money and not having the kind of identification the school wanted. So, when I didn't find my way to Building 36, I just walked back home. I've been working for farmer Hicks ever since. I've got the ten dollars saved up now."

Mother came back into the conversation. "Wait. Why was my son told that he could not go to school unless he had money? Why didn't someone take him to Building 36, or at least show him where it was?"

"Mrs. Lincoln told me—when they asked me to find out where this boy had disappeared to—she figured that that new boy could find his way anywhere and did not need to be tended. Perhaps she was wrong. In any case, it will not do for him to miss any more school, Mrs. Salter. Mrs. Wilkie is ready for him and we need to get him into class right away."

Mother looked at me and I looked at her. The tobacco shed work was finished for me. There was snow on the ground and J.R. was ready to let me slip out of his farm chores picture. The truant officer told us a bus would pick me up and drop me off since the Fayetteville Road had a lot of farm kids who took the bus to the brick world of this new consolidated school. Plans were made. The man made me promise to get on the bus the following Monday morning. He said he would tell the driver to stop for me but that I had to be at the end of the driveway and ready to get on the bus by exactly 7:10 a.m. He said it would bring me home, too.

I caught the bus the next Monday. That ended the special episode of "Home Non-Schooling."

Joel's Gibson and the New Shoes

In Kentucky there was the continuing uncertainty about where household dollars would come from. Dockie never lived in Kentucky with Mother and me. At different times, one sister or Joel would come a stay a bit. Those were times Mother and I worked to get the pantry filled as much as possible. There would usually be some dollars left when the family visitor left The Meadows (the name Mother gave our old two-story home and the surrounding farm fields and barn). Visits were both fun and vital.

Toward the middle of my seventh-grade year we left the Meadows and moved into an apartment in Lexington so that Mother would be able to walk to the library and the post office. I was able to stay in the same school and was elected to some student office for eighth grade. That required me to be a part of a quasi-formal ceremony at seventh grade's year-end program. I was told by my teacher that I could not take the stage for that event with the shoes I wore regularly. When I explained that it was the only pair of shoes I had, he said, "No matter—get your parents to buy you a new pair for the ceremony next Friday."

I started to say that there was no money on that front, but I did not want to, yet again, explain some curious home arrangement to another outsider who had no context at all for this white kid with seemingly good education but zero dollars. The way I handled the shoe issue was that I looked around my room at home to see if I could pawn anything. I had no material goods. Mother had no material goods that I could carry to a local pawnshop on the edge of Lexington. But then I saw the Gibson Silver Belle four-string banjo that Joel had given me a few years earlier. I had been working on playing it, but I was always in the shadow of brother Joel's great guitar and banjo skills.

However, I got J.R. to take me to a pawnshop on one of his trips into the city. I explained that I would find a way to get the money back, but I had to have some ready cash right now for a purchase necessary for school. He offered to lend me some money, but I told him that he had already done way too much for Mother and me. I wanted to meet this obligation myself.

He drove me to a pawnshop and I got eighteen dollars in pawn for the beautiful Gibson. I clutched the money in my nervous hand and asked if J. R. could drop me off at a shoe store that was not too far from home. He told me he had some errands and if I wanted to buy my shoes and wait for him twenty minutes, he'd be glad to drive me home, especially since there was no banjo now to make room for in his cab.

I picked out a pair of shiny black patent leather shoes (they were spiffy with a glow), paid for them, stood outside the shoe store, and J.R. picked me up in twenty-five minutes. When I got home, I put the shoes under my bed and tried to figure out the best-looking set of clothes I had for the Friday ceremony.

But, in fact, we moved again before I could play my role with my shiny shoes. I was able to get enough money to reclaim my banjo from the pawn shop, so I left Lexington with my new shoes and the wonderful banjo brother Joel had given me. We moved back to Wisconsin where I finished seventh and began eighth grade.

◆

One other episode that is so descriptive of Mother is this scene that came from her move to Berea, Kentucky to fill a new teaching position in English at Berea College.

[Thanks to Sister Pat, I have learned of this story.]

MOTHER IN BEREA, KENTUCKY

In the 1930s, when Mother had three daughters and a very young son, (brother Joel), her B.A. from Oberlin, and a generally absent husband, she and her four children moved to Berea for a teaching job she had been offered. After getting established and getting the daughters in school (Joel was too young), she went to a neighbor's house and knocked on the door.

A young woman, about Mother's age, came to the door with a child in her arms. Mother introduced herself and said that she had just moved in next door and wanted to say hello. The woman, reluctant for just a second, then asked Mother to come in. Almost immediately the mother with child in arms proclaimed something like, "I know my house is not tidy. In fact, things are all over the place, but I have very young children and I have just read something that says it is *okay* to have a somewhat messy house when you are raising one or more small children. In fact, here…" She handed Mother a copy of *Parents Magazine,* and said in a rush, "You might find this useful because perhaps you have young children, too." The lady looked relieved to be able to present some printed support of her position relating to housekeeping.

Mother looked at the article and smiled, saying, "Yes…I see. I know exactly the argument that the author was using in this article." Then after a short pause, she added, "In fact, I am the author of this article." She handed back the article and Mother and her new neighbor shared a moment of mutual amazement.

◆

PATRICIA LEARNED SALTER (1923—2021) My sister, Pat was the middle sister of the trio of girls born soon after Mother and Dockie got married. They all followed very distinct life patterns, but Pat has played the most important role in my life. There are two major reasons. These episodes define those reasons.

Ripon, Wisconsin

One factor that makes Pat so special as I think of my life is that I lived in Ripon, Wisconsin with her and husband Diete Roetter, and daughters Katharine and Helen for part of seventh and into eighth grade while Mother settled in Madison.

Although I was their uncle, I wasn't that many years older than the girls. We lived more like a family than an assemblage of kin. Diete was the Dean of Men at Ripon college during the school year and worked as a bartender at a roadhouse outside of Ripon during the summer months. We lived for a few months in a big old house in which I was given a spacious closet for my room, but then moved to a single-family home over by the campus. I not only had my own room, but I became part of the family in terms of chores and opportunities and learning.

This was the first time that I can remember living with a mother figure, father figure, and two younger siblings in my entire life.

Diete was a tall and very good-looking German who had come with his younger brother (Jurgen) and parents to Madison in the late 1930s from Germany in flight from the growing Nazi menace. Frederik Roetter—Diete and Jurgen's father—was a lawyer and had written a powerful anti-Hitler monograph that made it essential for the Roetters to leave Germany hurriedly. One of the sons went to London but the rest of the family came to Madison, in part because of a program that my mother was involved with. It sought to bring German families to American cities to escape the persecution being experienced by so many at that time in Germany.

In my wonderful Ripon period of my life, I learned about a family kitchen. Pat did the cooking, as I had never lived in a scene with regular cooking and kitchen work. I fell right into dishwashing and a very minor kitchen prep role. Most of all, what I really learned was how much it means to the woman making kitchen meals to have ready help, especially if it is good-spirited and actually does something. By this time, Mother had already become largely focused on her vox pop writing and our kitchen seemed to have little function. Dishwashing and kitchen tidy-up in Ripon were a whole new world for me and I loved feeling somewhat useful in helping to actually get meals on the table. Plus, the fact that I did these tasks working with younger Katharine and Helen gave us a great trio of shared interaction and family growing up together.

◆

Dietrich Roetter (1920-1967) My sister Pat's husband, Diete, introduced above, was a powerful presence in my Ripon years. He turned thirty during my time living with them and this next episode is still bold in my mind, for I had never before been exposed to any such masculine role player in my young life.

On Becoming Thirty

At the end of seventh grade, living with sister Pat, Diete, Katherine and Helen, was the first time I had lived with a man in the house who played the role of husband and father in any sort of understandable way. It was a grand period of my life.

The most singular event of those ten months came about this way. One morning Pat and the girls had gone somewhere, and only Diete and I were home. I think I was doing some work at a living room table. Suddenly Diete burst into the living room, just from the shower, totally nude. He walked to the center of the room, puffed up his very impressive barrel chest, flexed both his arms and said in a deep voice, "*This* is what thirty looks like, Kit. *This* is thirty years old!"

I about fell out of my shoes. Diete was an enormously handsome man from top to bottom. I got the feeling that he was someone I should strive to be like someday. He then grinned, ruffled my hair, and walked back toward the bathroom. Nothing was ever said about this "demonstration of thirty," but I have grinned to myself for over fifty years as I recall his bold birthday testament of what thirty looked like when worn by Diete Roetter!

Pat and the Tenner

In moments of review and contemplation about the direction one's life has taken, it's possible to recall a few events that clearly have significantly shaped the journey. This is one of the most singular such events in my life and I recall it with thanks. My middle sister, Pat, and I were walking one day in Madison, Wisconsin, and she asked me this question. It was 1955 and I was a high school junior.

"What about college, Kit? What are your plans?"

"I'm going to stay in Madison and go UW here."

"Have you applied anywhere else?"

"No–why?" I asked. "I've got no bucks and Madison will work...and I can stay at my job at Tri-Dairy with Sam Jacobson."

"Why not apply to Oberlin?"

"Haa...How would I cover such costs? As it is now, most of the money I make at Sam's convenience store goes to Mother just to keep us in groceries."

"Apply for a fellowship. You've done all sorts of extracurricular stuff and your grades are good. Tell them that your mother and father went there." Then after a tiny, life-changing pause, she reached into her purse and pulled out a $10.00 bill.

"Here, take this. This will cover the application fee. Give it a try!"

I was stunned. To get a tenner was a big deal in 1955, especially from Pat who was a long way from any easy funds.

I did what she suggested. I applied. I was admitted. I was granted some support funds. I got a board job. I went to Oberlin. I hated and loved the experience and my entire life has described a different trajectory because of that conversation, Patricia's exhortation...and that tenner.

◆

JOEL SALTER (1927-1976). Another family member who played a role early in my life—prior to Ripon—was brother Joel. He was eleven years older than me. He was an outlier in the family because our three sisters were all so close in age that they were a strong female unit. Joel, more than three years younger than Jean, our youngest sister, had his own circle of friends. Once I was part of the family scene, I was always the kid of the group, was probably more cared for by the girls than ever by Joel or even Mother. However, I have two episodes that focus on Brother Joel.

1610 Adams Street

I think that the earliest events I recall in my growing up were a pair of incidents that happened at the big old white house at 1610 Adams Street in Madison, Wisconsin, before Dockie took his Stanford University job. One day in around 1943 or 1944, Joel was doing some work on a car by the curb. He had run a long series of extension cords from the inside of the house that meandered down to the trouble light he had rigged under the hood of his old Packard. I was about four. I remember that I walked back and forth between the house and the car, trying to figure out some way to find some entertainment at either end of the extension cords. On one of these excursions I reached down to pick up the extension cord to run it through my fingers. As part of my funky karma, I happened to pick up the line exactly at the junction where one line was loosely plugged into the next line. I got my sticky fingers right on the hot copper and it fried my little bod for a nano-second. Nothing really happened but I recall the zing that came from that wire grab.

The other incident that I recall from Adams Street was that Joel—already an artist by this time—had created a painted football. He had done a spooky face on the ball and for some reason, I found nothing but fear in that plaything. At one point I remember being under a bed and Joel leaned down at the edge of the bed and jeeringly rolled the football toward me. Maybe it was the fact that footballs roll in an unpredictable manner, but whatever it was, I was terrified by the approach of this leering face rolling erratically toward me in my not-very-effective hiding place.

THE SALTERSTONE RING

It was always great to be able to show off my older brother as I was growing up. He played the banjo, piano, guitar, and sang. I recall times when I would bring friends to one of the musical gigs he performed at. I glowed in the reflected glory that I felt from his musical talents. However, this particular recollection came from a side show of such events. When I was in about eighth grade, we moved to an address that allowed me to go to a Madison Westside Junior High. One day Joel came to me and asked me if I wanted to see his new ring. As he asked, he extended his finger and showed a fancy class ring on his left hand. I had never seen such a stone. It had more texture than I ever thought of as ordinary in personal jewelry.

"What sort of a stone is that, Joel?" I asked.

"That's a Salterstone," he said with pride.

"A Salterstone?" I asked.

"Yeah...in fact, this is a totally unique Salterstone. Not even you could have a Salterstone like this." I reached out to touch it and jumped my finger back when I felt the skin-like texture to the stone. Joel laughed. "That's a wart, Kit. I got this old ring at St. Vincent's Thrift Shop and took out the cheap stone. I scrunched the empty ring over my wart. Now I have a unique—in fact, *the* unique Salterstone ring."

After that, I got great mileage out of being able to show off the Salterstone ring to my buddies whenever they came by and Joel was around. This probably went on for five or six months.

◆

My relationship with Joel was hard to absorb. He had been the most solitary of the first four children, strongly leaning toward becoming a loner early on. He had talents in art and in music, and those skills took him out of the family and put him into universes of nighttime playing and drinking that sometimes morphed into romantic nights, and finally he met his first wife, Maggie, in a bar in Madison. They broke up after a year or two, and blessedly, had no children. Joel met a second Maggie, the *real* Maggie of his life, the mother of their seven children (all born within a seven year period, beginning with Annie and Nannie (twin girls), and followed by Joel, Danny, Nathan, Heather, and Sam.

Difficult Times with Joel

In the summer of 1971, I went to Wisconsin to visit Joel and Maggie and the kids in the Baraboo Hills. The visit was, as was so often the case, a mixed bag of emotions. Joel was then working as an artist for the Barnum and Bailey Circus and for the Circus Museum at Baraboo. He was so very, very black in his view of the world. He saw so many things as wrong and painful for him and his family. I remember him telling me that he was working full time at a job that seemed to be an okay job, yet his salary did not lift his family out of the U.S. Government poverty level category. Pointing out an article in the *Capitol Times* from Madison, he told me, "Look at this, Kit—seven kids, two parents, $25,000 a year and I'm damn near at the level of a bum on the streets of Washington."

This was my next to last visit with Joel. I was there alone, and I ended the visit early by telling him that I could not afford spiritually and emotionally to visit him anymore. "You are so goddamn bleak about everything, Joel. There's not a thing I can do or say that you do not find to serve as a source for complaining and lament. Why the hell didn't you get some of my optimism and I get some of your artistic talent? It seems so stupid to have me so love life and be engaging it with no artistic skill… and you, you are overflowing with talent in art and music and you cannot find any brightness in anything you face or do?"

He responded with something like, "Kit, you're too stupid to see what hell life is!"

I replied by reminding him of when a buddy and I hitchhiked from Oberlin down to New Orleans where Joel lived and made a life from his guitar, piano, and singing—and he fed his soul by continuing his work in oils. That had been around 1957. When Hok and I finally reached his address after some days on the road, he let us into an apartment in which the windows were all covered with black paper. And, to make the darkness even more powerful, he had a loop tape of Tchaikovsky's Symphony No. 6, "The Pathetique," playing continually. Tchaikovsky had composed this near dirge the year he died, and I felt as though its music would guide nearly anyone inclined toward depression further into the depths of a hellish existence.

Hok and I decided not to stay there because the burden of Joel's ambient sorrow was too, too heavy for two Freshman college kids exploring the Big Easy for the first time. I left telling Joel that the visits seemed as though they were really bad news for both of us.

The Salters of Rice Lake

When Joel's circus mural and poster painting job ended, all nine of them moved to Rice Lake in northern Wisconsin. In that setting near water, the family had a full house, with Maggie working at a roadhouse bar and also being celebrated as a dynamite softball pitcher in the local women's league. Experience.

A couple of years after his death, in 1978, Cathy and I visited Maggie and the seven kids in Rice Lake, Wisconsin. We were pleased to find that the Community College had named the handsome campus art gallery the Joel Hayden Salter Gallery where Joel had taught art before he died. They exhibit a rich collection of his work on its walls.

Maggie, recently a widow, now served as the engine that kept the household functional. She was amazing. I have these three powerful images still deep in my mind. Natano would take the kitchen compost out to the bury pit on a unicycle. Sam, the youngest (about five years old then) came to the kitchen when Cathy decided to make a pie for dessert that night. Sam said, "I know where things are." And he got up on a counter and sat ready for questions. As Cathy asked, "Pie tins?" Sam would point. "Flour?" Another focused arm and hand. And the whole preparation was a dessert in three hands: Cathy with two and Sam his one, pointing.

The third image is that of Maggie—seven kids, father Joel already deceased, and the steady flow of kids in and out, wash in and out, clothes pulled out of the dryer by one kid, left on the floor while that current king of the washer and dryer put

Episodes in a Life

his or her wet laundry into the machine. There was the hum of steady activity, almost all of it wrapped in nice spirit and amicable interaction among all—including Cathy and me as newcomers. It was also in that visit to Rice Lake that we saw Maggie clobber a strong softball team with her rocket-fast slow-pitch underhand throws.

◆

Dockie (Jack) Salter, (1898-1973) the Distant Father. After Dockie had fathered three daughters in four years at the very beginning of his marriage, it became apparent that he was not interested in being a parent. He found no joy in the labors of raising, or even helping to raise his children. The girls had a strong alliance among themselves fortunately—and Mother was still mothering actively in that time of her life. Joel, born three years later than Jean, the youngest daughter, developed a keen sense of independence early on. I know of no rapport between Joel and father Dockie, but I was not a part of Joel's growing up. I came eleven years after him. Mother had been forty-two when I was conceived. By the late 1930s, it was Granddaddy (Mother's father, Harry J. Hayden) who played the most important role in keeping the Salter family home and family together through his financial and emotional help.

As I write this, I am perplexed by the love that is evident when I read some of Mother's poetry and sonnets written in the 1930s when she and Dockie were living in Oklahoma, and other places. The affection that she felt for him is like a call from a distant galaxy to anyone who actually overlapped the final decades of their marriage prior to Dockie's death in 1973 at the age of seventy-four. So, for the record, know that *my* images of Dockie derive completely from my small bit of family time with father Dockie present.

Dockie was tenured fairly quickly at the University of Wisconsin, Madison. His field was Political Science (Ph.D. from University of Pennsylvania, B.A. from Oberlin College (where he and Mother met in the early 1920s). Once he had tenure and a growing family, it seems he searched for and found a way to stay professional but not necessarily share the family household. His plan was to agree to fill empty teaching positions in other universities. These most often occurred because of sabbatical leaves granted to faculty at other schools. The episode that I included about Tucson occurred during Dockie's Stanford year as a sabbatical replacement.

Let me set the stage for the relationship I had with Dockie with the following episode.

Dockie's $3000 Figure

In 1956, during my first year of college at Oberlin, I was home in Madison and went to my father's office on the University Wisconsin campus. I had a bone to pick with him and I wanted to not do it in front of Mother. I recall his South Hall office as a small nook stacked in every possible corner with books, newspapers, and student papers. He had a scroll or two hanging by the windows. Dockie welcomed me in and gave a realtor's arm sweep to show off the space. "This is my office. It is in a good location. It is small but it's a good place to work. I only pay $3,000 a year for it."

"You have to pay for it?" I asked in amazement. "I thought professors would at least get their offices for free. You really have to pay for it?"

He looked around at the tight quarters, turned to me and said, "If I were to add $3000 to my annual salary, I would almost have a living wage. I assume the University does not pay me that $3000 because I feel they are charging me rent for my office."

"It's funny you chose $3000 as the supposed rent. I'm here about three thousand dollars, too, but my figure is not imaginary."

My father looked at me curiously, "What imaginary $3000 are you talking about, Christopher?"

"I'm talking about the $3,000 figure you put down in the parental approval form sent to you by Oberlin College. That information is used to determine financial aid. I found out that Oberlin had planned to give me full tuition support, but when your form finally came back to Oberlin for determination of my financial aid package, you had declared that you would provide your son an annual $3000 toward Oberlin costs."

I paused at this point because my father and I had a cash-free relationship that related mostly to the fact that he not only did not play any fatherly role when living with Mother and me, but he also seemed to provide her with nearly no money to live on. It was clear to my siblings and me that it was Granddaddy Hayden—Mother's father—who had kept the unit of Mother and Kit afloat through the early years of my life. After his death in 1944, the siblings and other family members had to help the home unit out.

I continued with my irritated response to Dockie's promised contribution to my Oberlin college costs. "When Oberlin got your letter, they dropped my fellowship by $3000 and this meant that I had to get a board job at Dascomb Hall. You'll be proud to know I'm now a pot washer. You want to be sure to mention to your friends that your youngest child has become the head pot washer at Oberlin's largest dormitory dining hall."

I stopped just a second to let that bit of imagery settle in and then went on. "Why in hell did you promise $3000 when you haven't ever paid that much to Mother's maintenance for years as far as I can tell!"

Dockie was clearly stunned. "You mean you're really a pot washer at Oberlin?" It was clear that the import of my lament was not that he had reneged on his promised support, but that Oberlin had replaced that absent money with a job that would not give father anything to share proudly whenever he chatted about faculty children and their educational and professional progress in conversation with colleagues.

Dockie responded to my question. "I had to write something down, Christopher. It was too embarrassing to have both your mother and me be Oberlin graduates and for us to have no money at all to send you anywhere to college, much less to Oberlin. And I just felt that $3000 would satisfy them but not be so much that they would diminish your fellowship support."

"Well, you were off by $3000, Dockie. As I figure it, in my five nights a week of one to two hours of pot washing and cleanup in the Dascomb kitchen, for about forty weeks of school, I'm earning about $6.00 an hour, or, in your economy, I'm earning enough to pay for your University of Wisconsin faculty office. Does that sound about right to you, Dockie? You're a professor at the University of Wisconsin and your eighteen-year-old son, who's been working since eighth grade at a convenience store to help give his mother some household cash, is now doing pots for a wage of about $6.00 an hour. How does that equation work in terms of your parental embarrassment?"

Episodes in a Life

Dockie seemed unmoved by any of this. He asked, "Have you gained any honors in your first semester?"

"Yes…I was made 'head pot washer' just recently and I now get to dine on whatever I can forage in the kitchen." I could not bring myself to tell him that I had, in fact, just been bumped up to 'head waiter' to work with a crew of thirty college coed waitresses in the spring semester. I wanted to play the pot washer card as fully as I could. It all led to nothing.

◆

I must add one other recollection of Dockie to further explain my sense of him having little interest in parenting his final child.

Fishing with Dockie

When Mother, Dockie and I were all living in Madison in a single home for a short while, Dockie asked me one day if I wanted to go fishing. I was quite surprised this question ever came my direction, but since Madison was a city four lovely lakes, I had had some fishing times with buddies. I told him that would be fun.

We got a little gear together. I do not recall how we got to the lake because Dockie never owned a car that I can recall. Maybe one of the older children agreed to drop us off at the edge of Lake Mendota or Wingra. In any case, we had gotten some worms and put them on our hooks and walked out on a public pier and dropped our lines in. For maybe twenty minutes nothing happened, and I cannot recall any conversations that we had. I was probably still surprised that I had been asked to go fishing with him at all.

Then I got a bite. Dockie so far had had no action on his line so both of us grew interested in the bobbing bobber at the end of my pole. Soon I felt that I had the fish caught and very carefully I pulled him to the surface. We both looked carefully at the first/only prize of our first ever father and son fishing experience. When the fish broke water as I arched my pole and pulled my line up, we could see that it was a flounder. Dockie was the first to speak.

"A flounder. That's a stupid fish. Let's go home now."

That first ever fishing trip became the only fishing trip. I took the flounder off the hook and dropped it back into lake. Somehow Dockie and I got home. It was, in so many ways, a singular experience.

And I want to add to this episode that has Mother and Dockie both involved, one in a very real way, the other in a virtual sense.

MOTHERS AND SONS

When I got back in the fall of 1956 from three years of English teaching at Tunghai University in Taichung, Taiwan, Mother was living by herself in Oberlin, Ohio. I went to visit her. As part of my effort to get us out of the house (where the general agenda was being asked why I had not read more of Mother's manuscripts), we walked over to the very beautiful new Seely Mudd Center, the new Oberlin College library complex.

We went up into the stacks because I was trying to write something about Margaret Sanger, and I wanted to see if Oberlin had *Women and the New Race* (1922). As we walked through these neat aisles in a China section, I stopped and looked at the spines of some books. I pulled one out of the stack. I do not even recall what book it was, but I know that it was one that I had heard of and I was glad to see that Oberlin had it. I opened it and, out of habit, I flipped to the back where there was traditionally a small paper pocket where the book's library card was usually kept.

I pulled the card from the sleeve and noted that only one person had ever checked this book out. My eyes got big and I turned to Mom and said, "Look at this…look at this. The only person who ever checked this out is none other than J.T. Salter."

And there it was…his special and so-recognizable signature right there at the top of the card, standing lonely in more than a quarter century of only a single check out. The book may even have gone back to the 1920s when Mom and Dockie were students at Oberlin. I was astonished. I might be the only other person who ever pulled this book from the stacks in consideration of reading it, or at least in consideration of checking it out. Mother looked at it and said, "Yes. Dockie sometimes checked out books."

She clearly was not captured by the sequence of things here. She looked at some other books. Just as we were leaving the inner stacks, I turned away from Mother, pulled the library card and put it in my denim shirt pocket. As we headed toward the stairs, I brought the book along to check it out. The new library had gone way beyond library cards. There were computer codes in the front of the book. I do not think Oberlin had gotten to bar codes yet, but I knew that library cards were just tradition.

We went down to the checkout lady. She was a woman who might have been sent from Central Casting if a director had said, "Send me the classic college librarian. Send one who is old and stern." Mother stood next to me while we checked the book out. The library lady looked at the book, noted the computer markings on the front, and then turned to the back of the book. Looking at the sleeve where the library cards used to live before computer codes were used for checkouts. She said, "Hmmmm. I wonder where the library card is?"

I replied, "They're not used any more are they? Are the old cards still part of the checkout procedure?"

"No, we do not need them anymore, but I always just check to see if the card is there. We stopped using them about four years ago. I wonder where this book's card went." I kept silent. Mother, however, had suddenly become curiously interested in this conversation.

She said, "I know where the card went. It is in this young man's pocket. It is in his shirt pocket. He took it from the book." There was no real inflection, just a matter of factual observation.

The wizened library lady looked at me and asked, "You have the card? You have this book's library card?" Her eyes were in a tight focus on my reddening face and my shirt pocket.

"Well, yes…there was only a single signature on it. It was my father, her husband who died three years ago, and he was the only person who had ever checked the book out. It was his signature. I thought it would be a great souvenir of my dad as a student here at Oberlin." I talked longer than I probably should have.

"You have the card that went in this book?" she asked again, unmoved by any of my narration.

"Yes, I do."

"May I see it?"

"Yes." I pulled it out of my shirt pocket. Mother was disinterested in the entire conversation. She, for the second time, spoke up.

Episodes in a Life

"It's time to go, Kit. I need to get home." The lady behind the counter studied the card, slipped it back into the sleeve on the inside back cover of the book, and pulled it out again.

"This card belongs with this book," she said. "If I check this book out to you, young man, will the card come back with it?"

My response was, "What happens to the library cards if they are lost?"

"Nothing. We do not utilize those cards any longer. We have a new system in our library now. The cards used to be critical. Now they are just relics." She spoke without an iota of feeling. What she said seemed to have no relationship at all with the prior ten minutes or ten sentences.

I spoke up again. "Just to be certain I understand the new Oberlin College library system, if I check this book out and if it comes back and the library card is missing, Mother will not be fined and the library will not have any trouble reshelving the book—is that correct?"

She paused and then replied in a flat voice. "Yes, things will be in order. I, however, will have a pretty good idea of where the card has gone. So will your mother, I believe."

Mother re-entered the conversation. "Yes, I know where the card was and probably if it does not come back with the book, my son will have kept it. I certainly will *not* have taken it. I have no need for any more recollections of J. T. Salter." Mother turned and walked away two steps to accelerate our departure.

I looked at the dry eyes of the desk lady and looked at the book and looked at Mother. The entire event had given a wholly new meaning to the term "library service." The whole event made no sense. I handed the red covered book to the library lady, opened it so that she could see that the card was still in its artifactual sleeve and concluded, "Thank you so much for all of your help. Thank you both. I do not need the book anymore." There may have been just a quiver of sarcasm in my voice.

Mother and I left the library. I tried one sentence on her as we were walking across Tappan Square. "Mother, why did you tell that lady where the card was? Why?"

There was not even a second of pause. "Because she asked. She wanted to know where it had gone. I knew where it was." She walked ahead saying, "We need to go to the Post Office, I have to buy some stamps."

◆

JURGEN ROETTER, (1924-2003) Husband of my sister, Jean. My sisters Pat and Jean married two brothers of the Roetter family that came to Madison in the late 1930s. Diete, already introduced, married my middle sister, Pat. Diete's younger brother, Jurgen, married my sister, Jean. Jurgen had earned a doctorate in Russian Literature, had fought in the Battle of the Bulge for American forces in WWII, and was a brilliant and serious man. All our family knew that when you visited Jean and Jurgen in their long-time home in Amherst, Massachusetts, two things always happened. One: you got a beautiful meal, and for the first night of the visit, were freed from kitchen cleanup. Two: you became involved in a serious and always interesting post meal conversation led by Jurgen and his amazing knowledge of American politics and current events. The combo was delightful and demanding. I offer up the next episode from my early encounters with the two of them. They were great moviegoers and the three of us (they would often pay my admission as a kid) all had a sweet tooth for a specific candy, Jujyfruits.

Jurgen's Anatomy Lesson

Once when I was about ten or eleven years old, I was visiting Jean and Jurgen at their Madison apartment on Brierley Street. I had just bought them a bulk pack of 24 small (1950s movie-sized) boxes of Jujyfruits. All of us loved those nickel boxes that came from early candy counters at the Majestic Theater just off the square in Madison. We would sometimes go as a trio and my gift was meant to thank them for covering my ticket costs for so many shows. As we were waiting to go out to the Majestic, I think I became invisible by the side of the room. Somehow the conversation between the two of them got to anatomy. Jean had said something about "the curse" as a real bother for women—something that men had not only no knowledge of, but even less understanding of.

Jurgen, never a man to get caught in the short end of a conversation responded.

"Well...you ought to live your life with a penis and a bag of balls hanging down between your legs. Women have *no* idea how awkward that is sometimes. And," he continued, "Men have to deal with it day and night, not just monthly."

I still remember my eyes getting *so* big as I heard these two references to a topic I had *never* heard anyone in the family talking about. As Jurgen spoke his mind, I remembered that every now and then I would get an erection in school and my greatest fear was that at just such a moment, the teacher would call on me to go to the board and write something out. *But*, to hear Jurgen actually reference the man's privates was a whole new conversational theme. We never again approached that topic as a trio, but I keenly recall that startling moment.

◆

This other Jurgen episode is more reflective of the manner that Jurgen used in his interaction with family and the general public.

Jurgen's New Shoes

I was visiting Amherst one time in about 1975, and sister Jean's husband Jurgen and I had a few minutes to walk together in the nearby town of Northampton, Massachusetts. We were chatting as we walked by a shoe store.

"Wait a minute, Kit. I need to buy a pair of shoes." He walked into the shoe store and sat down in one of the many open seats. A lady came up and Jurgen said, "I would like a new pair of shoes just like these."

"We have a number of styles in Florsheims, sir."

"I do not want to see other styles. I want a pair just like these. I wear size ten."

"Fine." She left and went to the back of the store. When she returned she had two shoe boxes. The first box she opened was of a shoe that was similar to Jurgen's shoe, but with a little more flare.

"Don't you have the Florsheims that I am wearing?" Jurgen asked in a steady voice.

She nodded and quickly closed the first box. She opened the second box. This pair was exactly like the shoes on Jurgen's feet.

Jurgen tried one on. It seemed to fit. "Fine. This is fine. I will take this pair, please."

"Do you want to at least try the more stylish new one, sir?"

"Have I asked about new styles?" Jurgen queried.

"No." A very short pause and then, "I'll ring these right up."

Episodes in a Life

"How much are they?" Jurgen asked, reaching for his wallet.

"Fifty-five dollars." she replied. (Don't forget that this was more than forty years ago!) Jurgen stopped reaching for his wallet. He stared at her in some surprise.

"They are our very best shoe, sir…but you must know that from earlier purchases." Jurgen did not say anything but did extract his billfold from his rear pocket. She walked with the box of shoes to the counter, put the box in a bag, and made out a bill for the shoes. Jurgen walked over and paid her in cash.

She thanked him. He thanked her and took the bag with the box of shoes. When we got out to the sidewalk, Jurgen said with a combination of resignation and firmness, "*Never* buy clothes because they are cheap. *Only* buy clothes because you need them, and they are exactly what you want. You will end up never wearing clothes you got because they were on sale. They will stay in your closet for years and then you will give them away." We continued our walk and met Jean for lunch.

◆

This additional Jurgen experience needs to be inked in as well: Jurgen and Jean were great country road walkers. When one visited the Roetters in Amherst, you had a good chance of a two-hour bike ride, or a walk perhaps just as long. The walk was always preceded with a necessary car drive to the beginning of one of the many walking trails that the two of them used with healthy frequency.

FRITZIE'S MANDATE

On the particular drive to a walking point that I am thinking of, they had their small dog named Fritzie with them. I do not recall the breed, but I do keenly remember it had a piercing bark. It would dance around the back seat, where the visitors sat, and go particularly crazy when the car passed a home that had a dog in the front yard. The outside dog was sometimes tethered, sometimes free ranging. The pattern was simple. Jean's dog in the car saw the other dog—almost always much larger—outside the car and Fritzie went wild with aggressive yapping, barking, and slathering on any nearby person.

This particular day, Jurgen, driving, pulled over nearly in front of the larger barking dog. He turned to me and said, "Kit, would you open the car door, please." I looked at Jurgen, looked at Jean, and looked at the yapping dog dancing on my groin.

"You want me to open the car door so that either Fritzie can leap out and get eaten or the big dog can leap in and take Fritzie and my arm off?"

"Part of that is correct. I am so damn sick of Fritzie barking wildly when we pass dogs outside the car that I want to stop and give Fritzie a chance to see what she is threatening with that stupid noise."

Jean broke in. "Do not touch that door, Kit. Do not even think of opening the car door with that wild dog now even more eager to meet and eat my little Fritzie."

"Then do something to shut her up if you feel you need to bring her on these drives to our walking trails," said Jurgen with clarity and a sense of resolution on his face.

"Right—Fritzie does not need to come on these trips. I will tie her up in the back yard and she can drive the neighbors crazy while we are out exploring the beauty of quiet nature."

"The only neighbor that will complain about Fritzie's noise is Emily Dickinson and she's not home right now."

"There are many other neighbors who *are* home now."

"What do you say, Kit? You have the deciding vote."

"No open door. No Fritzie on the approaches to your tranquil trail walks. Plan to keep adorable and noisy Fritzie in the basement where I sleep when I visit. I can perhaps teach her to be more like Emily."

Jurgen turned the engine on and we drove the additional mile or two to the walking trail. Fritzie never did learn how close she had been to mortal combat en route to a tranquil morning in the countryside.

◆

KATE SALTER (1922-2009). Kate was the eldest of my three sisters. She had the most dramatic life of all. She was a photographer and writer for *Life Magazine* in the 1940s. She followed her graduation from Mills College with two years in the Pentagon as a researcher in the Office of War Information. This was followed by two years spent working at the Rhein-Main Air Force Base near Frankfurt in Germany. She covered the dynamics of post WWII Army activities. At the end of that tour, Kate booked a solo six-week trip on a Danish freighter from Rotterdam to Manila, where she was going to meet Dockie. He was a Visiting Fulbright Scholar at the University of the Philippines. Kate spent half a year there teaching English and then returned to the states.

It was in that period (1951) that she met Sayed Ahmed Mahmood. At about this same time, *Life Magazine* offered her another position (1952) that caused her to move to New York City. She, however, had that full time work deferred as Sayed came to Manhattan and proposed to her, asking her to return with him to Pakistan. She did, and she and Sayed raised a family of five children—two from his former marriage and three born to them in Rawalpindi. Sadly, on Christmas Eve, 1964, Sayed was killed in a dreadful car accident while on his way home for some holidays.

Kate and her family—with ages ranging from five to twenty-four—all moved to the United States. This first episode on Kate comes from her home scene in Hamden, Connecticut where she settled as a professional realtor.

KATE AND THE KEY ALARM

In 1975, Sister Kate had a home in Hamden, Connecticut that she adored. She named it Halcyon and she lived in that house as though it was exactly what its name defined. My favorite recollection of that place is her 'Security System.' At the front door (the main door to the home, and there was a small porch buffering this door from outside weather), she had a bunch of flowerpots and clutter. Under one of the terra cotta saucers, she had a key sticking out. Maybe half an inch of it was visible, or possibly a little more. If you lifted the plant carefully and moved the plant, you could pick up a loose, flattened key ring. There were approximately fifty keys of different shapes and sizes on this ring.

Kate's theory was that when a robber came to case her place, he would spot the partially hidden key. He would pull the ring out from under the planter and begin to try to figure out which key went to the front door. None of them did. Kate's philosophy was that if he went from key to key to key, trying each one, she would be able to hear this process and call the police. If she was not there, this process of exploration would take enough time that she might see him from afar and call the police. In either case, there was no key to any door in her house on that ring, just a set of old keys from houses of the past. She never was robbed and although she never had to call police because of hearing the key ring search, she slept better knowing that she had this security system in operation.

The MS *Mongolia*

As a bold expression of delight in leaving her work in Germany in late 1949, Kate booked passage on the Danish freighter, MS *Mongolia* for a six and a half week voyage from Rotterdam to Manila. She hoped to teach English as a second language there.

On the journey to Manila, Kate spent many creative hours writing in a trip journal in letter form on onionskin that she mailed to her family and closest friends. In that eye-opening series of port stops, short day trips, and countless hours in the sun and leisure of time on the Mongolia, sister Kate portrayed a highly varied handful of travelers on the Danish freighter. Her pages of daily observation became a fascinating memoir. In 2017 this amazing trip became published as *Dream Trip to the Orient*.

In the Afterword to that liberating book, Kate's daughter Kashya wrote these lovely paragraphs on her mother's life.

"Our family's initial response to observing the disease [Alzheimer's] slowly erase her memory was to read aloud from the lovely onionskin letters she had saved, carefully recounting each and every event of her MS *Mongolia* voyage. She always had a broad smile on her face, as each recollection seemed to ignite an ember of fading memory.

In her final years it became evident that [Kate] had an uncanny ability to live in the present. A light gust of wind on her face, the dawn of a new day, a stroll along the lake, and the comfort of her family were what she coveted most. She did not simply dream her dreams, she boldly lived them. This remarkable talent for accepting what 'is' with such grace and dignity allowed her to live to the venerable age of eighty-seven." —Kashya Mahmood Hildebrand.

◆

JEAN SALTER. (1924-2017) My sister, Jean, the youngest of the three daughters was different from the other two girls in so many ways. She married Jurgen Roetter, her first major love. They made a household and had three daughters and settled into a very stable life. What those sentences hide is that husband Jurgen, having just spent years completing a very demanding undergraduate degree and doctoral program found the five of them 'trapped' at the University of Cincinnati, trying to live on his teaching salary of $6000 a year. I know some of this anguish because I had hitchhiked down to Cincy in 1956 or 1957 on my way south and I was there when the two parents were deep in the "what ifs" surrounding the potential of a major career change.

Jurgen and Jean's Career Change

Jurgen—from the first days of his education—had always been a thorough and demanding student of the issues he was studying or, later, teaching. At the University of Cincinnati (his first major teaching position) he found himself working fifty to sixty hours a week. He felt that he would not complain about such long weeks if he saw that there was some financial reward for the intensity of his academic dedication.

I do not quite know how to give real value to $6000 a year for a family of five in 1957 (it would be equivalent to about $54,000 today), but I do know that the whole framework of early academic employment in a life of university teaching makes you realize that you've got to accept the stress and the challenges of student indifference, academic custom, and endless interaction with issues and people that may not be the ones you want to spend your life with. To be bilingual in German and English and have strong skills in Russian, and a doctorate in Russian History would tend to lead a person to be looking for a school better known, and better salaried, that his first employer.

At the point I arrived in Cincinnati at their home that December, I had just completed three semesters at a small liberal arts college in the northern part of the state. Listening to a man I very much respected talk about walking away from the college or university life for which he had been training himself for years seemed to be a real shocker to me. I had lived on so few dollars for so long the concept of a real wage in any setting was still unknown by me. I'd done part-time work in an early convenience store in Madison in my junior high school years.

The only real checks I had ever seen were summer construction jobs in Wisconsin, but they only lasted eight or nine weeks, and most of that money had been put into Mother's household and the first car I'd ever owned. Let me shape this next episode into the sort of conversations I expect had occurred prior to my arrival, and also some during my visit.

In talking with a good and longtime friend that fall, Jurgen had been asked recently about leaving academics completely, undertaking some financial training, and becoming "Dr. Jack Roetter, Investment Broker." The Roetters had had hardly any money since their flight from Nazi Germany fifteen years earlier. Jurgens' college and graduate work had kept his family stone broke. The sudden idea of Jurgen working in a business that might reward his skills and dedication to his profession (whichever one it was) with a larger financial compensation than teaching was a tantalizing consideration.

Jurgen and Jean were deeply serious about the potential of a career change. A car was critical in this equation, too. The same friend who asked Jurgen his thoughts about being a finance broker of some sort told him outright he would have to get a very different car. The friend said, "Jack, you cannot expect a person to give you their money to invest if they see you're driving a ten-year-old Dodge or something like that. You have to learn to show your potential customers and clients that you have at least been successful enough to buy a nice car for you and your family."

"But how can I possibly buy a new or even a newer car? I can barely meet insurance and maintenance costs on this old junker we now own!"

"I understand that, Jack. I would not have even suggested this major a change in your life if I did not have a strong sense that you could do very, very well in stocks and financial

Episodes in a Life

management if you made that your full focus in professional development."

"That's very nice, but I cannot use that flattering assessment of my potential future…" Jurgen was interrupted by his friend.

"Of course. I know all of that. And you do not have the money to move, to maybe even look at a house you might want to buy, and deal with all of the hidden costs that loom just out of sight as you think of changing careers"—he put his hand up like a policeman saying "Stop!" and went on. "I am willing to finance a good part of this transition—including a new or much newer car—as soon as I hear you talk to me about the likelihood of you walking away from the academic setting that you've been working toward day and night for a decade. Are you willing to talk about that? About considering the one-way road you'd be on if you left the university, a school that I'm sure is expecting you to stay for the tenure battle and beyond?"

Jurgen was silent for a bit. Jurgen always thought before he gave his opinion. In that pause, the man asked Jean, "How would you feel about Jack leaving academics and going into brokerage, Jean?"

"Well, anyone growing up in the Salter family knows a great deal more about the academic life than the life of a stockbroker. The money management skills we learned in our family were—shall I say, modest?" She paused just a second but then hurried on. "You and I both know Jurgen is a man of great intensity and integrity. I would think that those two traits would mean a great deal in the world of finance. I would say that if Jurgen declares true interest in this new career then I would support him wholeheartedly, as would the girls."

Jurgen looked at Jean and the friend with a sense of relief on his face. He gave a particularly warm smile to Jean and then turned to the friend with the questions and said "This is a question of lifetime significance. You raise it over coffee as though it were just floating in your mind—but its implications are absolutely monumental to me, my family, our whole being and future being."

"And? How do read the signs in the life that you have been living for the past year compared with the time and energy you have invested into that life for the past years? How does that equation seem to you as a life mode for the next forty years?"

"Well, let's talk. Let's open all the doors of the future and show me, show us, what might be achievable for Dr. Jack Roetter in the life of financial management. Educate me. I'm fully ready to listen to all that you have to say."

At the end of that first academic year, the Jack Roetters moved north and east and began life anew. It is a change that sister Jean often described to her children and friends as "the best move they had ever made—both in terms of Jurgen's career, and in terms of a New England base for raising the three daughters and watching Jurgen's (Jack's) career grow to solid success.

Patricia   Jean   Kate   Joel

CHAPTER TWO

THE BUILDING OF A NEW FAMILY

LINDA LOUISE GRAEF (1939-2019) and I met at Oberlin College in the fall of 1957. I had been promoted from pot washer to head waiter at Oberlin's largest dorm the prior semester. I was a sophomore and Linda came in to the Dascomb waitress board job as a freshman. It was the beginning of a new school year and I had returned from a good summer of construction work and a funky two-week raft trip on the Wisconsin and Mississippi Rivers. I was looking forward to my second year at this demanding but stimulating liberal arts school.

A NEW LOOK

The Dascomb dormitory scene where I had my kitchen board job was the largest girls' dorm on campus. We had thirty tables of services for ten in our dining hall, set at lunch and dinner for the three hundred women and men from the larger campus. We had a wait-crew of fifteen coeds; each waited two tables. Linda Graef was new to this line of work and had a good spirit. Like all of us with board jobs, she knew that the kitchen waitress job was a vital part of being able to stay in school with its provision of both part time income and meals.

On the third day of the new fall semester, suddenly every waitress's outfit had a different look to it that evening meal. Their customary blue and white outfit had buttons going up the front and a smooth back with a tie apron for the waist. That night, each waitress had a smooth cotton garment, high in the neck, with the small aprons tied just below the breast line of these college coeds. This surprising reversal gave the outfit a saucy look. I studied the crew, some new, most veterans of my first semester as head waiting the prior spring. Who was it, I wondered, who had turned things around—literally—in my dining room? Who was the change agent? Then watching the girls move through the kitchen in delight at student reaction to their new look, I determined Linda Graef had probably been the innovator who had talked the girls into showing a little sportiness in their drab college dining room outfits. No new uniforms had been called for. No new aprons belts had been purchased. Nothing indecent in the new look—but the impact of the novelty in appearance was very powerful.

In any case, I talked with this Linda Graef from Fort Wayne, and it became clear to me that she was going to be a significant new role player in my Head Waiter world. Ironically, at that semester opening time, I had the immediate task of selecting a new Head Waitress to keep the crew fully represented in our dining hall management policies. It took me about five minutes to realize that having the newbie Linda play that role might be frustrating to some of the senior waitresses, but the fact that Linda had so quickly and effectively talked the girls into an 'about face' in their uniforms sealed the deal in my mind. Linda was made Head Waitress and she and I worked together in kitchen events and daily serving of more than seven hundred meals (including extra catering events) for three years. That cooperation and sense of sharing the college school world *and* the café, dining hall, and food service worlds led to our romance and marriage in June of 1960.

We then each received an Oberlin Shansi Fellowship to spend two years teaching English in a foreign university. We were initially assigned to a pair of schools in India that would have required us being Dorm Father and Mother in two different school settings. Still in our first year of marriage, we rejected the India option. We kept the Fellowships but were given positions at Tunghai University in Taiwan, the Republic of China. We did two years and were asked to stay a third year so 1961-1964 took us to the edge of the Chinese Mainland. We lived in a campus duplex and returned to Oberlin in 1964 for Linda to finish her undergraduate degree in mathematics and philosophy. I took a few classes, worked as a food service employee managing the snack bar in Wilder Hall, and—ultimately—going to Yale University to study more Chinese.

Here is a second episode occurring in our first year of marriage living in an apartment in Oberlin.

TANDEM FOOLS

In Oberlin in 1961 one spring night in April, Linda and I and some friends were talking in our apartment about what happens when you dare to do a foolish—not a bad foolish, but a silly—thing. This episode is about how such a whimsy happened in one experiment. I had proposed that some silly adventures could work out, even though early odds were very much against it working. I suggested that in order to test my optimism, I would write a letter to a bicycle company in Ohio and ask for a free bike in order to test my theory. In a bike shop I had seen an ad for a Huffy Tandem bicycle. It was a new product from Huffy Manufacturing in Dayton, Ohio.

The small group's response in our apartment was, logically, "Oh yeah, someone's going to send you a free bike!"

"Sure," I replied with a confidence that I did not feel, but I thought I would pretend I did in the spirit of that evening's conversation. So, that night I typed a letter to Huffy and I offered to do a trial run of their new tandem. I said that my wife and I would ride the Huffy tandem from Oberlin, Ohio to New Haven, Connecticut because we were going to study Chinese at Yale that summer. In my letter I said that we would write a report on the good and the bad aspects of their new product. Then Linda and I walked down to the Oberlin post office (and this was years before Mother had blazed a trough in the concrete sidewalks with such a route!) and mailed the foolish letter.

About ten days later I received a business letterhead envelope from Huffy Manufacturing. I stared at this formal business letter and opened it with considerable surprise. To even get a reply seemed unlikely when I rethought the proposed stunt that had initiated my letter to them.

The essence of the letter was, "We like your idea. How much would you charge?" I was dumbfounded! *"How much would I charge?"* Wow! Linda and I talked a minute and then I wrote to them saying that we would do it for eight cents a mile, plus expenses for getting the bike to us, and for any tandem repairs that we had to cover while on the trip. They would also have to collect the bike from New Haven at the end of the trip. I grinned all the way to the Post Office. In the last week of the 1961 spring term, a vice-president from Huffy drove up to our apartment in Oberlin with a small trailer attached to his big sedan. After we had greeted each other, he pulled out the partially assembled tandem bike, did the final assembly himself, and presented us with a shiny new Huffy tandem bike and a card with phone numbers and addresses.

We shook hands and both us smiled as though we were getting away with something really unusual. We ultimately logged 815 miles on the bike en route to New Haven and Huffy paid us about sixty-five dollars plus a little expense money. They took it back to Dayton and broke it down to assess the sort of wear it had experienced. To top off the fantasy of this whimsy, *Life Magazine* had seen a photo in a *Christian Science Monitor* human-interest story toward the end of our ten-day tandem trip.

The final craziness from the foolish offer to field test their new Huffman Manufacturing tandem came with Huffman sending the bicycle to Taiwan for us.

Life assigned a photographer to go to Taiwan to take photos of this young American couple teaching in Taiwan—and riding a tandem about the island. Huffy never got the bike back, but I did send them an eighteen-page report. The *Life* article ended up on the cutting room floor.

◆

Our first child, Hayden, was born in the year that I was doing my master's at Berkeley. This episode (related to me by Linda for I was not present at this work site, or mother-to-be site.)

Truimph at the Karmann Ghia Exit

When Linda was pregnant with Hayden in 1966, we had an old Volkswagen Karmann Ghia convertible. One day she was on her way to a doctor visit. She must have been in her seventh month or so. She found a parking place not far from the doctor's office and pulled into it. Across the street was a stone wall with about a dozen construction workers sitting on it, eating out of their lunchboxes, and commenting on the passing scene. As she was still behind the wheel getting her stuff organized, the guys began to shower her with comments about "Hey, why not have your lunch with us?" or "If you want to park that toy car in my driveway, I'd show you where I could put it," or "Come on over and we'll show you the rooms we're building."

Linda gave them a big smile and returned a little of the banter. Then, before, she opened the door of the Ghia, she called out "Do I know any of you?"

The faces grinned and a few said, "Oh, yeah, lady. Yes, indeed!" With that she opened the door and stood full up. The clarity of her pregnant condition was evident for all to see. She stood tall and asked one more time, "Which one of you do I know?" Silence.

She smiled and gave them a small wave, crossed in front of the Ghia to the sidewalk and walked on to the doctor's office a block away.

Linda and I stayed together long enough to bring our daughter, Heidi, into our world and until the mid-1970s when we decided that marriage was no longer fun for the two of us. Our mutual goal was to make life for Hayden and Heidi as comfortable and secure as possible.

I taught at UCLA from 1968 to 1988. In the middle of those two decades, I became involved in an educational innovation that seems so obvious in retrospect, but that seemed original at the time of its inception.

◆

CATHY LYNN RIGGS SALTER (b. 1945—). Cathy has been the most important and loving force in my adult life. From the moment I met her, I was taken.

"AND I SUPPOSE YOU'RE DIVORCED AND HAVE TWO CHILDREN."

In the 1977 NUVUES Institute (New Understanding of the Value of Urban Environmental Studies), we had a one-day field trip that David Alpaugh and my graduate student Bill Lloyd (the professor who shared the lecturing duties with me) and I had organized. As the bus was rolling down Westwood Blvd toward downtown Los Angeles, I suddenly realized that I had forgotten to take my morning insulin shot. I leaned over to the driver and told him we were going to do a short stop at Westwood Park, a four-acre plot behind the massive Federal Post Office building in the heart of Westwood Village.

As the driver did some reluctant route changing, I told the forty-five students and schoolteachers of the unscheduled stop under the guise that they could think about environmental modification and the amazing designation of very expensive real estate for public park space. My intention was to let them all out to ponder this geographical consideration while I secretly ran over to the apartment building at the south edge of the park where I lived. This would give me a moment to rush in, take my shot, and then return to bring the group together for ten minutes of discussion on these park issues.

As the bus was moving toward a spot where it could park and wait for this unexpected detour folks began to stand up. I was at the head of this line, eager to remedy my missed dose of insulin. Just behind me were some of the teachers (who always sat near the front of the bus). As the bus parked, I heard some comments about divorce and single parents. I turned to the teacher immediately behind me in line and said to her—with no agenda in my mind at all, "And I suppose you are just divorced and have two children in grade school. Right?"

The shy woman blushed a little and said, eyeball to eyeball, "Why, no. I've never been married."

The bus door opened, and we all flowed out into the small park. That shy woman was, in fact, a teacher from Audubon Junior High School named Cathy Riggs. As I looked back at the column as I stepped off the bus, ready to give them one last pitch before I raced for my insulin, I saw the teacher behind Cathy give her a big elbow to the ribs and a large smile, saying, "Ohhhhh...I've never been married!"

The trip was underway again within twenty-five minutes. Cathy and I began courtship about five weeks later after the end of the 1977 NUVUES Institute.

◆

SOMEONE LIKE THIS

In the summer of 1977, I was selected to be part of the first-ever American delegation of geographers to be invited to the People's Republic of China. I had to leave one week before the end of that program. In the last week before I left, I met and talked with—for the first time—a teacher from Audubon JHS named Cathy Riggs. She had been the ace NUVUES teacher, but she was shy and there was a lot of class group activity and not much time for any leisurely conversations. A few days before I flew to Canton, China, Cathy showed up at my office, bringing me a metal file box. She was blushing and told me that this was a Care Package so that I wouldn't forget the Institute teachers and students while traveling on the Mainland. Inside that file box were 45-rpm records, country western songs mostly, a lovely note about taking care of myself and some other assorted things. It was a special and unexpected event.

When I got back from China, there was a world of mail stacked up in my UCLA office. As I went through this stuff talking with David Alpaugh—the NUVUES Institute co-organizer—I came upon a post card with small, delicate handwriting. It was a card of Lake Havasu Falls in the Grand Canyon. It was a beautiful teal green and the images in the prose message were more wonderful than the photo images. The writer talked about the stones, the rush of water, experiencing crisp even cold air in the Canyon mornings, and the fact that this card was being sent on the nation's last Mule Mail route. As I read and loved this note I lamented to David, "David...why don't I *know* somebody like this? Why don't I know anyone who writes and sees the natural world like this?"

David replied coolly. "You do, stupid. She was in your class. That card is from Cathy Riggs!" We began a lovely courtship within days.

Oh, what a good decision!

First Dates

The series of events that began an emergence from a life without romance toward a genuine love affair for life began soon after the conclusion of the NUVUES Institute. A geography professor at Bakersfield Community asked if I would bring up a couple of faculty and one teacher from NUVUES. He proposed a day-and-a-half miniature Institute for local teachers in the southern end of the Central Valley. I still recall his big selling point (there was no money involved) was, "Kit, I promise to limit the house to no more than a hundred teachers! Really. We'll put a lid on it!" I talked with David about which teacher I ought to call. "Which teacher? Duh! Call the one who wrote you that neat postcard you liked so much from Lake Havasu." I responded by calling Cathy Riggs and asking if she had time to do a two-day trip and workshop to Bakersfield. I explained that the professor that was inviting us promised me that we would have no more than a hundred teachers in attendance.

When I told her the dates, Cathy checked her calendar and said that she would be glad to participate. We worked out details and, in a week, I picked her up. That gave us a group of one teacher, the two people who had helped organize and do some teaching in the Institute and me. We all fitted in my Volkswagen van (license plate NU VUES) and headed north toward Bakersfield. We had a box of handouts and we stopped and got a bunch of doughnuts. By then I had done enough workshops to know that a little sugar was vital to fuel these volunteer teacher workshops.

As we pulled into the Bakersfield Community College campus where Professor Wake had instructed us to park, we were in good spirits and ready to give an energetic two- to three-hour Friday evening opener to the two-day event. We walked into a nice sized auditorium carrying paper supplies and many doughnuts. One of us remarked that we hoped we had enough materials for the house we'd face.

We did. In the whole hall we saw the organizing professor and—count 'em—eight teachers! Before we could even gasp, Professor Wake walked up the steps toward us saying, "I'm sorry—so sorry—it seems that someone forgot to do any advertising for this environmental education workshop. This is our full house, at least as of now." I looked around and laughed, saying, "Well, at least the ratio is good. Eight students. Four presenters! And doughnuts and handouts in abundance!"

As teachers so often do, we read the scene and made the best of it. We gave a solid hundred minutes and then ended for that evening, promising to have the second day finish up by two. When you're anticipating dozens and dozens of attendees and are faced with fewer than a dozen, everything goes faster, or is it slower?

As the four of us walked back to *NU VUES*, we laughed and thought that doughnuts would be our dessert and our breakfast and treats for all who showed up the next morning. We decided that we needed to find a place to reorganize our heads, having driven the hundred miles from Los Angeles anticipating a demanding and rewarding evening for this gig. I had noticed a nice-looking place named Hart Park along the highway as we had approached Bakersfield. I found it and there was a high-water tank (not on legs, but a great round cylinder atop a small hill) that had an open chain link gate at the base of the hill. I nudged *NU VUES* through the opening, drove up the small rise, backed the van close to the base of the ten-foot-high water tank, and put on some nice Bach. We took out a bottle of wine we had brought along for contingencies and all sat on the grass with our backs against the cool metal of the water tower.

In the dark distance we could hear the Kern River below us. In the closeness to the van we could hear the Bach. The soft light of the cool star-filled sky was all around us. We chatted two hours about the stupidity of excessive anticipation for something like this. Since we at had at least our travel costs guaranteed, we mostly chuckled at our hubris at expecting a full house ("I promise you no more than 100 teachers, Kit!") for a two-day geography education workshop. It was good conversation and there was no bitterness except for the money we had spent on way more doughnuts than any of us could even imagine.

About midnight we felt that it was time to bunk so as to make it to the nine o'clock opening of day two in good time. I pointed out that the van was a pop top, giving a full bunk up top and a full bunk down below. I offered this idea. "David and I could sleep up top and you ladies can have the bottom bunk."

David responded, "That's a nice plan, Kit. But, as you've known for two years, Lucy and I are married, and we'd actually like to sleep in the same bunk."

Cathy looked at the three of us, smiling, and said, "Hey, I was in the Peace Corps for three years and we always had curious bunking situations when we traveled as a group. Kit and I both have sleeping bags so being up top together will not embarrass any of us!"

And that was how it worked out. We went to sleep hearing

the flow of the river, still pondering our expectations as we drove north and entered the auditorium. The lessons had played out acceptably and the four of us enjoyed a nice evening of conversation and getting to know each other a little better. In the morning we did the Saturday session and drove back to Los Angeles, still loaded with paper goods, but many fewer doughnuts.

After that weekend, Cathy (often called Chloe in this book) and I had begun to spend more time together and into the following spring. By that time, I had purchased a small Cottage (only about 800 square feet) in Beverly Glen Canyon. The kids were still living with Linda, but were increasingly part of the cottage scene on Beverly Glen Boulevard. This two-mile long, two-lane Los Angeles Street wound uphill from Sunset Boulevard in west LA to Mulholland Drive, and then continued down into the San Fernando Valley. My spring 1978 question about her moving into the cottage with me led to the next plateau of our friendship.

COTTAGE LIVING

When Chloe and I had been courting almost ten months and I asked her if she would move into my small cottage, the kids were still living with Linda at a place we called The Moon in Beverly Glen. I had been able to scrape up enough funds from our division of community property in our divorce settlement to buy the tiny cottage. Blessedly, it had two levels and two bathrooms.

In 1978 when I asked Cathy about joining forces with me (and the frequent presence of ten-year-old Hayden and eight-year-old Heidi, she pondered a minute and then said, "You and the kids are very, very close. I'm not sure that I can find a place in that trio." But after a tiny pause, she then added, "What about this—let's have the four of us take a trip in your VW van. If we can operate effectively and pleasantly in such tight confines, then I'm willing to give The Cottage a try."

NU VUES with its pop-top was a great road van. The four of us had taken some overnight trips as a quartet and they had worked out pretty well—but Chloe was talking about a more ambitious junket. So I planned a 6000 mile, six-week trip from L.A. to Boston and back in *NU VUES*. After two initial days of getting our routines figured out and meshed, the quartet eased into a grand summer of exploration, road songs, camping out, river swimming, and ultimately, family discussions that moved across all diagonals of our four travelers. At the conclusion of the odyssey, Cathy said that she would love to move in with us and The Cottage became our home for a decade—longer than anywhere I had ever lived in my entire life.

In this exploration of travel together over miles and time, we all learned alot about each other and about the demands of travel. When we began to head west toward Los Angeles, we got into quilt country in Pennsylvania. This led to antique store stops, something we had not dabbled in during on our first 3000 miles of eastward travel. However, as the van began to feel the power of the western states talking to it—and we felt the associated sense of 'homemaking' that was now in the near future of the four of us—we stopped more often 'to take a look around at this stuff.'

Hayden and Heidi soon realized that there was not much in those shops that caught their attention. But the real impact of this change in our travel pattern led to this edict from the back of the van as Chloe and I climbed in after an antiquing stop.

Hayden spoke up from the back. "Hey, you guys. Heidi and I have been thinking about the way this trip is shaping up.

We see that you're thinking about things for The Cottage that makes us very nervous."

There was a pause to let the two adults up front ponder that assessment coming from the young squad in the back of the van. Hayden continued. "Here's the deal. We're glad we're going to be living in The Cottage all together. We know that means more paraphernalia or whatever. But Heidi and I are in limited space back here and the recent arrival of a chair and picnic basket that has nothing to do with our trip now makes us real nervous."

Hayden did not pause long enough for us to begin a response. "So, this is our deal. You two can get whatever you want in the junk shops...anything you want for The Cottage. But whatever you buy stays up front with you two. Nothing more comes back here in our bedroom and kitchen and living space for the next 3000 miles. Okay?"

I'd been playing with images in my mind as the rules of acquisition and travel were being outlined. My quick reaction was, "Oh, so that means if we want to collect, for example, stamps, that would be okay?"

"Yeah... as long as you kept them up front," was the quick reply.

Cathy said, "Or, quilts? Could we collect quilts, too?"

"Quilts would be a lot more welcome than chairs and baskets. We might even agree to having one or two quilts kept in the back with us—right, Heidi?"

"Yeah, but they'd have to be cozy ones—not those crazy wool ones that scratch on both sides. Cozy ones would be okay in small numbers."

"And what else?" Cathy asked.

It was clear that the kids had been thinking about this a lot. Hayden and Heidi rattled off the following items in quick order. "Harmonicas, but not to be played. Flags, but only folded and then only one or two. One or two books, but not massive dictionaries like Dad gets at the Goodwill. Sets of marbles. Maybe a few pairs of socks, but not underwear. No toothbrushes. No tee shirts—we have our cubbies already filled with tees. Pens, pencils, small school supplies, but not old geography textbooks from a hundred years ago."

By this time, Cathy and I were looking back over the front seats and the kids were leaning against the back van window, looking like two merchants who had just negotiated a great deal for their business. The van was silent, although the motor had been running in place for nearly ten minutes.

I looked at Cathy and we both grinned and nodded. She focused on the kids and asked "Okay...but what shall we do with the wicker chair we got yesterday?"

"Why not try to sell it at the next stop?" suggested Hayden. "We've seen a lot of people bringing in junk in their cars when they come to these places."

"Do you two want to set up a 'Furniture Sale' at our next stop? Do you want to sit outside by or in the chair and offer to sell it to people who come in?"

"What would we have to get for it?"

"Cash money...at least thirty dollars."

"How much of that would we get to keep?"

"We'd do an even split. But you need to get at least thirty dollars. If you can get more, we get fifteen and you two get the rest. Whaddya say?"

In fact, the chair came home with us. The front of the van became full of quilts—no stamp collections and no harmonicas—and acquisitions became less a part of the trip as we headed into the Midwest and left the images of quilts to states east. The quilts became friends for all of us as we got into the more open spaces of the Great Plains and west. We would cruise into the nighttime dark with the kids wrapped up in all sorts of Amish and Mennonite quilts with the van radio playing an occasional Mystery Theatre if we were lucky.

◆

Cathy's family lived in San Antonio. Her father was in the Air Force and had retired there in 1974, after completing his career as the head of the Strategic Air Command in Offutt Air Force Base in Nebraska that year They lived in a small garden town house that had one guest room. Since Cathy and I were not married, but were living together in LA, there was an issue about where we would sleep when we came to visit. The awkwardness of having their unmarried daughter sleeping with a man still not divorced from his first wife was partially resolved by Florence, Cathy's maternal grandmother. In this episode, it became clear that it was time for some changes in our relationship.

ONLY THE BEST OF INTENTIONS

When Chloe and I were courting, I had just come out of an eighteen-year marriage to Linda and initially the idea of remarriage was not attractive to me. I knew keenly that I wanted to marry Chloe, but because our living together with the kids was working out very comfortably, I did not put a second marriage high on the conversational agenda. She was teaching full time at Audubon Junior High School, was Department Chair, and deeply involved in a world of outreach activities as part of both her teaching life and my academic

Episodes in a Life

life at UCLA. In the context of Los Angeles, our current living arrangement seemed to be working out fine.

However, we visited Chloe's parents, sisters, and grandmother in San Antonio periodically and the situation that occurred was in a 1982 visit.

We were billeted at Cathy's grandmother's lovely large apartment in a sweet part of San Antonio. Bill and Alice, Cathy's parents, had not grown comfortable with the idea of overseeing the two of us bunking together in the one guest bedroom they had in their small home.

Florence, Cathy's white haired, eighty-year-old, rye and engaging maternal grandmother told Alice and Bill we could stay with her. She gave us a room and told us to not bring up the fact that we were both spending the night in the same room, in the same bed.

We could honor that, we said. At our first breakfast on Florence's expansive screened porch, the three of us were eating fresh melon, having coffee, and planning activities for the day. It was warm but not yet San Antonio sticky, and the greenery surrounding the porch of her second floor apartment was just beautiful. Florence had gotten up to get some more coffee or something and as Chloe and I were completing a sentence, I suddenly felt surprisingly firm hands on my two shoulders. From behind, a voice—also surprisingly strong—intoned this question. "What, exactly, young man are your intentions with my favorite granddaughter?"

I obviously could not read her facial expression as she asked this, but Florence's tone was rich in a blend of seriousness but reasonableness. Looking at Chloe, I could see that she read this inquiry as a very real question coming from Florence at this moment, but actually coming from the entire family.

"Marriage, of course, Florence!" I responded almost instantly.

"And when do you think that will be?" she continued.

"Why, your granddaughter and I were going to talk that over today so that we could all determine a date that might let you come to Los Angeles to be part of the ceremony at The Cottage. We hope to have a garden marriage." I was patching together shards of earlier conversations Chloe and I had had, or I thought we'd had. Reading my love's face as I spoke, I saw nothing that told me I had wandered into real *terra unexpecta*.

Chloe then spoke up, "Yes...your timing is—as it always is—impeccable, Granny. I think that we will bring some date possibilities to dinner this evening."

We were, in fact, married on December twenty-first of that year. It was the birthday of Cathy's wonderful father. No one from the trio of Bill, Alice, and Florence came to the wedding, but Molly, Cathy's oldest sister came. Florence played an active role, however, in prompt decision-making. For that we are both thankful.

"CLOTHESLINES"

One of the most endearing qualities of Chloe is the power of her writing. Although, as I said earlier, her skill in a 1977 postcard narrative was huge in getting me to focus on this Junior High School teacher working in south central Los Angeles. But—and we have now been together more than forty years—it has been her work with imagery, storytelling, and charting the consequences of human actions that has been such a joy to be close to. I want to add an episode of one of her earliest columns. It is the first one I laminated and kept in my office as a reminder of where Cathy Salter takes words.

Cathy began writing for the weekly *Boone County Journal* in late 1993. She had been involved in Hartsburg's recovery from the damages caused by the Great Flood of '93. She had published one essay on the rebuilding, then underway, in this small agricultural town. In 1994, she was approached by Jane Flink, editor of our local weekly newspaper—*The Boone County Journal*—and had asked her if she would like to do a weekly column. Although Chloe had never really been a formal writer, she was a tremendous correspondent and the idea of a scheduled effort caught her fancy. She began *Notes from Breakfast Creek* that spring. She now has written nearly 1300 columns. I am including this one in its entirely because it so thoroughly exemplifies her style, spirit, and wordcraft. Each time I reread "Clotheslines" to a class, I realize yet again how our lives have been enhanced by the writing that she has done in the past quarter century. I am proud to bring this early column to these pages.

> Life is a tapestry of lines and patterns woven into a journey. On a map, lines are routes traced by the feet of past explorers. On a face, they are a lifetime of human experiences. Telephone lines and rail lines crisscross the American landscape, humming with a steady energy that can be felt and heard just as surely as a human pulse is read when a finger is pressed against a vein. Lines connect us with each other and with our past. Reading their patterns on the landscape can be a journey back through a part of America's story that still has a foot in the past as well as the present. Some lines are disappearing. Cities try to bury cables, eliminating the need for poles and the busy network of communication and transportation wires that converged over city streets. Rail lines bypassed by history have become

walking and biking trails, though the lines still remain on the land and in our memory. Though they have not disappeared, their utility has changed with the times

Clotheslines, too, are a part of America's story. They remain much as they have always been, a part of the landscape of rural America. Prairie women harnessed the winds of the Great Plains that blew relentlessly across the vast spaces that must have seemed like an ocean separating them from the distant worlds they had left behind. Each Monday, washday, sheets were transformed into sails, and the landscape was awash with white ships anchored in the backyards of rural farmhouses. A woman's domain was the home and the job of taking care of it filled most of her waking hours. At the turn of the century, there were still relatively few laborsaving devices in the American home. Women prepared food, cooked three meals a day, scrubbed the floor, raised the children, did the ironing, and hung out the laundry.

By the time of my mother's birth in 1919, the exhausting task of standing over a washboard and washtub was being replaced by power-driven washing machines. On farms, gasoline or kerosene engines regularly used for pumping were borrowed by the women on wash days. The time spent washing six wash tubs full of clothes, an average wash load for a family of nine or ten persons, was reduced from six hours to four. Eventually, the electric storage battery or a direct electric current from a public service line running through the rural countryside enabled farm women to run their washing machine with an electric motor. Power washing, as it was called, was thought to be such an improvement over hand washing that it might single-handedly banish the chronic fatigue of the housewife, thus leaving her with surplus energy at the end of the day for the piles of ironing that followed wash-day.

Being a child of the mid-1940s, I have no memory of hand-powered washing machines, but I do remember my mother's clothesline. In 1955, we were living in a duplex in western Massachusetts. The two living units shared a utility room that housed a washing machine constantly in use. Winter memories of our two years in Massachusetts are of ice skating and shoveling through the deep snowdrifts that grew into mountains around the house. Spring and summer memories are of roller-skating and our clothesline.

It was a collapsible clothesline, designed to fit into a small yard. Like an umbrella, it could be closed during the winter months when it was not in use. When open, its four concentric lines grew out from a single pole anchored to a cement pad. On days when the line was filled with billowing sheets, it made the neighborhood game of hide-and-seek a grand adventure.

Mother had a large wicker laundry basket and a blue-and-white striped clothespin bag that she hung on the line and pushed ahead of her as she worked her way from the inner reaches of the clothesline to its widest outer ring. I saw such a clothespin bag recently at an auction but didn't bid on it when the moment came to act. I have thought about it many times since that day, and regret that I don't have it to use on the makeshift rope clothesline strung across our basement.

While washing clothes by hand would be tiresome and tedious today, there is a quietude and peace connected with the solitary exercise of hanging up the week's laundry. It is an outdoor task, done ideally on a day when there is sun and wind moving through and around the clothes and the woman, warming them both as she stretches and bends between laundry basket and clothesline. As each item of bedding or clothing comes out of the basket, it is given a firm shake before being pinned onto the line. Patterns begin to form, and colors fall between white spaces like a quilt being pieced together. Each wash day a new and unique pattern is created and taken apart in the time it takes for the clothes to dry.

Like a quilt, what hangs on the line is, literally, the fabric of our lives. Like the telephone line and rail line, it connects us to another time. It is a line that stretches between our youth and our present age. It is a place where we played in our childhood and stood next to our mothers and sisters. It is an exercise in silence. And it is a connection that I feel to all the women who have ever stood at a clothesline and let warm breezes carry their quiet thoughts and dreams up into the fresh and open air, to be carried... who knows where?

© Cathy Salter 1994. Excerpted from *Notes From Breakfast Creek,* originally published in *The Boone County Journal* May 5, 1994.

Hayden Forrest Salter b.1966. Hayden was born in the Kaiser Permanente hospital in Walnut Creek, California on October 22, 1966.

Racing to Walnut Creek

I recall the night of Hayden's birth particularly well because I was in San Jose teaching a three-hour evening class of Evelyn Wood Speed Reading. Linda and I knew that she was close to her due time, but we very much needed the extra dollars this class provided. The organizers told me that if I did at least half the class, they would pay me the whole rate for a single class. I shared this news with the class that evening and told them that I was going to call Linda at break time, which would be at eight-thirty, and if she felt that she was moving toward the breaking of her waters, I was going to cancel the second half and race north to Orinda. The class became a part of the keen drama that timing and location came to mean that night.

When I called, a neighbor friend told me that Linda was absolutely ready to go to Walnut Creek, but that she wanted to relax herself so you would have time to be there. I told Jolene (the neighbor) to tell Linda I was on my way. I excused the class, grabbed my briefcase, and ran out to our old Karman Ghia and headed north. The drive was so frustrating—I exceeded the speed limit on the interstate as much as I could, but I felt armed by the single line, "Officer—I'm racing home because my wife is about to have our first child!" I assumed the officer would maybe say, "Follow me. I'll put the lights on." Or, at least, "Okay, kid—you can get away with this line once, but for your second child, you've got to plan better and not be seventy miles from your wife when her water breaks."

I did not hear either of those lines. No cop stopped me. I drove as pell mell as a Ghia can go, pulled into our driveway, ran into the house to see the mother-to-be sitting at the harpsichord her brother had made for her. She was playing some Bach, but the two neighbors were hopping from foot to foot nearly yelling, "Linda! Stop! Get up! Get the brown bag and your hospital stuff and go with Kit to Kaiser!"

She did. We went. Hayden was born in three hours and has lived a timely life for more than fifty-five years since that evening.

SIDESTEPPING

One day in 1976, Hayden and I were walking on the lower part of the UCLA campus on our way to play raquetball. Hayden was about ten. The sidewalk we were on was one of the reluctantly installed new walks that ran counter to the original design of rectangular campus grid spaces. Our route then was a narrow concrete cap over a pedestrian route that had been a diagonal grass path long used between two formal sidewalks to get to the John Wooden Sports Center. Hayden and I were walking single file (there was not space for side-by-side walking) and I was in the lead. We were having a conversation. A solo person was walking toward us. When he was ten feet away, I stepped off the concrete and walked along the edge of the narrow sidewalk. Hayden did the same. We continued our conversation while making this lateral move. After the three of us passed, him heading north and the two of us, south, Hayden paused a second and interrupted, asking, "Dad, how come we always get off the sidewalk? How come we move? Why doesn't the other guy get off the walk?"

His question came like a bullet. I had no good answer, although somehow images of Granny and her consummate kindness in parallel situations flashed across my consciousness. I think I might have said, "We do that because it's polite," but I may have said nothing. It is a specific question in a very specific scene that I have wondered about for decades.

I have pondered this three-minute mini-exploration of "the meaning of life" many times in the four decades since Hayden asked that specific question at that exact location. It has served in my head as the reminder of the power of small events to set in motion responses that grow in your mind over time. I do not even recall whether or not Hayden and I had a more profound discussion of sidewalk protocol after our racquetball, but I have used the moment as a hallmark of the way in which parenting is so often made up of snap comments that seem to fill the need at the moment, but that, in fact, should be the basis of a much more serious talk between a parent and a child. My guess is that the event is not even nested in Hayden's bag of family commentaries—especially since he has a trio of his own children in Madrid, Spain to provide daily interaction face-to-face on via email or Marco Polos.

In parenting there are endless things that seem vital to understand in dealing with the demands of making good decisions for a child. This episode is a short recollection of the open highway with Hayden. He was about ten or eleven and I was about stupid.

Changing Lanes

In the summer of 1976, I was in Amherst doing some writing in the basement at Jean and Jurgen's home. I was lucky enough to get access to Boston's Joslin Diabetic Clinic for a week of diabetic training and because of this, Linda flew Hayden across the country to drive home with me in December. I still recall our driving the old VW bus for this trip and at some point, in New Mexico, I had let Hayden scoot into my seat, sitting just ahead of me so that both of us were behind the wheel. This was to give him his first feel of driving.

At one point I passed a very slow truck (this van passed almost *nothing* on this 3000 mile trip) and as I was passing it, I told Hayden, "Okay...you can pull us back into our lane after we finish passing this guy." Hayden said, "Neato!" Just as soon as the van was past the truck (perhaps one foot or two) Hayden turned the wheel and pulled directly, immediately, precariously in front of the truck. The whole concept of gliding, of going in at a diagonal to take over space in front of the car or truck you just passed was nowhere in his mind. No. I floored all 54 horsepower of the van and waved to the trucker, who looked alarmed, but nothing happened. I did not put Hayden at the wheel again for hundreds—maybe thousands—of miles, but I did spend a lot of words talking about how driving is a process of smooth transitions.

Prodding Makes Perfect

When Hayden finished Brown University—where he had also taken courses in architecture and architectural engineering at the Rhode Island School of Design—he applied to Harvard and Rice for graduate work in Architecture. He got admitted to both schools but was promised a larger fellowship at Rice. He was moved by the money offered by Rice since Cathy and I had said that we would cover all of his undergraduate expenses, but not his graduate school costs. And Brown had been an Ivy with an expense structure to match.

At Breakfast Creek, in mid-Missouri, where Hayden visited us post-Brown graduation, Cathy and I both lobbied hard for Harvard. Having been teaching more than twenty years, I knew how much the place you take your graduate degree has major significance for the rest of your professional life. He finally organized a federal loan and went to Harvard. It was a dynamic two years and one of his favorite roles was being the Teaching Assistant for an architect named Jose Rafael Moneo. Moneo had just won the 1996 Pritzker Award—known as the Nobel Prize in Architecture.

Hayden worked closely with Moneo as his Teaching Assistant. Suddenly, school was over, Hayden graduated and came to Missouri for a few days as he thought about the next steps in life. When we had conversations over this vital theme to parents and children alike, we finally got Hayden to outline his favorite possible scenario. "I'd like to work with Moneo. He is brilliant and brings a beautiful grace to the buildings he creates."

"Then ask him about work."

"There's no point. He's never had an American working in his shop."

"Did you two get along when you were his T.A. at Harvard last month?"

"Yeah—that's the crazy thing. We got along very well. That's why I want so much to work for him—and then someday—work with him."

Chloe turned to Hayden. "We have a fax machine in the bedroom you're staying in. Why not write a simple letter at least asking about possible employment with him?"

Hayden paused. Chloe went on "If you write the letter right now, I'll send it by fax while you two do those errands you were talking about this morning."

"Really—do you think he'd consider it?"

"The only way to know is to try it. Write your letter and we'll take off. Get at it."

Hayden wrote the letter and gave it to Chloe. We gathered up the stuff we needed for our errands and she told us she would fax it right away.

Hayden and I returned about three hours later. As we drove up and parked in the driveway and walked up the steps into the front door, Chloe met us as though she was just there by chance. Looking over at Hayden as she gathered some of the bags, we were bringing home, and said, "Hayden—there's some stuff on your bed that you might want to take care of." There was no electricity in her voice, just an aside to call attention to some little chore or something.

Hayden left the hallway and walked into the bedroom he was staying in for the several days visit at Breakfast Creek. After about sixty seconds he ran out of the other room, saw the two of us still in the small foyer. All six feet of the kid jumped up in the air and sissored my waist with his long legs, saying in great excitement, "Moneo's willing to hire me! He's willing to pay me! And he is sending me travel money to get to Madrid!"

The air had left the room. Hayden was now, literally, launched toward his lifetime dream. He left for Spain in less than a week.

This next episode gives a sense of what he began to do with his degree, and with Moneo's commissions around the world.

Cathedral of Our Lady of the Angels

Soon after Hayden had moved to Madrid and taken up full time architecture with architect Jose Rafael Moneo, he was given the task of moving back to Los Angeles. Moneo had been commissioned in 1998 to build the first new Catholic cathedral in the United States in a generation. Hayden and his wife Ana and their young son Nicolas all moved to a small home in Echo Park as Hayden began a thirty-month role as the Architectural Engineer for this $189,000,000 project. Chloe and I visited this magnificent project several times and those three visits are still fully etched into the life layers of my mind.

•• *The enormity of the construction site.* After the monumental removal of earth to create a deep basement in the heart of the five-acre downtown cathedral site, a trailer office for Hayden and some other engineers and clerical staff was perched on the edge of this substantial excavation. This building site is adjacent to the Dorothy Chandler Pavilion and the Mark Taper Forum—two of the cultural gems in the heart of Los Angeles. This surprisingly large parcel dedicated to the new cathedral had been assembled by trading various city owned parcels with the Los Angeles Unified School District and other city offices. Chloe and I knew the spot because it had long been a sought-after parking venue for downtown cultural events.

The decision to replace rather than rebuild the 1871 classic Catholic cathedral was forced by the city disallowing the nineteenth century landmark cathedral to be rebuilt after the powerful 1971 Southern California earthquake. It was nearly breathtaking to stand to the side of the office trailer and peer down into the excavation as thirty-two deep cylindrical holes were carefully being bored into the earth to accommodate earthquake-resistant columns for the secure support of the new cathedral.

Overhearing Hayden in and out of conversations in English and Spanish with contractors and engineers Chloe and I reminisced about the small construction projects Hayden had created on the living room floor in his years living in The Cottage. And he and Heidi even undertook some small water diversion projects on road trips.

• • *The view from the top of the growing structure.* More than a year into the construction we came back again to Los Angeles to get a view of the growing structure. Hayden helped us negotiate various lifts and scaffolding to finally reach the top level of the cathedral. From there we could truly feel the power of the cranes and other support technology that had been building this beautiful and impressive structure layer by layer. We, again, were dumbfounded that this kid we had known in so many more modest dimensions of life was now again in phone and walkie-talkie communication in two languages with the crews that were bringing this cathedral to sacred and secular life.

··*The dedication of the Cathedral of Our Lady of the Angels.* In September 2002, there was a four-hour dedication service of Our Lady of the Angels Cathedral in downtown Los Angeles. Hayden got a few of us tickets for great seats up toward the front of a large crowd of people eager to witness the dedication and to see the inside as well as ponder the exterior of this monumental structure. There were many aspects of the dedication that glow in my mind, but these two images are the strongest:

One. Cardinal Roger Mahony, near the end of this four-hour multi-cultural process of dedication, was charged with the specific task of ultimate consecration of the massive six-ton altar of Turkish marble for the completed cathedral. For the ceremony he leaned over the surface of the enormous stone and slowly, carefully, but with strength, polished each square inch of the marble surface. With the backdrop of a choir singing, he burnished the altar surface into the cathedral's official presence. There was great power in the image of this tall, red-gowned priest giving the new role to the several ton block of stone from halfway across the world.

Two. At one point, while the dedication audience was still outside in the fall sun, we sang some robust hymns of adoration and welcome to the structure. Directly in front of the seats Hayden had gotten us, was Angelica Huston. After one consecrating chorus, Ms. Huston turned in her seat and looking straight into my sunglasses, said "What a great voice! You gotta get into a church choir!"

◆

One of the most evocative images of Hayden in the present era is the intensity with which he parents his son (Nicolas) and two daughters (Ines and Catalina)—currently twenty-five, twenty, and eighteen. He and his beautiful wife, Ana, both work actively in professional roles. Ana is an active caterer. Hayden's work with Pritzker Award Winner Rafael Jose Moneo (based in Madrid) for a quarter of a century has led to a great deal of travel with commissions to be managed in China, Switzerland, the United States, France, Spain and other foreign venues. His son has just finished a year with Sciences Pos in Paris. Ines, the eldest daughter is currently at Stanford University for a two-month Chemistry internship. She has just been admitted into Cambridge University to study medicine. Cata, the youngest child is deep in preparation for exams that will open doors for her to participate in some of the external academic experiences that both her siblings have captured. And in school theatre as well.

Heidi Louise Salter (b.1968). This as an introduction to my daughter Heidi, now more than fifty, and always fanciful, artistic, and creative. Many people watched Heidi grow up and those in teaching used to feel that she, with her mix of artistic skill and human compassion, would be a great teacher. Since Chloe and I have both been teachers for decades, we were the ones most likely to face her with "What about teaching, Heidi?" as conversations in high school revolved around ideas about careers. I present this episode to chart one of the conversations regarding the future Heidi.

Conversations that Count

One of the unwelcome hallmarks that has always been a part of my teaching world is the frustration at not knowing whether or not you—the teacher—have any real impact on the lives of the students you spend your lives engaging. When I was teaching at UCLA, I would sometimes, not always, but sometimes, bring home the question "Does any of this really matter? Do any of these lectures really intersect a student's life?" As Heidi grew older and we were all living in the tiny Cottage, it became clear to Chloe and me that she would be a great teacher. We dropped the hint now and again that she ought to think of such a life.

"Not a chance," she would say. It was never picked up upon as a career possibility, at least in conversations with us.

Years after she had gone to Berkeley for her BA and had made up her own major in English and Humanities, she and I were talking one day and I asked her, for the umpteenth time, why she wasn't thinking about teaching. At that time, she was in Oakland, California in her fifth or sixth year working as a counselor for city and or state agencies. She was working to get teenage kids to break drug and drinking patterns. Heidi seemed to intersect them just before they were scheduled to go into the California Youth Authority (teen jail).

One day Heidi said to me, "Dad, you've always said that in teaching, you never really know whether or not you connect with your students' lives. One of the reasons I do what I do is because I know every night, every day, that I have touched a life. If I can bring a teenage girl in off the street—even if only for one or two nights—I know that by her being clean for those nights, she has a reminder of what it was like, or what it could be like, to stop doing tricks or drugs or drinking. For those days that she—or he—is mine, they are seeing a different world. I am the reason they are, even fleetingly, seeing that other world. I *know* that such a view can have an impact on them. That's part of the reason that I'm not teaching. I *want* to feel and believe and know there is a payoff with so much energy being put out to try to bring about change in individual teenage lives."

Happily, Heidi decided after eight years of social work on the street in Oakland and San Francisco she wanted to try teaching. Subsequently, she got her M.A. in English from San Francisco State (at the top of her graduate class) and she is now a tenured full professor at Diablo Valley Community College in Pleasant Hill, California.

And when I told her that I was writing this episode, she responded with, "And now I have great conversations with students almost every day. I work with students who came to a community college because they feared they couldn't make the move from street life to serious school demands. Many even feel pretty good about being launched toward some sort of career. I've even got some headed to graduate school." Then she adds with a grin, "*But* I know that my street experience has given me 'credentials' in the eyes of some of my students from the street world." (1999, 2018)

Here are two other nuggets that fit into the description of Heidi, her creativity, and her role in the student and teaching world.

Rediscovered Art of Childhood

When Chloe and I return from time to time to Los Angeles for a speech or meeting, we are lucky in that we sometimes stay with Don and Suzanne Dunaway in Beverly Glen. They have one of the most spectacular homes that either of us has ever seen. It's in a setting of chaparral, open sky, soaring red tail hawks, and a swimming pool and roses unmatched in any garden Chloe has ever tended.

On one such visit, I nicked myself shaving. Hoping that the guest room bathroom might have something useful for my clumsiness, I opened the mirrored cabinet door of the medicine cabinet. No luck in the one straight ahead, so I turned to the adjacent mirrored door and found all the shelves totally empty—except for a small collection of tiny clay figures. I stood tall and looked at the seven or eight creations. The largest of these was maybe one inch high—and suddenly I realized that these were figures that daughter Heidi had made for the annual Beverly Glen Community Art Fair that the neighborhood organized each June.

Heidi would use Play-Doh to craft little bears, dogs, cats, and exotic creatures, bake them in our Cottage oven, and then display and sell them for one or two dollars apiece. Her booth was one of the 'hot' spots in the Art Fair and she usually sold out her zoo before noon. She would then sit there and make things to order. She would let people take them home and bake them themselves.

So, here, in Don and Suzanne's fabulous home was a stash of her wondrous fanciful animals from about twenty-five years earlier! They looked great. They made me think of a small flock of mutants that had been hiding out and now looked nervously at me as I discovered them. I stared in amazement at how well Heidi's fanciful figures had survived two house moves for our hosts, and a quarter century of time passage! Great stuff, Heidi! Great planning, Don and Suzanne!

Changing Social Contracts

Around 1980 when Heidi attended Emerson Junior High School in Los Angeles, I had carpool detail off and on. I recall two encounters that have stayed in my parental mind.

Lesson one. The first time I was taking Heidi somewhere just by herself, we were bound for a school function. This was *not* drop off for a school day, but it was drop off for a school party or dance in the gym or something. We were chatting and driving along in my black Volkswagen Rabbit diesel four door.

Suddenly Heidi said somewhat urgently, "Dad, you can let me out here. This is fine."

"Hey, we're two blocks from school. I've got time to take you to the front door."

Heidi spoke with more force. "No, Dad, *this* is *fine*. Right here. *Right here.*"

Although I slowed the car, I was still protesting. "But we're a block and a half away from school. It's no problem to get closer."

"Yes, there *is* a problem. It is dorky to get dropped off by your father. Here *is* fine!"

I pulled over. "Dorky? Dorky? It's *dorky* to get dropped off to a school function by your father? Huh?"

"Dad, never mind. Thanks for the ride. I'll get a ride home

with Mandy's mom." Bye," and she was out the door.

So, lesson one. It's dorky to be a helpful Dad.

Lesson two was more powerful. I was driving Heidi and some friends home from junior high school. I had Heidi in front with me and there were four girls tucked into the back seat of the Rabbit. I heard this conversation:

One of the girls in the back seat said, "Melissa—I didn't get my social studies assignment written down. Do you have it?"

"Yeah…but it's buried in my backpack and I can't even move my arm. I can't get it out now. Why don't you call me tonight?"

"Okay," said Brenda, "what's your number?"

There was a nanosecond pause and then Melissa continued talking. "Okay…let's see. This is Wednesday. I'll maybe be at my mother's place. That number is…" (and she gave a number) "but sometimes we go on Wednesday nights to my Mom's boyfriend's place and that is (number)." A slight pause, then, "*But*, this is the third Wednesday of the month and that means that Mom might go to a place for a massage and then I just hang out in the waiting room and I don't remember that number…*OR*, maybe she'll drop me back at Dad's and that phone is (number)."

At this point Heidi broke in. "The assignment was to read the stuff on the Indians and the first Thanksgiving. I think it was pages 45-50 or something." Brenda got an arm extracted and wrote the assignment down on her hand with a pen from Jennifer.

As I drove, I realized that I had just heard the very essence of the new social contract in American culture and its complex maze of divorced and recollected, reconfigured families.

◆

I spent a number of years in different national teacher consultancies. This usually involved putting workshops on aspects of Geography Education and taking them to classrooms that had a little money for geography. Most were one day hits, but some spilled over to a second day. The pattern of this Louisiana workshop was built around two days and provided this episode of both Heidi and my own serendipity.

Published at Nineteen

For a few years I was a member of The National Faculty. This provided me opportunities to go out on the talk circuit and give one-day or two-day geography or environmental workshops for sixth to twelfth grade teachers all across the country. At one point, I was in northern Louisiana for a two-day workshop, and had completed a day of work on geography education for thirty teachers. I was dropped off at a motel at the end of the day by the event's organizer and he said he'd pick me up at seven the next morning. We would go to a diner and get breakfast and then head for the second and last day of my workshop. This driver and teacher (Fred) was the school's curriculum coordinator so it was interesting to get his views on the school scene.

Fred showed up a few minutes late, driving a big station wagon, filled with boxes of books and maps and charts. I got in the passenger seat and as I was fastening the seat belt, I turned and saw a pile of books tipping in my direction. I reached back to straighten them and, lo and behold, I knew well the book that was on the top of the stack.

"What are these books, Fred?" I asked.

"Oh, those are the books that I have had the most success

with in my efforts to get reading going. I have tried lots and lots of titles in an effort to get my teachers to use literature at every possible level of instruction." He paused a second for his meritorious intention to soak in. He then went on. "That stack that is about to crush you is the crème de la crème. Those are the titles that have been the most popular across a whole bunch of grades."

I looked at him as we were getting into traffic.

"You mean you've not done some special rearranging to get any particular book on top of the stack?" I asked.

"Well... I did make an effort to bring just—in that particular nervous box—the titles that I have had the most success with. That took some special rearranging. The ones toward the top are the real winners."

"But, the very top one is just there by chance, right?"

"Yeah...what are you digging for anyway?"

"The book you have on top of the stack is the book that our daughter, Heidi, wrote and illustrated. It won the Landmark "Written and Illustrated By..." Book Contest three years ago." I said this in a mixture of pride and amazement. "That's why I wondered if you had somehow found that book and put it on the top of the heap so that your National Faculty person for today would feel all puffed up from seeing his daughter's book in your car."

"You mean the Taddy McFinley book is your daughter's book?" I pulled the book off the heap and had it ready to show him as he turned into a small strip mall with a diner. "Hey... wow.... that book is a BIG hit. Lemme see the title page... Heidi Salter...what the dickens, you're right. So, Heidi's really your kid?"

I was able to tell him about the fact that when Heidi was eighteen, she came and stayed with Cathy and me in our home in Washington, D.C. when we were working for National Geographic. She got a job with National Geographic too for a while and was motivated by news that Chloe brought home from a Wyoming talk she had given. She had learned about a competition for books called "National Written and Illustrated by..." for young authors. Heidi had two months before she reached the cutoff age of nineteen to compete in the contest, and she had an enchanting book that she had written and illustrated the prior year. She redid it, submitted it, and Chloe and I got a call four months later telling us that Ms. Heidi Salter had won the national first prize for her age cohort.

The publisher and contest organizer lived in Kansas City and wanted to tell Heidi herself. At that time, she was in Spain working on her Spanish. We gave the publisher and contest organizer all the numbers we had for her. After two days, he called back saying that he had finally tracked her down and had made a tentative time for her to come to the Landmark publishing house in Kansas City for the final edit. Seven months later Landmark published *Taddy McFinley and the Great Grey Grimly* (1989). Heidi was then a published author and she even made a few dollars on it.

Dad was very proud to have her book have made it to the top of the stack of books loved by students in Fred's station wagon in Saint Francis Parish in Louisiana.

◆

CHAPTER THREE

TRAVEL AND THE FORCES OF MOBILITY AND CHANGE

It seems to me that I was in motion nearly all of my first three decades of life. In early years, the action came through household moving. In the decades since college, my motion has been professional and personal travel. In the Hitchhiking Chapter that comes next, I will have motion in the context of uncertainty in pace and place. In this travel chapter, I turn to the ups and downs that we all know by trying to change one place for another on a short time basis.

ADAM AT 6 A.M.

During the 1970 filming of the movie *Adam at 6 A.M.*, actor Michael Douglas was playing the role of a professor at a major university and it was decided that the Palm Court in Bunche Hall—where the UCLA Department of Geography is located—was a great visual setting for a short segment. The crew got an okay from the University and a location person walked up and down the eastern corridor (which opened out onto a really lovely palm courtyard), searching for the perfect office.

He came to my open office door—and looked in and asked me if it could be used for a couple of quick takes.

"Will I need to leave the office?" I asked.

"Yeah…we think so, although we're not doing any interior shots."

"Well…it's yours if you'll let me stay in here at my desk. I promise not to race out and get my three seconds of fame while the camera is running.

"Okay…it's a deal. Michael Douglas will come and open your door and walk in as though it's his office—twice, maybe three times."

"Okay. I'll sit tight." And, as promised, the movie filming occurred, and young Douglas opened the door firmly and walked in two times. The first time he closed the door, looked around and seemed surprised to find anyone inside. I said something like, "Hi…. I'm an autograph seeker and I broke into this office to be here to greet you!" I then laughed and told him that was a lie, that it was just my office and I had been allowed to stay at my desk during the shoot.

He looked around some more and asked how come it had so much stuff in it, so much stuff on the walls. I explained that I was a geographer and a traveler, and it was good karma to always bring something home from a gig. He nodded and backed out.

He came in again at the end of another outside shot in about five minutes and said, "Still want an autograph?" I said, "Yeah, put your name on this paper I'm grading, and the student will think that the low grade is easily trumped by having the real Michael Douglas's signature. He scrawled his name on the student paper and left. It was a nice encounter. His greatest movie, *Falling Down*, had not yet been shot yet so I could not laud him for that work, but it was nice to meet him.

He is *not* 5'3"— maybe a little taller.

Dimple and Flame

In the late 1980s and early 1990s I was on the road a lot for National Geographic. This means that I built up a world of frequent flyer miles on American Airlines. On one trip from Los Angeles to D.C., I upgraded to First Class (funny how it seems imperative to upper case First Class). I was in the last row of the first-class section, but in the aisle seat so I could see the whole cabin. I noted after I was seated that none other than actor Kirk Douglas boarded with a fine-looking young woman as his travel companion. They took the two front seats on the starboard side of the cabin. Kirk Douglas had been one of my heroes for a long, long time. I told myself that I had to think up a way to talk with him. Once we were in the air, I came up with a plan and I crouch-walked up to the front row after drinks had been served but no food had come yet. We had the following conversation.

"Mr. Douglas, my apologies for bothering you two, but I see this sixty seconds as a way to resolve a riddle I have had to carry for some thirty years." He gave me a look that ranged between irritation and curiosity. I hurried on. "In high school a bunch of us would always see any film that you were in. We loved 'em all...but you set a unique tension in motion as van Gogh in *Lust for Life.*" I took a breath and went on. "You surely remember the scene when you are trying to get a potato farmer to grant you permission to marry—or at least court—his daughter. The farmer wants none of it. He's not interested in you as a son-in-law at all. You're frustrated and, as always, passionate. You then see a small candle on the farmer's table. It's the only light in their drab dwelling. You extend your open palm over the fire and tell the farmer, 'I'll keep my hand over this candle until you give me permission to at least see your daughter.' Your face was showing some pain, but more fully it was showing clear resolve."

I paused just for a second. "Okay...my long-time tension comes from the fact that my buddies and I saw that scene—we probably went to the movie twice or three times just to see that scene. Half of us said you were so damn tough that you just endured the pain for the shoot. The other guys said that you were so stupid that you endured it for the scene and just figured that portraying that image truly required some pain. Can you tell me what went on there? I am still in touch with a few of those guys and I could solve the riddle and set the record straight."

By this time, Mr. Douglas was openly interested in this little drama. He gave me a big grin (and his dimple is quite real) and said, "Hell, kid, I am tough. I am certainly *not* stupid, but I am not as tough as that scene looked." His grin took over his entire face. "The special effects men—and we had them even then—ran a length of clear plastic quarter-inch tubing up through my pants, through my shirt, down through my long sleeve and had the open end come out just at the underside of my wrist. When the shot was being taken, the camera angle was high enough that the clear piping could not be seen. Through the tube they forced just enough air so the flame of the candle was blown sideways. This minimized the burn and the pain on my hand. It was real flame. It was a real scene. But it was not as brutal as it looked."

He stopped and looked up expectantly. "Do you think that'll square the argument? Will your buddies believe that?"

"Oh, you bet! Especially the ones of us who figured you were tough *and* smart. They'll love the story. My apologies for the interruption.... I'll have fun writing the letters to settle accounts." I turned to go and then spun back around for just a second and added, "Incidentally, your son, Michael was in my UCLA office for a shoot of *Adam at 6 A.M.* a few years ago. They needed a scene with him ducking into a professor's office near dawn and mine was in just the right place. I just went on working and he stepped in a few times. I wish I could have told him that I had met his father. Oh, well.... Thanks again."

Now, some thirty plus years later, this is the first time I have written this story down. I could only track down one high school buddy who might have ever thought about *Lust for Life*. I called him after this first-class encounter, but he didn't believe the story I have just given you. That's the problem with films. You never know what's real and what's just wonderful and wished for. I'm glad to have finally put the caper to ink. It is as real a story as Kirk's dimple.

GUERRILLAS IN CUBA

In the late summer of 1960, Linda and I traveled through much of Central America in a random sort of journalistic exploration for Oberlin College. I had been awarded a tiny stipend to cover a portion of the travel costs if I would write some articles for the *Oberlin Review*, the college paper. The incident I recall so very keenly from Castro's Cuba (the U.S. had not completely closed the door on Cuba yet, but was planning to that fall). Linda and I were walking around the front of the school building where Fidel Castro and his ragtag guerrillas made their first attack against the Batista regime on July 26, 1957. We had gotten there by hitchhiking from Havana to the eastern end of the island. There were some 'guards' in front of the Moncada barracks. We were looking for rumored bullet holes.

The trio that stepped forward to ask who we were and

where we were from must have been about sixteen at the very oldest. The leader of the three had a machine gun slung over his shoulder on a shabby and awkwardly carried leather strap. He, for whatever reason, found that having two kids from the U.S. (we were maybe three years older than him) to be a very offensive thing. He started teasing us about being from the Big Country that thought it could run Little Cuba. The line that still sticks in my mind—and all of this discussion was in Spanish—was something like "What if World War III began right here at the Moncada? What if it began with the three of us (the Cuban trio of heady youth) shooting these two gringos? We could sure as hell begin the fighting if we shot these two!" He glistened with the excitement he felt at seeing such an opportunity suddenly be so very proximate to his own person. Linda and I were dumbfounded at where this kid's mind had wandered in the ninety seconds that we had all been part of this very special quintet.

Fortunately, his two buddies told him to forget it, saying, "We want the Americanos to see the really great things that Fidel has done, and what the Revolucion is doing. These two are not worth anything. Leave 'em. Let 'em go see everything and then go home and tell the Americanos to get ready for real revolucion!" Somehow it all worked out. We spent about eight to ten days thumbing on the island before coming back to Oberlin.

The Street as Learning Center

One of the great joys that Chloe and I share is a love of the street as a "journaling" locale. No matter where we are—stateside or abroad—if we have some flexible time, we will head for a coffee shop or a bistro or diner. We position ourselves with a street scene that encompasses horizontal as well as vertical variety, demographic as well as architectural diversity, and we nurse a coffee and take the time to capture such images (always leaving a generous tip for the use of that niche).

This common travel love is one of the reasons that we journey so well together. The broader love of the street is a major factor in my having decided on geography as a career. There is so, so much you can observe and ponder in street scene geography that such a career choice has made a great deal of sense for my system. The term for this that I love most is one that Jean and Jurgen taught me in 1975 when I was living in their basement for a month, doing a writing project. I would go regularly to a local McDonald's and set up my coffee and notebook (actual paper) and spend hours working through thoughts and paragraphs and then come home and edit and type such words into a text. Jurgen told me one night that I was a classic *boulevardie (a* person fascinated with the life of the city street). I have been happy living up to this term ever since. I offer these two experiences.

In Madrid, Chloe and I have stayed a few times at an old, small hotel right in the center of the city. A part of its neighborhood includesa handsome traffic circle designed around a massive statue. As Chloe was studying the window of a nearby attractive jewelry shop, I stood back from her the way the second cop does when two cops stop a traffic violator. The first cop is doing the talking. The second one is at the ready, keenly observant. I was the second cop, watching Cathy's purse handbag hang on her shoulder as young men flowed all around the doorway of the nice looking shop. She finished her viewing and we moved into pedestrian flow again. "Good," I thought, "I protected her from any funny stuff in that doorway!" Within maybe two minutes a young small man rushed up to me, fell to his knees to my right side, and began brushing an invisible powder or dirt off of my lower pant leg, all the while apologizing for having spilled something on me. As I tried to figure out what was going on, a man bumped into me from behind and rustled my vest (I always wear a multi-pocketed travel vest abroad) and then walked on quickly, going in the same direction that Cathy and I were walking. As I felt my vest to see if anything had been lifted from my inside pocket, I realized my sun glasses case was gone and at the same instant, a young man in a fine looking suit walked toward me, grinning, and handed me my glasses…and he walked on, going the opposite direction from us.

Wow! It was ballet. A three-person cast, each delicately choreographed, and each with a very specific role in the wallet lifting. No wallet was taken (a vest is a great travel investment), and why they returned my glasses was a question until I figured out (assumed) that what they were doing was showing me what a useless 'second cop' role was in skillful Madrid pocket picking or purse snatching. I figured that they had seen me guarding Cathy at the window and decided to do their ballet on me. If they captured a wallet the second person (dressed in khakis) would dish it off to the guy coming the other direction (in the suit) and I would still be trying to figure out where the pant leg guy had gone. But, since the only capture was a rumpled soft glasses case, they decided to let the whole ceremony be international theatre. I got my glasses back. And I have had a good Madrid story for more than a decade!

Another real favorite learning moment on the street came in downtown Los Angeles. I was teaching a nighttime class at USC in Los Angeles. It met one night a week and this particular term I had about eight or nine students. All were coeds but one guy. The girls were mostly classic southern California lovelies. I don't know what requirement my *Landscapes of L.A.* class met, but it must have had met some magic requirement for the Modeling Major or Fashion Planning.

We had a field trip to downtown L.A. one class night and we drove in the male student's old SUV and parked by the Greyhound Bus Station. I was wearing—as has long been my habit—a Panama hat and I began to walk this little cluster around the innards of the city. They stayed very close because this was the first time any of them had been close to the real downtown of Los Angeles.

In just a few minutes two Anglo guys in their early twenties began to hassle us, asking the girls especially to 'help them out; what about some spare change?' As I saw his field trip taking shape, I realized that with my hat and the gender nature of this small group I must have looked like a (high class?) pimp moving his squad through the wrong part of the city.

I stopped us at a good-sized doorway and told the two street guys, "Okay...okay...back off. Here's the deal. If you'll let us interview you for fifteen or twenty minutes, I'll pass my hat around to the class and you'll get all of the cash in the hat, and I'll start the process by throwing in a fiver. Whaddya say?"

The guys loved the deal...and all of us felt relieved that a little structure was added to this awkward situation. We did twenty minutes—mostly learning that these two college age Anglos had been captured by the idea of being absolutely without responsibility! They lived hand to mouth, slept in the Union Mission when they could tolerate the preaching, and otherwise used doorways and abandoned buildings they had spotted and felt okay in. The hat gained them nearly thirty dollars, and the class and I headed forward in our nighttime walk a little more confident in our comprehension of the culture of the street in downtown L.A.

CROSSING TO THE HEMINGWAY MARINA IN HAVANA, CUBA

In 2003, Chloe and I were invited to take a cruise on a twenty-eight foot motorized sailboat by Hank Waters and Vicki Russell, then Editor and Publisher of the local *Columbia Daily Tribune*. This paper had been in Hank's family for more than a century and it was a plum to be able to negotiate the ninety miles of the Straits of Florida and the Gulf Stream in late spring with them. We had all gotten hotel space in Key West and were planning three days of exploration in that southern tip of Florida when, to our surprise we got a call from Vicki on the night of the second day telling us: "Whatever plans you had for Key West, forget them. There is a major storm headed to the crossing zone to Havana so we're going to cast off in two hours—meet us at ..." Oh, boy—that sweet moment in loosely planned travel when adventure comes to your door, but it will not tolerate ambivalence. We had already had to pay for three nights at this great motel, so we were square there, and we had only a little luggage, so we got our stuff, checked out, and went to a café we had noticed on an earlier walk in the day, got a light dinner, and headed to the meeting place in the harbor to be ready, even ready early.

There are only three things I recall from the crossing.

Hank and Vicki were the first actual Lewis and Clark type of co-captain pair I had ever known. Brother Joel had been in the Navy and he came back from his tour absolutely positive that a boat or a ship can *never* have a shared captaincy. The power of decision-making is must be singular and often immediate. Hank and Vicki worked in shifts but with smooth cooperation in decisions about our nighttime crossing.

Chloe is a world-class sleeper when it is time to sleep. When she whispers good night and turns on her side, she is asleep in minutes and hardly moves—or gets up—during the night. When we were shown to the minuscule quarters in the hull of the *Missouri Traveler*, she curled right into her bunk and I began the longest night that I could recall in my entire life. About the fourth hour of my reliving our 'light dinner' and the nature of my digestion program, I was lying on the deck of the Traveler at the very face of the mounting seas. I recall giving serious consideration to slipping over the edge into that rumbling Gulf Stream, but swear that my only constraint to that terminal plan of action was "Damn, if Hank loses a passenger overboard, he and Vicki will have endless paperwork to wrestle with in two languages—and they'll be irritated at both me (no longer an issue) and Chloe—who has not done a thing to generate their certain irritation with their earlier decision to invite the Salters on this cruise. I held on and held back and continued only to send my innards seaward. In reflection upon regaining wellness later that day, I loved life but hated the sea.

Here are some of the episodes that came from seven days of urban exploration in Havana in 2003.

"Harvested" on the Havana Malacon

On one of our long days of urban exploration in Havana in our last trip to Cuba, Chloe charted a marathon walk from our Hotel Inglaterra at the edge of Habana Vieja. She mapped out a walking approach to the University of Havana, the Plaza of the Revolution, and the Malacon. The latter is a seven-kilometer long sea wall at the edge of Havana Bay. The curving coastline describes a long arc. Built along this wall is a parallel sidewalk. Fronting this wall is a four-lane urban roadway (never as busy in Havana as any other big city we have seen) and for several miles there are two- and three-story apartment buildings, somewhat like row houses in Baltimore. On our walk, we came down to the Malacon to walk along it and admire the great cascades of surf that splashed up as massive waves. We stood in front of the deserted-looking apartments and watched people dodge the splash. We grew pensive about the beauty that this city had in its setting. We could imagine people at one time sitting on their terraces on the second or third floors, gazing at the sea and beyond. The urban skyline went from the Morro tower (in the oldest plaza of the city) all the way around to distant suburbs that look over the edge of the bay to the west. The view reminded us of just why Havana was so powerfully popular with American tourists prior to the Cuban Revolution in 1956.

Suddenly—it seemed sudden at least—a short woman of about sixty appeared from nowhere and spoke to us in Spanish and asked where we were from. This is a standard opening line of so many conversations. It segues to offers to sell cigars or other stuff, or lamentations about how poor they were and how much they would be benefited by just a few U.S. dollars. This woman, however, did not take the conversation in that direction. She asked if we would like to talk with a regular Cuban family. She told us it was her daughter's birthday, "She is a student in the Law School at the University of Havana." and she would like us to meet her. I explained that our evening was already booked but thanked her a lot. She said that it seemed so important for Cubanos to have some real conversations with people from the United States since so much depended on both populations understanding how it could be that these two neighboring countries were so very distant because of the two governments. We chatted a few minutes, told her our hotel in response to a question, and then walked back to the long avenue that led to the University.

The next afternoon we were planning on going to Hotel Nacional for our final afternoon and for a long drink and a discussion of the MOL (meaning of life). MOL discussions can best occur in settings that are peaceful, for such discussions need a sense of pensive leisure. As we were planning this final day, the phone rang (the only time in five days). It was Eva, the lady from the day before by the Malacon. She invited us for some of her daughter's birthday cake that evening. Chloe and I decided it would be a good chance to see a home and have such a chat. We got the address and realized that we could walk the mile and a half or two miles after our MOL discussions and stay for a little bit and then go back to finish packing.

Well...the Malacon neighborhood home of Eva Delfin her husband Jorge, son Hector, and lawyer-to-be daughter Maria was up a steep set of stairs with all sorts of wires strung along the walls. This stairwell was in a building that we had walked by the prior day. It seemed to us at first glance to be probably deserted or abandoned. But not so! As we were led into their apartment, we saw and visited their four bedroom, kitchen, bathroom, living room, small dining room, and terrace dwelling. We talked with all the family and stumbled along in a nice and engaging exchange of two families awkwardly searching out lines of confluence and overlap.

We spent some two hours there and finally—in an almost nonchalant manner—were given a list of things that were critically needed for the family—things that they wanted us to send them if we possibly could. They ranged from over-the-counter medicines to used clothes. We got shoe and clothing sizes and a list of some of the simple medical needs they had. As we left in the darkness, after sharing a piece of birthday from Maria's birthday cake of the day before, we found ourselves feeling that it was all a wonderfully innocent response to the prior day's conversations with Eva as Chloe and I walked on the Malacon. But, in my mind was just a touch of suspicion, wondering about whether or not if we had just been 'harvested' by observant Cubanos. Chloe rejected this reaction and I felt it had been good social time in any case.

We put together two big boxes back in Missouri over the next two weeks and took them down to the Post Office. There (duh) we quickly learned that we could mail nothing that weighed more than four pounds. So, we just sent medicines and a blouse or two. The overall experience, however, of that happenstance was positive and interesting.

EVIDENCE OF KIT'S YOUTHFUL DARING!

In the summer of 1977, I was invited to be a member of the first American delegation of geographers to tour China. Thirty years after that 1977 tour, I wrote "Swimming with Mao." As they say in film, 'Based on a true story.'

"Swimming With Mao"

It was a time of new beginnings. The day was just beyond dawn. The month of August 1977 had heated up to the fullness of a traditional Chinese summer. I was a member of group that had just finished the first week of a four-week official tour of the People's Republic of China. And, that morning, our American delegation had just been delivered to a riverbank in Southeast China.

We were China's first officially invited delegation of American geographers and not one of us had been to the Chinese Mainland before. Curiously the two Chinese government tour guides—urban planners—had never been to this region either. They were now in Guizhou Province, the home of spectacular landscapes created by limestone mountains and hills jutting up into the sky in wild abandon. This karst landscape is a familiar image second only to the Great Wall as a restaurant and calendar icon for The Middle Kingdom.

The first week of the tour had been spent visiting densely crowded urban centers in eastern China and this swing down to the Li River and its dramatic karst region was intended to be a refresher for the entire group. There was a breath of freedom felt by all of the travelers that August morning.

When the bus stopped, the ten academics gathered up their small packs and filed out to stand in an uncertain circle near the gangplank of a two-deck river ferry. The tour guides had a head-nodding exchange with the boat's representative. Then the head guide turned to the geography delegation and said, "Captain Wen has sent word that we are a little early. He has to await another important delegation before we leave. He has provided watermelon seeds and hot tea, and hopes that you will be comfortable."

"Hot tea and watermelon seeds." These were the markers of our tour circuit. We had begun to talk of "T & S"—our shorthand for "Tea and Statistics" as the secret weapon of Chinese tour guides. Whenever the guides got exhausted with continual delegation questions, they would suddenly find a commune or a factory. The bus would be stopped, and we would be ushered into a conference room where a local representative would greet us, and have tea carried in along with bowls of *guadza* (dried watermelon seeds). These dry seeds would be positioned much like baskets of unshelled peanuts at some American bars. The delegation would then sit and listen to a local spokesperson sing the praises of the Chinese Revolution—the lyrics being statistics of recent production increases—while piles of empty or ill-opened guadza husks mounded up by each of the captive delegates.

At the river's edge this particular morning, the idea of another hurry-up-and-wait event did not play well. Frustrated, one of the geographers asked the tour guide a question.

"What if we have a quick swim here while we

wait for the other group?" The guide's response was instantaneous. "Not possible." No explanation, just *Bu keyi*.

"Why?"

The guide replied, "Snakes. There are snakes in the water here. There may even be nasty fish that could bite you. No....no swimming. I am sure the other bus will get here soon. Have some more tea."

"Snakes?" the delegate, a Californian, asked in amazement. "You say there are snakes here in this river...and that's why we can't have a quick morning swim before we saddle up to share another three hours of tea and statistics?" The tone was not whiney but the other delegates did feel a slight awkwardness in the air.

At that moment, a second bus came into sight. The momentary consideration of swimming was replaced by quick official preparation for departure. There was relief felt on both sides of the conversation.

The boat was loaded. People searched out spaces at the railings on both upper and lower decks. There was a clear hope that T & S would be replaced by quiet time for enjoying the awe one felt in looking at the bold karst landscapes. The hills seemed to thrust out of the well-farmed earth, carrying terraces and small streams and even peasant households up the flanks of the karst hills. Solo observation was a refreshing and much welcomed pattern break.

After nearly three hours on the river, the geographer who had asked about the swim was on the upper deck. He had heard that the destination of the tour was a town on the banks of the Li River that had undergone much change because of rural development. He was looking perhaps a mile ahead at a settlement with some small industry or harbor facilities on the right bank. "Is that the town we are meant to tour?" he asked a tour guide standing nearby.

"Yes...I think that is Yang Zhou. Let me go and ask Captain Wen." The guide then walked to the small control cabin and knocked on the door. At that same moment, one of the Visiting Delegation's members turned and said to the questioner, "Yes...that is Yang Zhou. I made this trip four months ago and I recall its breakwater."

This is the moment, he thought to himself. He turned to a delegation friend and asked, "Greg...will you do me a favor? I am going to dive into this 'snake-infested river' and swim to Yang Zhou. Would you hang on to my pack and clothes?" As he talked, the geographer stripped down to a pair of Speedo underwear and handed Greg his gear.

"Hell...you're nuts! You don't know what's in this river."

"Will you watch my stuff?" he repeated as he was climbing up over the railing.

"Yeah.... But I still say you're nuts!"

The geographer dived off the railing. There was about a ten-foot drop into the murky river water and then he disappeared.

And this marked another of the new beginnings of this day.

As he cut into the water, he relished the first real freedom in seven days...but his under shorts began to slip off his body. As his shorts were racing toward their own freedom, he just barely angled his ankle in time to catch them. He stayed underwater getting his shorts back in order and pulled back on. He then resurfaced and, without looking back at the ferry, began swimming. He thought, *I'll stay away from the tour boat. If I get tired, I can go to the left river bank and walk to Yang Zhou.*

But it was not to be. As he got into his stride, he could not help but see what he had left behind. The ferry was executing a laborious full U-turn. Behind the ferry there was an empty dinghy. The captain of the ferry was swinging into position to drop a man into the dinghy. The lone sailor's task, clearly, was to come and reclaim "the bad element" from the American Geography Delegation.

The swimmer quickly realized that he had few options. *I could get out and walk on the bank, not acknowledging the one-man dinghy rescue crew—but that would make the Chinese sailor lose face. I could continue swimming.* He felt good about his stride now—but that would cause the whole boat's crew and captain to lose face at allowing a foreign guest to swim in the snake-infested Li River.

No. It was the swimmer's choice. When the dinghy and sailor pulled up next to him, he reluctantly climbed aboard the small craft. The sailor did not greet him, just began to row them back toward the stalled ferry.

Thirty Years Later...

In 2007, there was an academic celebration of the First American Geographic Delegation to be invited to China. It was held in an upscale hotel and one of the speakers alluded to "the American geographer who swam with Mao in the Yangtze." People in the audience clearly wondered who among the small population of professional geographers had even been in China when Mao did his famous 1963 Yangtze swim. Unexpectedly, I was asked to step forward and spend a moment reliving that swimming drama.

Stunned, I stood but energetically explained that I had *not* been with Mao, the river in which I swam was *not* the Yangtze. I proclaimed that the group was confusing me with someone else entirely.

Amid laughter and back slapping, the group stuck to its lore and asked me what had happened to my underwear and how I had survived the snakes in the river.

That morning I left the meeting still confused but resigned to my new mythic role as the American geographer who went swimming with Mao. I remain convinced of the following verity: *Truths are harder to promote than those myths for which people are hungry.*

◆

There are spontaneous moments in foreign travel when you experience something that you have not anticipated. One such trip was to London with good friends Larry and Diana. Here is the episode of serendipity that recalls that good fortune.

SERENDEPITY IN LONDON

On a trip with friends Loghead and Diana, Chloe and I went to London for a week of city exploration in about 1997. We found Saint Martin-in-the Fields, a church that we had always heard of on our local NPR station, KBIA as a source of lovely Baroque music. There was a cafeteria in the basement of the structure where we had a surprisingly choice lunch. We then explored the Gift Shop (always a vital aspect of city work) and I found a fun pen called the Alibi. But...most wonderfully, we then went upstairs and into a vast and grand sanctuary. In that space was a chamber orchestra and a choir of perhaps thirty voices. They were practicing Easter music. We sat down and listened to them rehearse for twenty-five minutes. The music filled both the whole space of the dome and of our minds as we suddenly were reminded of the power of place, especially in a religious setting. We did not talk. We did not photograph. We sat and listened and felt very lucky that we had chosen this day, this time, this moment to visit here.

◆

Another spin on travel is always the road trip taken with family—and most often in domestic landscapes. In this episode that follows I used a road trip as a means of trying to diminish my guilt over *not* giving Mother the time she so wanted to have me read her political vox pop writing—or even to listen to her as she gave me impromptu lectures in her home on Pleasant Street in Oberlin, Ohio. A full decade after returning from Taiwan and soon after being hired by University of California Los Angeles, I had driven to Oberlin to see Mother and try to make her feel that my move to California was not simply to be distant from her waving of manuscripts in my face exhorting (no, demanding) that I read them. This episode portrays the high costs and hijinks of a therapy road trip.

Mother and the Yellowstone Connection

One of the most amazing trips I have ever taken was a summer trip in 1973. I was driving to Oberlin alone to visit Mother. As I approached her home on Pleasant Street, I was mulling over the guilt that I always carried to Oberlin. My paramount life task in Mother's eyes was to read the manuscripts and letters that she had been writing for decades in her battles with various American institutions. She would often meet me at the front door, manuscript in hand, asking me if I had read this yet. I steeled myself for a repeat of this common scene as I walked up the sidewalk from my VW to her front door.

This trip was no different. As the front door opened, Mother (full name Katherine Shepherd *Hayden* Salter) made a request of me even before the door was fully open and I had put my small bag on the floor. "Kit, would you take me to Yellowstone Park?"

In high surprise, I asked her why that particular wish, that particular park?

She reminded me that her great uncle was Ferdinand Vandeveer Hayden. In the early 1850-70s Hayden had been involved in the New York Geological Survey. In 1871 he headed up a team of fifty people to the Yellowstone region in northwest Wyoming to investigate the rumored exotic landscape elements. Wisely—and with great significance, Hayden invited artist Thomas Moran and Civil War photographer William Henry Jackson to be part of the Yellowstone team. When, eighteen months later, the Hayden Survey made its report to Congress, Hayden organized a stunning display of the landscape images of Moran and Jackson in association with the Survey's report.

Subsequently, Congress declared Yellowstone to be the first U.S. National Park and dedicated $25,000 to establish this park, intending to thwart development of this amazing world shown in the graphics on display in the Capitol Rotunda.

Our investigation team of 1973 consisted of Mother, gracious and ever-supportive niece, Helen Roetter Marshall, and me. For our field vehicle, I had my VW convertible and it was pretty new and quite dependable. Helen was a grand spirit and she was able to adjust her schedule quickly to clear about seven or eight days. I did the same. Mother, Helen, and I set out in Ohio summer weather for points west.

Ah, the delight of a road trip. Ah, but it was not really realized on this junket. Mother sat in the front seat and this means that Helen sat in the back seat and I drove. Only a spirit like Helen could have tolerated the buffeting and demands of fifteen hundred miles each way in an open car. Mother, seeing her son as a profoundly captive audience selected a series of detailed genealogical discussions to bring to the front seat of the car. Helen could feign inability to hear in the wilds of the back seat and I was thereby the recipient of many, many, hours of monologue on family matters. It got so I drove longer hours each day. I could at least keep my eyes focused straight forward and give careful attention to signs, parked cars, litter, abandoned tires, hitchhikers, and all things roadside at the moment. When the three of us were in a motel room at night, it was trickier to patiently absorb Mother's ongoing monologues.

After about two or three days, we came close to the Park. I decided that we would want to see Old Faithful, the Falls on the Little Yellowstone River, and maybe some bubbling mud holes—and some landscape feature with the Hayden name. As I type this, I cannot believe that I was so very selfish a son to get

Katharine Hayden into the Park and then just fly around and hardly see anything. I know, however, that I was at the very edge of my sanity. Spending such close and unbroken hours with Mother's highly expressive presentations on the political issues that had been bubbling in her busy and energetic mind the prior twenty-five years was unprecedented in my life. In fact, I felt that I was close to giving the car to Helen and asking her to drive Mother home, leaving me to hitchhike *anywhere* else. But, we continued our desultory sightseeing in this most extraordinary national park in our country.

The event that broke the spell was that at one point we were crossing a high pass to see some other wonder spot and we got caught in a major snowstorm! This must have been in late May or even July. It served as a reminder that life was uncertain and that we had better get back to our regular patterns before things really went crazy. We descended below the temporary snow line, left the park, and headed back for Ohio. For most of the drive back I felt like I was in the Chevy Chase movie where the family spends crazy time and money to see the Grand Canyon. Upon getting there, Chevy (the father) looks over the edge for perhaps ten seconds and says, "Okay... fine. We've seen it. Let's get going. There are more things to see." I cannot recall the trip home except to say that Helen was never more a joy than on the swing back. We put the top up on the VW and for a lot of the time and Helen did a grand job of chatting with Mother and keeping the car cool and social. As we reached Indiana and Ohio again, Mother's powerful need to educate *right now, right here* diminished in its intensity in the tight little car.

It occurred to me again and again that the passengers in a car conversation really had no options before headphones. Now, at least, a person can bury himself or herself in headphones and closed eyes. In this trip it was all very immediate and very proximate. Prayers of thanks go to Helen as I recall that week! And I think Mother had a fine family time.

HEMINGWAY'S CUBA

Ernest Hemingway lived in Cuba for about twenty of his near sixty-two years. He was there in the 1920s as a young man who loved fishing, loved the people of the sea, and grew to love the city of Havana. He lived for about two years in a hotel called Ambos Mundos (Both Worlds) down by the harbor. He had a room on the fifth floor (Rm. 511 is so marked) and he could see Havana Bay, the Morro tower built in the 1600s, and some of the oldest trees and structures of this early Caribbean city. There was a bar on the top floor of the hotel, graced with a grand view of the harbor and the earliest plaza of Havana. The hotel's location on Calle Obisbo gave the writer easy walking access to his favorite bars and cafes in Habana Vieja (Old Havana). The hotel is one of the early places given a deep renovation by the government in an effort to make Old Havana attractive to tourists (the major cruise ship slip is only 700-800 yards from Ambos Mundos) and to promote Cuba's willingness to support and promote international (and UN) calls for the preservation of much of Havana's dramatic early urban landscape.

On Calle Obisbo is the Florida Hotel—another one of Papa's favorites—and, more importantly, it is the home to the Floridita Bar and Café. It was in this bar that, supposedly, the daiquiri was invented. Hemingway drank there often and thinned the amount of sugar and upped the amount of rum, creating what is now called the *Papa Daiquiri*. It is cited and touted as a hallmark of Hemingway's Havana and Cuban presence. This has great economic import to the Floridita for it had some of the most expensive drinks we found in the city, and yet it was always, always crowded.

Traveling with newspaper people this trip, I imagined the following conversation. It opens with four journalists new to the Floridita Bar. One of the four speaks to his friends around the small table.

"All right, we are going to modify history."

"How?"

"Well, you are journalists with a newspaper resource and are known to even occasionally do some research. One of you will find a letter from Hemingway—or, if necessary, from a friend of his who wrote to someone on your paper's staff fifty or sixty years ago."

"Okay...maybe, what does the letter say?"

"It will recount the exciting time this person had with Papa at some bar we have not yet found, but it will be one of the elegant but not-so-busy ones in Habana Vieja."

"Yeah, but so what?"

"The 'so what' of this is that the letter will talk about the invention of the still-unknown drink. We will call it...(the speaker pauses for just a few seconds) the Habana PapaRon (*ron* is rum in Spanish). This letter will explain that Papa and your father's friend dreamed it up at this yet-to-be determined bar on a lazy Habana evening, but Hemingway left the city soon afterward and moved on to Key West. The PapaRon was never capitalized upon. Now we can score with it."

"How?"

"Easy, look at all of the places that talk about Hemingway drank here, wrote here, visited here, danced here...there are endless examples of places made sacred by his mid- 20th century presence. If we can make the drink sound interesting, we can score big time!"

"What's in the Habana PapaRon, oh dreamer of innovation?"

"Well.... how about a good shot of rum and...citrus juice and a generous splash of Scotch? That would sound almost reasonable and it might work."

Well...this conversation never happened as far as I know, but the concept is full of merit. Some journalist or exploring traveler just has to 'find' the letter... Everywhere you go in this city you gives you some idea of how sacred Ernest Hemingway (Papa) is in Cuba. Marina Hemingway is the largest marina in Havana Bay and it has a nice restaurant where Castro and Hemingway had their single meeting in 1960. It was during the annual marlin fishing tourney and the restaurant—called Papa's—has photos of the meeting and a story line about the encounter. And if you go to Finca Vigia—the lovely home some twenty miles from Havana where Papa lived with his final wife, Mary Welsh Hemingway for over a decade, you feel as though you have come to Mount Sinai or Lourdes. The stage is clearly primed for the 'finding' of the PapaRon.

◆

Sometimes the travel image in our mind is distant, long-haul, and highly complex. But sometimes, it plays with your mind very differently.

ROAD MOVIES

All through my life movies have been of major importance. The "road movie" is special in that such a theme combines the delicious suspension of disbelief (required of all movies) with the drama of what happens, and might happen, on the road. *Thelma and Louise* is, in fact, the first movie that rushes to my mind as a person asks, do you like road movies? *Thelma and Louise* is the instantaneous image as I shape an answer. But, go beyond that dramatic movie (can you recall much besides the ending?), and you'll probably hit upon various Chevy Chase *Vacation* movies, *The Grapes of Wrath, The English Patient, Breaking Away, The African Queen, The Mission, Road Warrior*, and—well countless others. As I stare at the few titles here, I realize that such an inventory is endless. My mind, however, is not captured by a movie, but by the concept *of a movie* when involved in a life and death scene of my own. Because this occurred in a foreign setting, I include the event in this Travel chapter.

Mountaineering Mount Yu Shan

When Linda and I spent three years in Taiwan, great recreation was found in mountain climbing and hiking. In 1962, I organized a small climbing group of two Chinese guys and me. Our plan was to scale Mount Yu Shan (Mount Morrison). With a height of 13,113 feet, it is the tallest mountain in Taiwan and taller than Mount Fuji in Japan. Our trio had some rope, ice axes, a lot of inexperience, and dangerous bravado. We had no guide because the mountain appeared to be largely a walk-up from our novice perspectives. We spent one night camping out at about 8000 feet and undertook the remaining 5000 feet at dawn the second day.

I do not remember our approach very well except to recall that my two buddies stopped climbing about 1000-1500 feet short of the summit. We talked and they said they just didn't want to go any higher, but they would wait if I wanted to finish up the challenge. I felt good, and two years earlier I had successfully climbed about 17,000 feet to the peak of Mount Popocatepetl in the Valley of Mexico, so I felt okay about the solo ascent for the rest of the climb. They settled in at the upper edge of the tree line and I took off. I figured it would be about a three or four hour round trip.

I climbed at a reasonable pace and finally reached the upper lip of a cirque some 300 feet short of the Yu Shan summit. (A cirque is the rim of a dead volcano crater.) It appeared to be the last tricky feature to deal with before a final steep ascent to the peak. At the upper edge of this crater rim, I had developed a simple climbing process. I was afraid to walk along the very thin ridge edge since the surface of the cirque was icy and steep. At the lower lip, there was probably about a thousand-foot drop onto a debris pile, fed steadily by whatever it was that slipped on the icy surface or fell into that crater. On the other side of the edge was a similar option…so, I sat on the edge, chopped a foot hole for one heel with my three-foot-long ice pick, and then, slowly, oh, ever so slowly, edged my way around the top of the cirque, moving toward the peak and a more reliable topography. It was the *Salter lateral butt-slide* that I developed to carefully scoot and slide the 200 lateral feet to reach a more secure beginning point for the final ascent.

As is so often the case with repetitions, the repeated use of my maneuver grew into overconfidence. At one point I broke my routine of not moving my foot to the next foot hold until I had carved that new niche for secure footing for my climbing shoe. But, stupidly, I was lulled by repetition into moving my foot, slide my butt to the right—but had not yet carved a secure foothold. I had broken the critical attention to the new Salter Lateral Butt Slide! I began to slide down the 300-400 foot incline that would take me to the lower edge and then sail me down another 1000 feet to a quiet and cold death.

As I started sliding, I still remember with intensity my first reaction: "Hey...this is like the movies! The slide, the sun, the bright sky, the cocky climber....God...it's all perfect!" This thought must have taken about fifty feet of downward incline. The next thought was more sensible: "Shit....this is it. This is *for real!*" I twisted my head around and saw that ice and small rocks were following me in this downward flow. Below me some seventy-five feet I could see a small triangle of rock—maybe the size of a generous piece of pizza—was sticking out of the snow. The surface, otherwise, was a sheet of ice. I nudged my cascading body toward the triangle of hope. As I came toward it, I interlocked my gloved fingers and went over it and forced myself to catch on that tiny peninsula of stone no matter the pain. Rocks and ice slid into my face and over my head and then went on down to the bottom lip of the cirque, falling away to nothingness.

After thirty seconds there was nothing but silence except for the distant landing of debris that my slide had dislodged. I hung there breathless and terrified for three or four minutes and then looked up to see what my options were. Few...few indeed, but at least I was alive. The slope of ice above me looked impossible to negotiate but blessedly I still had my ice axe tied to my right wrist. On my left wrist I had lost my watch, but I had gained a thin, clean cut across the inside of my wrist. It had gone deep enough to give blood, but the incision was just a tiny bit too shallow to have cut the vein that would have ended my show right then. Even as I write this and look again at the ragged white scar, I feel lucky as hell to be writing this myself and not have it just be an entry in some record of Lost Shansi Oberlin Students.

I did not finish the climb. The midday sun had softened the ice and snow just enough to allow me to gouge out small footholds. I very carefully got myself foothold by foothold by foothold back up to the crest of the cirque, where I had stupidly broken my routine and begun the slide downslope. At the crest, I wrapped some rag around my left wrist, took one other look at the remaining mountain lying between me and the real summit of Mt. Yu Shan. With a clear wish to descend and not continue upward, I turned and hiked very carefully back down to my two curious and nervous friends.

They claimed that they were beginning to worry about me and were just about to come after me. I told them I had had a little slip but that all was well. It was then they noticed the cut across the top of my left wrist where I had grappled with the stone pizza piece. One of them had some tape so I taped it and we hiked back down to base camp and gave Mount Yu Shan its due for that day.

◆

Lessons on the road in travel need not come from a crisis. Taking advantage of the captive audience in a car cruising toward a commonly anticipated destination can make a seminar room out of car's front and back seats. There will be more about that in the forthcoming hitchhiking and freight-riding chapter, but here is one travel episode that I have thought about many times.

THEMES FOR WRITING ON THE ROAD

For Thanksgiving in 2003, Heidi and Sugie came to Breakfast Creek, as did Marianne Kenney (a teacher friend of Cathy's and mine for nearly twenty years who lives in Denver). The five of us made a trip to Kansas City on the Friday after Thanksgiving. Cathy and I wanted to show off the holiday lights of the Plaza in Kansas City. We could then easily get the California girls back to Kansas City International Airport for their trip home.

En route to Kansas City, I realized that I had bright minds in the confines of my west-bound Toyota Avalon and I posed this conundrum: "Okay...here's the problem. For decades I've thought of and talked about myself as a writer. But, for those same years, I have managed to fill up my days and nights with endless lists of little things that always seemed essential to do to meet job and professional obligations. But I'm always thinking, 'when I get this list done, then maybe I'll have a chance to write!' So I retire on December 31, 2002 and by January 15, 2003, I'm planning to outline and undertake a major (1000-1200 page) manuscript on human geography. Now here we are deep into November of my first year of retirement—and even though I have created a fine outline of my text (Human Imprint and Impact on the Earth), I have written only about ten to fifteen thousand words and I began it two months ago." I took a shot of water and continued.

"What's wrong? Why have I, yet again, filled up my life with lists of things I feel I *must* do before I can try to do any real writing?" I told my captive audience I would accept all their answers and ideas on writing that would help me come face to face with my quandary. Let the record show that included in the quartet to whom this riddle was posed were published authors, a doctorate in English, two English profs, a journalist, an artistic and productive teacher who has written many short units, and people who had known words and me for lots of years—and thinking people every one!

We spoke to this delimma for almost seventy-five minutes and these are the elements of writing that I have culled from that productive road trip conversation.

Theme one: There must be discipline. There must be a schedule for writing. You need to declare a day, or a time, that is only for creative writing. Heidi talked about Woody Allen saying that if you just show up, you have a good chance of writing. And all agreed that if you fail to show up at such a writing time, seldom will writing be accomplished.

Theme two: We talked about "the muse" concept. There was not a common voice on the muse concept. Sugie and Chloe were keen to have me come to grips with whether or not I really wanted to write the college text. If not, then it would be hard as hell to get the pages done. If, on the other hand, I really wanted to write the text (if I had the requisite drive in my heart or mind), then it was only discipline that I was lacking. I explained to the group that I did not really believe in the muse—although I have had some pieces of writing in my life that have just flown out from my fingers. However, I declared that I was willing to entertain the muse concept.

I reminded them of Faulkner's classic answer to a senior lady who asked him, "Mr. Faulkner, do you write only when the muse moves you, or do you write by schedule?"

"I write," he replied, "*only* when the muse moves me—and it moves me every day from eight a.m. until noon!"

Theme three: Never finish a smooth section at the end of the day." Sugie talked about the importance of—especially if you have momentum going—not bringing a flowing section to completion at the end of a writing day or time. It is better, she has read and believes, that if you have the mind moving well with an idea, put your mind on pause rather than bringing the hot passage to full conclusion. The object here is to come back to your writing the next day and be stimulated again by that good section that you have left as a work-in-progress. As you finish it on day two, you may then be infused with the excitement (again) of that realm of thought and be able to wrap it up, and then push on in good pace to the next segment.

Theme four: Also the group decided that it was a poor plan to make endless little lists. Do not let little projects (wash the sliding glass door, straighten the bookshelves, dry dishes in the dish rack, etc.) come into your writing time. When you sit down to write, stay in your chair! See the little things that fill up lists relentlessly as the enemy! When you write, *write*. Reward yourself by doing small tasks after you have written for four hours minimum.

One of the best lines that came from this road seminar was "Act your way into right thinking rather than think your way into right acting!" This came from Heidi and I think it is part of the wisdom of AA. The concept is that it is damn hard to ever *think* yourself into fully right deportment. Rather, just begin to *act* the way you want to act. Forget thinking your way into that deportment. If you want to write, sit your arse down and write. Don't talk about it. Don't plan on it. Don't put such an act on a list and work toward it: *Just do it!*

The buzz of ideas and beliefs filled the Avalon for many miles and minutes. The talk was great, just great. I still try to shape my writing efforts with these recollections in mind. An outcome of this road trip seminar was simple:

Work very hard to get rid of guilt at *not* doing lists! I have spent so many years being in the thrall of lists, I need *not* to let them lead me all the way to my grave. Give writing the spot it ought to have and make every day (or nearly every day) have some writing time that is uncluttered, focused, and unshadowed by guilt.

After all our road trip conversation and the stimulating feedback from my captive audience, I, of course, dropped the geography text. I'm sure that that decision was no surprise to anyone a party to our traveling road seminar.

CHAPTER FOUR

CHINA

In a sense, China episodes are really a sub-set to the Travel chapter just completed. However, the three years in China (1961-1964) were so profoundly different than any era of life I had been exposed to that I feel compelled to give the experiences and learning from those three Taiwan years and the seven or eight China Tours I led, or Cathy and I led from our Los Angeles UCLA base and from the Missouri base in the 1980s to'90s that they have to stand alone.

BEARING WITNESS

In my first year in Taiwan (1961), I was in constant awe at the range of strong customs I witnessed. Like so many outsiders, my life was touched every day by new things. At one point I was walking with a student on a long hike into Taichung, the nearby city. We were negotiating a fairly steep hill, alongside a major road with some intersecting smaller roads. All of a sudden, a bicycle load of bricks being carted downhill by a worker (a three-wheeled cart with one person peddling). It spun out of control. At the intersection we were just approaching, the cart flipped over as the bike-peddling driver tried to turn away from a truck that had just pulled out in front of him. The cart overturned. The bricks went every which way. The brick driver was piled beneath bricks, bent wheels, and the edge of the truck. After a second of dumbfoundedness at what we were witnessing, I made a move toward the guy—where a crowd was already gathering.

"No!" yelled the student, grabbing my arm.

"Come on, we can help," I yelled pulling my arm free. He grabbed me again and forced me to stop. This was quite unusual for a student interacting with a professor in China.

"I will speak in English. Listen to my words," There was a look of terror on the student's face. "If you touch that man, if you even get up close to him, it will change your life forever." I stared at him, relaxing my efforts to pull away a little. He went on. "In China, blame for the countless accidents that occur between carts and trucks and bikes is always argued. The only certainty is that if there is a *waigworen* (foreigner) close to the scene—and *especially* if it is an American. That is the person who will somehow be blamed—and expected to pay for the accident!"

I shook his arm off. "That's stupid… you and I were only walking on the side of the road. I simply want to see if I can be of any help."

"Are you a medical doctor?" the student asked with his eyes looming close to mine.

"No…you know I'm not, but still I can maybe do something to help."

The student looked at me with an intensity I had not yet seen in Taiwan. "If you touch that man or get any of his blood on your hands or clothes or even if you get close and try to talk with him or anyone else, you will be blamed. You will be sued. You will cause the University great trouble. You will probably be forced to leave Taiwan. Do not get any closer. Let us back away carefully right this minute."

I did. I have never forgotten the event. I do not even know if the cart driver lived. But I can still feel the burning intensity of the student's eyes as he fundamentally yelled the rules of life to me in my new setting.

The Unscheduled Village Visit

On one of the tour trips to China that Chloe and I led, we were scheduled to fly one leg not on China domestic airlines, but on a military aircraft. This came about—we assumed—because the tourism industry in China was growing so powerfully fast. In any case, it was outside of X'ian that we had our plane set down and were told that it would be at least three hours (which usually meant four or five) before we would be able to leave. It was mid-summer and the waiting room had the classic few high overhead fans that turned at a speed just high enough to keep flies off the blades.

Chloe and I looked at each other and stepped to the side of the room. "What about an exploration?"

"You're on!"

I told the national guide that my wife and I were going to stretch our legs and explained that we were going to just slip away so that we would not be followed by a dozen or so people curious about an unscheduled countryside visit. The guide could see the merit in keeping his/our charges safely contained in the military waiting room. I assured him that we would be back within two and a half hours. "Take three if you need them—we won't be going anywhere for probably four at the soonest!"

As we picked up our small packs and went for the side door, Betty—a sixty-year-old retired teacher from southern Illinois—slipped into stride with us. "I heard what you said. I want to come, too." I told her that we would be walking a lot and there would be dust and heat. She reminded me that she had been a high school biology teacher and had done many field trips over a lot of years, often through uncertain and unknown terrain. Chloe said, "Come on...we've got to make our move, or we'll be followed by half the group." The three of us left the building and headed for the long blacktop roadway that paralleled the edge of the base.

The day was just about perfect. We got through the gate and looked out across a landscape of summer soybeans, rice beds and little nests of adobe structures clustered around an earthen floor for the drying of produce and grain. Betty, Chloe, and I set out in easy and pleasant conversation along the road. There was no jeep, truck, or lorry traffic. Only a few bicycles were out in this mid-day July warmth. Although we had had some rural stops on earlier days on this tour, we had not yet had the perfunctory visit to a commune. Given the switch that was taking place in China with the nervous emergence of ever-more free local marketplaces, I thought the national tour guide might just bypass stops in the rural, small-scale countryside entirely.

Not this day. We walked maybe two kilometers observing and talking for a few sentences now and again with a man or woman working the fields and we fell into a quiet harmony with the beauty of the Chinese rural scene. The economy of space used for agriculture was quite stunning. The households and farmsteads seemed to take up no extra space. Fields ran right up to edges of buildings or adobe walls of the farmhouse. Kids would be sometimes playing with some of the ducks that were being tended, and they would spot the *'waigworen'* and look and then shout something and then all scamper back to a household doorway. It was one of these skitterings that caused us to stop and visit a real rural household.

A grandfather came out from one of the doorways that had been a haven to three or four giggling four- and five-year-olds who had seen us and then fled. Since we had been on this tour for a week or two already, my Chinese (plumbed up from who knows where?) had become reasonably useful again, at least at a low level. The man walked out to the edge of the lane we had been following.

"Are you foreigners?" he asked in Chinese with some a mixture of a bark and a real question. This question always intrigued me for it was visually quite apparent that we were not Asian in any way.

"Yes. We are. We are Americans," I replied, and then added, "We are teachers."

"What are you doing here?" This question, too, was a common one when Chloe and I encountered someone in one of our explorations off the usual tourist tracks.

"Our airplane had a problem. We had to land to get it fixed."

"You have your own airplane?" the old man queried. He was now surrounded by the returned children and maybe two or three other family members, all younger than him.

"No, we don't have our own plane. We are with a group of travelers and all of us had to stop at once." I always felt uncomfortable using the word 'tourists' to describe the groups that Chloe and I led.

"You mean the plane did not just drop you three off?" He laughed in an old man's way at the idea of just swooping low and ejecting the three of us.

"No...the whole plane stopped. The three of us wanted to see the countryside so we left the base and have been walking for maybe an hour."

"They let you leave the base just like that?" He expressed a little surprise in his voice and question.

My reply was, "When I explained to the Base Commander (what word did I make up for 'commander,' I wonder) that these women would protect me, he agreed that a walk was okay. He told me not to get out of sight of these women, especially the older one." The grandfather looked at the petite retired schoolteacher and the bright face of the innocent, Chloe, and he nodded.

"Yes...I can see you are safe. Won't you come in and have some tea? Even have some lunch?" This seemed to be an enormous leap for him—and for us, as well. The three of us agreed to the courtesy of the tea and we stepped over a small irrigation ditch and walked to the shaded doorway of the small structure. It was an adobe wall on top of a stone foundation base. Rice paddies came right up to the margin of his house.

The next hour was a family drama. The three of us sat in firm chairs while another five or six people (from six years old to probably mid-seventies) arrayed themselves around a crowded wooden table. All manners of food were produced and everything we were offered was keenly watched by ten sets of eyes watching us react to household garden vegetables, local spices, even meats of uncertain origin. I thought often of the most important thing I have ever taught a graduate student: "When you are abroad and invited to share a meal, *never* ask what you are eating if you do not know what it is! Ask later...

maybe three months later...but do not ask what it is at the table with the item in your hand or your mouth—and in the presence of the host!"

We spoke of life in the village versus life in the city and learned—as Cathy and I had so often in prior years of travel in China—how little interaction there was between the two settings. The people (and there were few people in their twenties here) of the village world knew of the rapid economic development of urban coastal China, but the closest they had gotten to such dynamics was a slightly more open local rice and pig market. Farmers seemed to be getting increasing independence in planting and marketing decisions and, for the rural world, there was nothing more significant than that. This peasant family had a black and white TV and this window on the wider world gave them images that were sometimes disturbing, but mostly they described them as foreign and unrelated to their lives here in this farming village.

We thought it was necessary to leave as soon as we could after this meal and talk. It was essential to get safely back to the military base and the waiting room. We felt perhaps farther away from our own home world in this rural home some three or four kilometers from the military airport than we had in our prior ten days of exploration of exotic China. We backed out of the major room, both bowing and thanking them all profusely. We promised to come again (think about the hollowness of that phrase in any situation!) and to send them some photos of all of us together.

Our return walk was at a faster pace. We talked a little about what we had learned, or at least what we had been exposed to. All three of us felt that we had pulled back the Green Curtain and had seen that the real heart of China continued to be solid rural folk working the land with traditions of grand intensity. This image, of course, is deeply argued by every urban experience we have ever had in China, especially in the really large cities like Shanghai and Beijing and Guangzhou (Canton), but on that day, in that place, within our trio, we all fully believed in the Chinese rural worlds keenly involved in an ever more self-reliant style!

◆

When traveling abroad, one has a heightened sense of observation. This episode that follows is one that Cathy and I fell into entirely. We were out on the streets of Beijing much later than we usually were. There was a potential for change in the air of the city because China was moving apace to find its way into the top global economies as well as dominant nations in terms of political significance. The continued role of Chairman Mao Tse-tung as the universal Chinese portrait was even occasionally being questioned in the second decade after his death in 1976. Although all the political language in the Chinese press continued to praise the Communist revolution (begun in 1949), the spread of market-driven capitalist enterprises was on the increase. You could see it in street vendors, expanding retail activities, and even in changes in land use within and around the urban edges.

So, this episode came on to us in full drama at midnight in Tiananmen Square in the heart of Beijing.

REPLACING MAO

In 1996 Chloe and I were leading our only Mizzou China trip. We had arrived late in the day in Beijing and were put up in an old but elegant hotel that we had stayed in once before. After my customary Optional First Night Seminar on Beijing, we sat around and talked a while with about a dozen of our twenty travelers. Beijing was evocative and discussions went just where a Prof wants such talks to go. When we finally broke up about eleven p.m., all of us seemed to feel that we had—really and truly—arrived in China.

Chloe and I left the Beijing Hotel to do a constitutional before we went up to our room and get materials ready for the next two days. We headed toward Tiananmen Square because that was a venue of late night activity. As we approached the square it seemed a perfect night for this exploration. The June 4, 1989 student demonstration and bloody governmental reaction seemed already lost in history. There were probably fifteen little pods of four to six people scattered about the massive square. (One hundred acres of old housing was razed and replaced with monumental and revolutionary architecture during the heyday of the Communist Revolution between 1949 and the construction of Mao's Mausoleum on the square in 1976). There was a little moonlight and there were perimeter lights still on. Chloe and I talked softly about all that had gone on around and within this massive square.

Just a little after midnight a truck with a long extension arm pulled through the arch into the Forbidden City and positioned itself just beyond the archway. Chocks were put out by the wheels on this large truck after it had come to a stop just yards away from the massive portrait of Chairman Mao hung high on the edge of Tiananmen Square.

A few of the pods of night people began to drift toward the arch. Recall that this is the arch that is the ceremonial entranceway into the three to five thousand rooms of the Ming and Qing Dynasties Forbidden City. You know the image best by the fifteen foot high painting of Chairman Mao Tse-tung

(Mao Zedong) that is suspended above the crown of the archway. Mao has looked out on the activities of the Square, the city, the populace and the nation from this unique position for at least thirty-five years.

The man in the basket at the end of the long cherry picker arm attached a number of ropes to the top of Mao's painting. As he did this, we began to wonder if maybe we were witnessing the absolutely unbelievable removal of Mao from his most powerful vantage point in the entire country. Slowly ropes were attached and then the man in the cherry picker basket gathered four of the rope ends and tied them together and hung the knotted cluster on the end of his basket. The arm rose up slowly and, even more slowly, the fifteen by eight foot painting of Mao was lifted off the wall. The universal image hung lifeless and then slowly spun below the man in the box at the end of this midnight arm.

Chloe and I tried to get a photo of the removal, but we did not have any flash and the light was too poor. "Damn!" we both thought as we realized we were very possibly witnessing the eclipse of one of the most powerful political forces of the twentieth century...and all we had to record this event was words—like so much grand history! We went over to the truck—and there must have been fifty people milling around by this time—and were able to get a short length of the silken white rope that had been used for the suspension of the painting. We were both nervous and excited at what we were seeing. We thought such an event would most likely be accompanied by some sort of massive demonstration to give Mao a grand sendoff that was more in keeping with his revolutionary stature and associated crowd frenzies.

But there was none of that. Looking up at the great open place—an openness that I had never seen in some nine or ten times across seven or eight trips to Beijing—we talked about the power of that particular Mao icon. That painting of Mao was surely better known than even the green-eyed Afghan girl on the 1988 cover of *National Geographic* magazine. Her face had been reproduced literally millions of times. We put the silken remnant in a pocket and grinned with nervous delight that we had been here, right here, at this moment.

But, at that moment, a large truck could be seen driving across the stone surface of the Tiananmen Square. The pods of people moved aside and flowed sideways giving full access to the truck. It was clearly bound for this now remarkably empty archway. The cherry picker truck was still there and its chocks were still fixed on the stone pavement while the removed portrait of Mao was being secured for travel. On the back of the truck just arriving was a massive tarpaulin. Four men were riding on the truck's flat bed, two on each side of a large item under canvas.

Right…you've guessed it. The truck stopped and two of the men worked hard to get the canvas off the new painting. It was a fresh, glistening identical portrait of Mao. With patience, the four ropes attached to the basket of the cherry picker were now reattached to large hooks on the back of the new Mao picture. It was then carefully lifted high, swung over to the archway wall where the old painting had been. The same man who had done the removal now spent some thirty minutes doing the reinstallation. Four of the ground crew took the old portrait and got it under canvas. I asked if I could slice off just a little from the removed picture for a souvenir, but he said no one should touch it or he'd get in trouble.

And by a little after one a.m., the new painting was up. The old painting was covered and hidden on the truck. Both trucks were gone. Chloe and I had a six-inch piece of silken white rope as a kind of evidence of the event. Half of the small group had left the square. Except for the relative brilliance of the paint on the new portrait, it was as if nothing had occurred at all in the prior seventy-five minutes. But it did. The drama—even for those minutes of misunderstanding—was quite heady. The Mao icon appears to be still there.

THE GREAT BRICK TREK.

A quick image. In one of my first days after arriving in Taiwan for teaching, I spent an afternoon wandering though the countryside of Big Belly Mountain (Ta Du Shan) where Tunghai University was located. On that outing I met a woman who looked to be in her seventies. She had gray hair wrapped up in a bun, blue peasant clothes that were loose fitting and covered with the mud of labors of the land. She had a bamboo pole of some three inches diameter and on each end of the pole, she had a basket with some thirty wet clay bricks. She was taking them from the shaping yard to the kiln to fire them.

We chatted a little because I was still working very hard in an effort to gain at least conversational Chinese. She was patient with me—for about three minutes. In an effort to thank her, I asked her if I could carry her load to the kiln she was bound for. She grinned at me and told me that I would not be able to lift her load. I—then twenty one or so and still of good frame and weight and recently active as an Oberlin

College wrestler—laughed and told her she was wrong. "May I take them for you?" I asked again. She told me that she did not want to embarrass her American friend by having me try to carry them and fail. She started to crouch down again to get under the carry pole.

"Wait....how about this? If I cannot pick them up and carry them to your kiln, I will give the pole right back to you and give you the pomelo that I am carrying as a gift for letting me try. (Pomelo is a wonderful grapefruit-like fruit that I would sometimes carry on hikes for moisture and energy.)

"You really want to try to carry these?" She was just a little edgy because I had broken her pattern of movement and work. "And if you cannot, you'll put them right down and give me your pomelo, too?"

"Right....exactly right." I felt myself pumping up, ready for this chance to give face to American college youth!

"*Keyi*....[okay]..." She backed away from the bamboo, which stayed at about four feet high because of wire bands that linked the carry pole to the two baskets of bricks.

I stepped under the pole, grinning to her and grinning to myself. A guy loves little strength victories, especially in the face of disbelieving women—even if they are three times the guy's age. Putting the pole on my shoulders and using my hands to steady each of the two baskets, I stood tall.

Nothing.

I awkwardly grinned again and resettled the bamboo on my shoulders and put my whole torso into lifting the two baskets. There was a little budge as one of them lifted off the earth and the other clung to its solid purchase on the pathway.

I set the pole down and carefully centered myself again and, this time, did not bother grinning. I had a whole culture's face to save in this next lift. I arched myself into my full height

(I was probably six inches taller—and forty pounds heavier—than the senior woman). This time both baskets broke their hold with the earth. I extended myself fully and had each basket maybe eight inches off the earthen pathway.

"Now you must walk. You must take them to the kiln that is over beyond that building. Come. We must go. I am late already."

Now, the physics of holding yourself erect with eighty pounds of wet mud more or less equally distributed at the two ends of a single pole seems simple to write of. But, when your face is in the crucible and your own personal pride is just barely off the mud in front of you, moving ahead in steady and balanced stride is just about impossible. I would walk forward. The baskets (each seemingly with its own trajectory in mind) would move laterally. Or, the right one swung ahead while the left one dallied and considered more backward movement. All the while, the erect torso is wondering what the hell is going on here.

I barely succeeded in carrying the load the seventy-five yards that I had promised, all the while trying to look as though it was child's play...and all the while feeling as though the woman was just short of slipping in under the pole and nudging my shoulders out of the picture while she finished another of what was probably fifty carries a day.

I reached the kiln. I gave her the pomelo. She was gracious and said I did just fine. I went on beyond the farmstead and out of sight just as fast as my stressed body could move.

It was a humbling and powerfully focused learning experience. I still feel that pole. I still feel complete awe at what this woman was able to do. I have never since that early time in Taiwan lightly offered to carry a peasant's bamboo shoulder of pole of any rural product!

ENGLISH LESSONS ON THE PACIFIC

To complete my dissertation, I received one teaching quarter off from UCLA in 1969. I bought a one-way air ticket from Los Angeles to Taiwan. I spent eight weeks doing the final field work for my manuscript on the Geography of Marginality: Agricultural Development of Eastern Taiwan. Eastern Taiwan is similar to the Appalachian landscapes of villages and isolation. It was a great field season. I then arranged to get aboard a Chinese freighter that was leaving Keelung in northern Taiwan and sailing to San Diego. There was a very small cabin that I was bunked in and I ate with the crew. This was not one of those flashy cargo ships that has middle-grade accommodations for the hearty traveler. This was a working freighter that I somehow got some space in.

I spent the bulk of every day with a true laptop—a manual typewriter that sat on my lap or any surface I could commandeer for hours of daylight. Twenty-eight days later, by the time I reached San Diego, I had about 315 pages of dissertation draft finished.

But that is not my story. In the evenings I began to tutor about ten of the Chinese (Taiwanese) crew in English. They were largely young twenty-year-olds from urban Taiwan. I asked the Captain if it would be okay if we spent an hour in lessons after dinner and clean up four or five nights a week. He okayed it, telling me that I would quit it in three days anyway because the men would stop coming to the sessions. I loved the challenge.

We did it for about three weeks, maybe for a total of a dozen lessons. There were generally about seven or eight crew members at the sessions, and we all felt there was some progress being made. It made a great break for me and I think that the lessons had a very specific purpose for the crew members.

A year after we had docked and I had returned to UCLA, I'd completed my dissertation and grown more comfortable in the Southern California world. I learned that the freighter I had sailed on was coming into port again in about a week. I drove down to San Diego and was able to weave my way through the masses of activity and hubbub that characterizes a busy harbor. Talking myself onto the ship because I recognized a man I had gotten to know in my crossing a year earlier, I sought out the captain to greet him. Walking along the working decks, another crew member I also recognized caught my arm and pulled me into a doorway.

"What are you doing here?" he asked with some urgency.

"I wanted to come and say Hi to some of the crew members that I got to know last year," I replied, pulling my arm away from his rough hand.

"None of them is here. No one you taught is here." He made this statement as though this observation was of some gravity.

"Where have they gone? What happened?"

He allowed himself a little smile. "You taught them too well. You made them feel that they really knew some English. The second night in harbor last year, eight Taiwan sailors jumped ship. All eight were in your class!" He then went on. "I would not seek out the Captain if I were you. He blamed the loss of so many completely on you. He called you some sort of—what do you call it? Pied Piper?"

I did not continue my search. I thanked him for the warning and stayed in shadows and made my way back to the dock and out of the harbor. As I drove north on Highway 405 that night,

I realized that teaching sometimes seemed to have a real power associated with it. I was both proud and embarrassed.

◆

In the episode below, Cathy and I were on one of the China tours that we led over a decade and half for UCLA. The tour groups were usually about twenty people, many of whom (but not all) were seniors. In coming to Shanghai, we were keen to find some sort of a venue that not just reek of China Moderne. We had heard of a Shanghai hotel that was unusual because, even while it had added amenities that were attractive to the ever-expanding tourist trade (and not just Americans), we had also heard of a hotel venue that sometimes had an unusual band like the one described below.

THE PEACE HOTEL DINNER BAND

In the era when Chloe and I were leading travel groups from UCLA to China, we always looked forward to Shanghai. It was the only city in China that absolutely was not the same as any other city. We would spend long hours on all sorts of rambling explorations. On a 1982 trip, we decided to have a dinner at the eighth-floor restaurant of the Peace Hotel because of the rumored band. Generally, we ate in fun noodle shops or street cafes, but this hotel eatery was fancier, and had nice ceremony about it. There was the patina of old elegance. The tables were dressed in oft-laundered and ironed tablecloths. The dining room had a comfortable space between tables, unlike the hyper-dense patterns most modern cafes and restaurants (even in China) seemed to feature.

The waiters were mostly senior men—probably in their sixties or seventies—and there was a quietude about the place that was also most unusual for a Shanghai eatery. At about nine p.m., five white haired men came out of some inner door and walked over to a small six-inch dais in the corner of the room. We had noticed but had not asked about the small set of drums and an upright piano. I do not know why we had not inquired about the possibility of music...but suddenly, there it was. These gray and white-haired men each wore a shabby but tidy tux coat and black pants. They took their places and without so much as an emcee's introduction, began to play tunes that felt as though they had been in storage for decades. The Ry Cooder Buena Vista Social Club film and phenomenon had not yet been released when this happened, but that was the experience we felt. These men had actually been part of or all of the Peace Hotel Dinner Band in the ragged years late in and after WWII. Once Mao had won and the Communist Party ascended to full control in 1949, the band was dropped completely. And, in the 1980s when we heard and met them, they were only nervously stepping back into a modest limelight to play again.

The music they played is what a dinner club would have had in the Nat King Cole era—not Glenn Miller—and it made for a delicious dinner and evening. We chatted a while and they, with some awkwardness, talked about the different things they had been doing for the thirty-five to forty years since they were disappeared from that early Mao scene. We never saw them again. We tried one other time to get to that restaurant, but it did not work...but still the images of these elegant seniors playing that night is evocative of *Lost Horizon* and Shangri-La, and Havana in the 1990s. It is one of my travel images that stays active when Cathy and I think again about some of the great China experiences associated with leading small tour groups.

◆

Years before this Shanghai experience, I had been teaching in a Chinese university in Taiwan. This episode nearly changed our entire Taiwan experience!

The Swimming Lesson.

In one of the summers Linda and I spent in Taiwan in our three years of teaching at Tunghai University, we passed a month of the summer break living at the Sun Moon Lake Hotel. This was a really lovely Japanese Inn-like accommodation on the margin of a one hundred-acre lake high in the mountains of the Taiwan Chung Yang Shan. We were staying in an out-cottage that I think had sometimes been used for restaurant help. It was tight but the setting was just tops. I spent my day sitting on a plastic milk crate with my typewriter on the back of a truck's tailgate. If I sat tall, the arms just worked for composing at the typewriter. I was writing *The Youngs Are Fortunate*, a contemporary novel about a fictional Central American country in revolution.

I was trying to gain some proficiency in Mandarin, so I spent a lot of time chatting up the wait-staff at the hotel. I became particularly good friends with a thirty-year-old waiter. He was about five foot six, had thick black hair, a winning smile, and just enough cockiness to make him rather unlike most of the young men who had stayed at the restaurant longer than they had planned. This was a very critical conversation we had. Know that all of the dialogue that follows was in a hasty and stumbling Mandarin and English—both off us using some of each. He opened the chat.

"I see that you swim often." You could not live in this complex and not be attracted to the swimming in the beautiful blue waters of this crater-lake like setting.

"Sure. I swim at least two times a day. This is a beautiful place to hit the water."

"Do you swim with confidence?"

"Probably. I have lived by lakes and rivers for a lot of my life. I like to swim. I guess I have confidence." I did not know where this was going, but it was great language practice.

"Would you teach me to swim?" He looked me straight in the eye.

I thought a second about this. Somehow in northern Wisconsin, if you get a request to teach someone to swim that means a few days in a local lake. In Taiwan, I had a little bit of nervousness because I was selfish with my time and did not want to get caught up in an impossible task. The man continued.

"I do not have enough time off to really learn, but I want to begin to learn. If you are a good swimmer, I could learn some from you and then work on the rest myself when the summer rush is over at the hotel.

This reassured me. "Right. I'll be glad to do the early lesson. When do you want to start?" I said this with a willingness to invest some hours in a swimming lesson.

"How about tonight? I will be through work at eight-thirty and there will still be light for a while." There was a clean efficiency about this guy,

"And where? Where is a place we can set this in motion?" I queried.

"Let's meet on the pier that I see you swimming from. I

will be there about eight-thirty in a swimming suit. Okay?"

That settled it. I spent the rest of the afternoon in my jury-rigged writer's studio at the rear of the pickup truck on my strong milk crate. I immersed myself completely in the battles of Campache in the Yucatan Peninsula in my novel's quest for structure.

I ate my dinner a little early, got on my suit and worked a little more. About eight-twenty, I closed up the typewriter box, put all of the papers and stuff in the milk crate, carried it back to the room we slept in, and headed for the pier. For whatever reason, there seemed to be no one at the pier that evening. I remember walking down the long set of steps to the lip of Sun-Moon Lake with my eyes focused simply on the long pier, the smooth lake surface, the broken landscape of the far side of this mountain reverie, and the one man on the pier. It was the waiter, dressed in a pair of trunks. As I put my feet on the pier and began to walk out, I looked around to see if there was a sandy beach area anywhere about that we could wade into for our first lessons.

"Hi…I am glad you are here. When shall we begin?" His voice expressed some eagerness. I was about forty feet from him.

"Now…we can begin now. We just have to decide where…." The splash broke my sentence in two. I looked at the end of the pier and there was no one there. There were the tell-tale ripples that you see when a diver breaks the surface of the pool with a poor dive. I ran to the end and looked all around to see if he had caught on to the edge of something and was waiting there for me to explain that we had to go to a shallower place to begin. No. He was not there. The ripples were moving away. He was in deep water. I felt as though we were in deep doo-doo.

The water at the end of the pier was about twelve feet deep. It was a long pier and the lake gained depth very quickly. The light was soft and generally the water was clear, but somehow this particular combination of twilight plus fright scared the hell out of me. I think I might have yelled "Shit" as I sailed off the end of the pier trying to figure out where he must have gone.

There is no real drama to conclude this episode with. I got him not on my first dive but on my second. I pulled him up by arm and trunks. I got him over to the ladder on the pier and he coughed a lot, and then a little, and then he grinned.

"What were you doing, for God's sake? What kind of a trick was that?" I yelled as much as my lungs and heart and fear would allow. "What were you thinking of? Are you crazy?"

He responded after a little more coughing. He was holding on to the ladder with strong and determined arms as he spoke. "You said you could teach me to swim. You said let's begin now. You were walking toward me. I decided you meant now, and I jumped in. I figured you would show me what to do." He grinned a little more, but he was sheepish in his look this time. He went on. "I have never swum but I have seen lots of swimming. I think I can do it, I told myself, so I did it. I knew you would be able to pull me out if I did not do it well enough to stay on the surface." He caught his breath.

"Do you see what it takes now to keep the body afloat? Do you now realize how it is not just like in the movies—it is real work until you really understand your body and the water and your strength. You are very, very lucky!" I stopped a second and then finished. "No, actually, I am very lucky!"

I told him to climb up the ladder. He said, "Is that all? Are we finished? Am I done?"

"No, not at all, not by a long shot, but you have to climb up the ladder and we have to walk to the other end of the pier to learn some basic stuff and later on—some other night—we'll come back to the deep end." I forced him up the ladder by swimming over and going up one rung at a time just behind him.

We spent another eight or nine days on swimming routines. The guy was quick, and he was relentless. I had to watch him every minute to keep him from doing his big jump into the deep end. But by the end of the third or fourth day, he had picked up enough skill in the crawl and in the dogpaddle to let me feel okay about him jumping into the deep water, at least as long as I was treading water near his target zone for his jumps...and then dives. I recall the fear that raced through my body as I searched and dived and then searched in water on that first afternoon. The event is one of those markers in your life that never leaves your consciousness.

◆

Another China event that seems so unlikely in my searching my memory for singular events, but this is a genuine surprise. Cathy and I had been leading a fifteen person China Tour for UCLA for some ten or eleven days. Our stop for these two days was Chongqing—a city then of more than five million inhabitants. It had been a hideaway for many of the Chinese Nationalists during the bloody 1940s decade of China's war with Japan and with the civil war between the ascending Mao Tse Tung Communist forces and the long entrenched and U.S. supported Nationalist forces of China Kai-shek. By the 1980s when our China tour arrived, Chongqing was almost overwhelming. Massive, industrial as well as highly commercial, it broadcast: "China ascending" to our small tour group of mostly senior Americans tourists.

One of the vital events of arriving at any Chinese hotel was having each and every tour member take one or two hotel business cards from the registration desk so that in case anyone became lost, the card could be shown to get help in getting back to at least the hotel that was our two-day base. This episode is the evidence of what happens when that precaution is not taken.

ALONE—IN CHONGQING (CHUNGKING)

In leading tours to China, Chloe and I learned that it was impossible to really know what to anticipate in the unfolding of a twenty-day trip. Even though we always had at least one get-together before we left Los Angeles, it was very difficult to anticipate how different people would respond to the various pressures and awkwardnesses of travel in 1980s China. On this trip we had the massive city of Chongqing (Chungking) included on our itinerary. This was a city of more than five million then when our tour was visiting. It is on the banks of the upper Yangtze River in west central China. It had been the wartime capital of the Chinese Nationalists and had benefitted from both the development of the wartime investment and the long distance from Beijing—which gave the city more independence. It was a coal-burning, highly industrialized, densely populated Chinese river city of traditional urban density, but also of hot food and endless alleyways and neighborhoods.

There was a quiet girl of about twenty-five on this particular trip. She seemed shy, or at least uncomfortable with much interaction. I worked my tours as gently as I could, but I was at them to see things so that they could bring ideas and images of China home from these junkets. I had optional 'seminar' meetings. I worked in as often as possible some reference to their particular lives and careers/jobs in an effort to make as many as possible feel that they were on a kind of family trip. And the ones that I was unsuccessful with, Chloe could often capture. Between the outgoing Kit and the accommodating and gentle Chloe, I think that most everyone felt comfortable with these three weeks of exploration.

But not this gal. I've forgotten her name. She was like the student in a field walk who always stands just outside of earshot, who always is looking south as you are pointing to something north and describing its importance.

On our first afternoon in Chongqing we booked into an amazing hotel. It had gardens, porches, massive lounges, and a site atop one of the many hills in the city. As was customary, I exhorted each person to take a hotel card from the registration desk and put it in their pocket in case they wandered away from the group or got lost on their own. The card in the eyes of a taxi driver was a Get Home Free (well....you had to pay the taxi fare) Card. It was essential.

We got to the hotel just after noon and there was a free early afternoon. We were to meet at four p.m. to take a nearby factory tour and then go to another place for a special dinner. The group—as was almost always the case—divided into three cohorts. One cohort fell into their hotel rooms and napped, wrote cards, and came to the lounge for tea or beers or something else. The second cohort unpacked, got into walking clothes, and—grabbing a card—headed out into the streets to see what a new Chinese city felt like. Recall that these were people with no Chinese language, but with often a good sense of exploration and interest in getting closer images of people and the place. The third cohort would come to the lounge with a book—often a guidebook on China—and stay close, reading about the city and the region that was going on just outside the door.

About three-thirty most of the various cohorts were back, hanging out in the lounges waiting for the bus and the four o'clock trip. We had not made this an optional trip, so Chloe and I were expecting a full complement of the group. At just before four, everyone was at the ready…except the quiet girl. I asked if anyone had traveled with her and might know where she was or why she seemed to not be here. No answers. No one had gone into the city or anywhere with her. In fact, nearly half of the group had no image of the girl I was trying to locate.

Now, what are the social dynamics of a situation like this? I was responsible for the whole bunch. I had a national guide who came on the entire twenty days with us, and there were local guides for each distinct city. But it was Chloe and I who had to be certain that the full set was present and accounted for every day, and for almost every event. If someone was sick, we knew about it and made arrangements. If someone just did-not-want (refused) to go see another factory or commune, we knew about it and organized the local hotel person to be aware of a loner. It was such a leadership role that made Hong Kong so very, very wonderful because (at the end of the China tour) we had two days in Hong Kong in which everyone was on free time. We did not have to know or worry about anyone! All true members had hotel rooms and keys and English was pretty widespread in that stunning city. That was a joy!

But this was Chongqing. This was a milling throng of literally millions of Chinese deeply involved in being Chinese and not being respondents to tourists' questions about anything. I asked the national guide to do the leadership on the four p.m. tour and had him write down the address of the fancy restaurant that we were scheduled to have dinner at in three hours. He was reluctant to have Chloe and me go to search for this girl, but I told him that she was my responsibility in this case. I also told him the group would be calmer if he was with them and would talk about the historic importance of Chongqing in the 1940s.

Chloe and I then spent almost three hours bussing and cabbing and mostly, walking through the various marketplaces in the center of the city. We had driven by a number of buzzing areas on our approach and I had seen a lot of interest in a number of faces in the bus. We each had several hotel cards, and we decided to split up and wander about looking for an American girl who seemed either absolutely out-of-place or quite comfortable in her complete incongruity with the Chinese street scene.

We spent two hours searching. It was a classic search. We had almost no information that would give us geographic direction. We moved with that mix of uneasiness at losing a tour member and by our own fascination at what we were seeing in the lanes and side streets and major avenues of one of China's largest urban centers. We had agreed to meet by six-fifteen and take a taxi back to the hotel to see if by any chance she had come in. We met. We both allowed as how we had seen no sign of her (we felt a little like Missing Persons police but without a photo) and we taxied back to the hotel on the hill.

And there she was. She was in the lobby and asked, as we strode in with that mixture of relief and fury that parents express when a child has broken rules and gotten lost, "Where is the dinner tonight? I thought everyone would be here."

"Where in the world have you been? Chloe and I have just spent more than two hours searching the innards of Chongqing trying to find you. Why didn't you come to the four o'clock trip?" As I asked these questions the relief began to soften my irritation as I looked at her implacable face and apparent disbelief that she had caused any disturbance.

"I was walking around. I don't really know where I was." Her reply was both tranquil and definitive.

"What were you trying to do—make us crazy?"

"No...I was just on my own. I didn't do anything to bother anyone. So, I missed a factory tour. Big deal!" She paused a moment thinking of something else she wanted to say. She then added, "I wanted to be alone. That's the whole reason I came on this tour. I wanted to be alone. I wanted to be away from people." She met me eye to eye.

"Wait...you decided to come to China so you could be alone? So you could be away from people? Hello——do you know where you have come to? Do you know where you are?" I queried in high curiosity.

"I was alone," she said, standing with less shyness than I had seen for days. "No one knew who I was...and apparently, no one knew where I was. I was exactly where I wanted to be. I was alone and it felt pretty good."

That was the end of the inquiry. The three of us took a taxi to the dinner restaurant and we agreed to let the issue go. I said that she ought to have a story to tell the rest of the group since there had been a lot of concern about her whereabouts.

At the dinner she said that she had gotten kind of lost in a market and got back late. She made a minor apology to the group and dinner played out fine.

And, in fact, this event seemed to break a sort of barrier that had been surrounding her in the prior ten days. She became a little more of a tour member. Chloe and I made extra certain that everyone possessed hotel cards at each of our next stops.

But the fact is that the shy girl had, in fact, taken a card...or I fear she would still be in the secret places of the old Chinese capital.

THE BICYCLE AS A FIELD AID

In my three years in Taiwan (1961-'64) I spent some time putting together my ideas for a dissertation topic in cultural geography. I was immediately in a swoon over the Chinese capacity to manage the rural landscape. The village scenes and individual farm households and small kitchen yard gardens, the markets in small towns...and the people and their productivity. All of these things were stunners for a kid who had lived on a farm for only a year outside Lexington, Kentucky in sixth grade. It was my simple awe at this traditional Chinese transformation of the earth that made geography seem the most obvious academic discipline to select to weave together these fascinations.

In moving through Taiwan, however, I had the continuing problem of how to observe and stimulate some interaction without being constantly trailed by bunches (hordes? legions? multitudes?) of young children. If I walked out of the town to the farm villages that surrounded every town, the kids fell in almost immediately, especially if I spoke a little Chinese to any of them. If, on the other hand, I organized a jeep and a government guide (I had been doing a number of articles annually for the *Industry of Free China* on aspects of economic development and that gave me a little link to government offices), then whenever I arrived at a farm household, the farmer was suspicious of my intentions. I realized that I needed some intermediate mode of travel. The bicycle became perfect for this.

The beauty of the bicycle was that I could move fast enough if I had to to outdistance the young kids. If I wanted to find farmsteads farther out of town, the bike gave me easy access to such distances. Being on a bike made me an item of some interest to the farmers and this opened conversations that would then, often, segue into interviews that were very useful to my explorations. I could also carry enough stuff in a big bamboo wicker basket on the back of the bike to camp out if I wanted to. I even got—on one long trip—the pack organized enough that I could secure my old manual portable typewriter in the basket. This made me a fully independent working unit. I loved it.

In a bar at the edge of town one night, I sat at the end of the counter with a little better light and I wrote a four-page article on, yes, "The Bicycle as Field Aid." I sent this to the *Professional Geographer*, and it was published, and it became known, casually, as the exposition of Salter's Cycle Theory. I loved that, too. A million good encounters came from being on the bike…and flight was always an option. A perfect situation.

THE GREAT WALL

There is no Chinese landscape feature as well-known as The Great Wall. From simple restaurant calendars to film efforts to conjure up explicit China imagery, there is no match for this stone wall to convey the certainty of "This is China." Wall-seekers take a two-hour bus trip from Beijing and then get off the bus in a muddy staging area in the shadow of the

Wall. In 1977 on my first visit, there were only a few busses and no tourist attractions, booths or vendors in this informal parking lot. When I last saw twenty years later, the bus lot had been expanded fivefold and there were scores of busses and some thirty stands, shops, and vendors. I recall then the featured the tee shirt that said, "My grandparents saw the Great Wall and all I got was this crummy tee-shirt."

In climbing up the limestone steps that give you access to the Wall itself, your senses are dumbstruck with what it must have taken to construct this world's most massive "public works project." It is wide enough to be able to have four horses walk abreast for guard work. Since it is at the crest of the mountains that weave eastward from north China toward the Yellow Sea on the east coast, the contours that the Wall follows are very uneven. There are many surfaces that go from one section of relative levelness rising to the next peak and then descend to another relatively level area...and then repeat the process for miles. In its period of greatest uniformity and steady maintenance from the Qin Dynasty (212 B.C.) and the Ming Dynasty (1368-1644 A.D.) it was more than 1,500 miles long. Currently, however, there are perhaps only three miles in good repair. That is where the busses go with their loads of both domestic and international tourists. This wall is a global hallmark of China's unparalleled effort to remake the landscape in a grand Chinese pattern.

The power one feels on the Wall is both humbling and expansive. At one point in the 1990s, a firm had set up a series of yurts—the yak-felt shelters were havens for the traveling Mongols who ruled this world in the thirteenth century. To stand on the Wall and look north and see fifteen large yurts in a landscape scene with power poles and roads on the horizon was effective in making one think of the landscapes of six and seven centuries ago...in fact, of twenty-two to twenty-three centuries ago.

The Chinese speak of the Yangtze Three Gorges Dam Project on China's longest river as "The New Great Wall." That phrase says it all—enormous human costs and expenditure of resources. However, speculation about ultimate utility of this maximum effort also invokes the uncertainty in how well it will work. The Great Wall did little to keep the Mongols and the nomadic raiders out of settled China. The Three Gorges Dam may or may not finally pay for its cost in taming the Yangtze and generating low-cost electricity.

I put The Great Wall as the most singular landscape feature that China has to offer. Explore the open segments that China features, but slip away from your tour group and head west. If you walk some two hundred yards, you get to the place where a simple cord closes off the old, unrepaired Wall and there you can see the reality of normal times. Great limestone chunks are all scattered, running along the further crest of Ming Dynasty structure (or earlier) and all going into quiet ruin. It is all worth seeing and thinking of as you take the nervous bus ride back to your hotel in Beijing.

There are many lessons that one learns after spending time in China that have a lasting effect, particularly if it is years more than weeks you invest in that amazing nation. Since I had not yet begun graduate school at UCLA, but I had read Professor Joe Spencer's *Asia, East by South* (1954) I had a great deal of respect for both Spencer and the two schools he was linked with—UC Berkeley and UCLA. In the mindset of the geographers who gave energy to those schools' reputations, field work was central. For that reason, I wanted very much to make a productive use of my time in Taiwan for I planned to go on to do graduate work after my three years in Taiwan was completed in 1964. The episode that follows was part of my field work education that has lasted for years!

THE PROPOSITION

As leaders of several UCLA-China travel tours between 1980 and 1986, Chloe and I had some great experiences. On one of our early tours, we had an eighty-three-year-old man in our group named Pat Peterson. He was our tour's senior member. We had just come to Shanghai and we were in a great old hotel somewhere near the center of the city. As was my tradition, I offered an optional seminar about nine one evening early in our stay. This gave us a chance to express early reactions and make some comparisons with the place(s) already visited. We were having our meeting in a social room at the hotel, and suddenly in burst Peterson, red in the face, bright of eye, and talking very hurriedly.

"Kit, Kit....I was propositioned! Really! Me, I, was propositioned by a neat looking young woman over by the river." He could hardly contain himself.

"You, Pat...really? Hey, you ought to feel proud!" The dozen or so of us gave him a round of applause and grinned at his joy.

"But you told us there were no, or maybe only a few, prostitutes in China now," he said, trying to make the whole narration more intellectual and less prideful.

"There aren't many now, Pat...but when a real hunk shows up, current custom falls away and old street traditions rise again." He was pleased. We were all educated by the incident.

SHANGHAI

Think of this as a Shanghai fear. This coastal city has a more powerful migrant pull than any other urban center in all of China. If anything new and opportunistic is going to take place in China, it will almost always begin in Shanghai. The city is a nearly violent migration magnet to rural populations all up and down the coast, and inland along the banks of the Yangtze River. For twenty years, under Mao, the Chinese locked the doors on rural migration and sent millions of 'surplus' urbanites back to the countryside for reeducation ("let the bureaucrats learn some rural reality!") in an effort to control the unattached urban unemployed.

But that is all another story. The one item I want to give you an image of here is umbrella fear. Shanghai has a street density like no other city. We have not been there since 1996 but my guess is that it is still in this city that you run into the highest densities anywhere in China. And I am not talking traffic densities or residential densities. I mean pedestrian densities. All the images from *Blade Runner* or *Star Trek* that were to evoke endless populations with neither order nor direction....all those images derive from and thrive in Shanghai. And the biggest fear of all that is umbrella fear. On rainy days, no one seems to stay home at all. The streets are just as crowded. But almost all of the people you see have black, unfurled umbrellas. And as they tend to be a little shorter than either Chloe or me, you walk through these crowds with your eyes at just about umbrella tip height. You fear that a lot. Your entire horizon is defined by a stream of eight-pointed umbrellas spinning out of control in heavy rains as the holders run and dodge and dart and leap...all the while leading with umbrella tips.

You develop a real Shanghai umbrella fear!

CHINA AIRWAYS

A quick image. Early in the tourist travel to China, we were always anxious when flying on domestic China Airways. I found that I watched very carefully to make certain that the pilots did not enter the cockpit with a parachute-like pack. Anyway, you get on board and sit anywhere (there was only "coach" in China until recently) and are given a stick of gum. There is nervous chatter and the plane taxis and takes off. Your heart begins to return to its normal rate as you look out the window and see that you are moving as a good angle away from the densely urbanized or farmed lands below you. You relax a bit in your seat and look at the interior of the plane more carefully than before. Then you see this.

Out of the passenger overhead bins, smoke begins to issue forth. At first, just little wisps seep out. Then more. Then still more. You have that awkward impediment of potential embarrassment that keeps you from yelling, "Hey...the plane is on fire!" So you nudge your seatmate and see that he or she has been noticing the same thing. Just a nanosecond before one of you decides to cry out, you hear a young girl's voice say in lumpy English.

"China Airways use modern dry ice for cooling. You will

see some of the vapor coming out of the luggage bins. Not to worry. I will bring some sodas now."

Ah…dry ice. Of course. The country that gave us gunpowder and fireworks can also give us a visual cue that seems related to such power.

A Harvest Ago

In Taiwan, as in China, the harvesting of rice and wheat is a multi-generational project. The actual grain is cut from the dry fields and left on the ground in wrapped sheaves. In the 1960s and '70s there would be a unit that would be dragged through the fields, and assigned family men (often but not always) would shove sheaves into the craw of the harvesting machine. This consisted of a metal drum about the size of a fifty-five gallon oil drum that had been attached to a heavy flywheel. The bottom of the barrel had been taken off by a welder and someone had hammered hundreds of nails through from the inside to the outside of the barrel. The barrel was suspended on its side and fixed so that a person could spin it around by means of a foot treadle. It was like an old foot-powered sewing machine. The drum would build up a high rpm, and the sheave would be thrust into contact with the spinning nails. Immediately, thousands of small golden dry grain kernels would be pulled off into a bin that lay at the bottom of this rig.

A person would put the sheave into the foot driven spinner five or six times, turning it a little each time. At the end of the circuit, it was felt that most of the grains were separated from the long grassy stems and the sheave would be thrown down and replaced with a nearby, unharvested one. When the field had been harvested in this first cut, the ripe grain was scooped up from the base of the rig and taken to the family compound and spread out to further dry on a tamped earth or concrete surface. The older generation—both male and female—would then gather up the shorn sheaves and carry them to the nearest road. There they would be spread out on the hard surface so that passing carts, busses, trucks, even bicycles would ride over the grassy pods and break free the remaining heads from their stalks.

After that second generation of harvest, all of the grain heads would be further dried in the sun by the farmhouse. There would be continual sifting and winnowing by, again, the grandparents of the household. When this third level of harvest was completed, the grain would be put in large burlap bags and taken to the local miller. He would run the dried grain through his gasoline or diesel- or electricity-driven mill, separating the white rice or wheat kernels from the brown, crisp husks and hulls of the plant. This residue—the bran—has most of the nutrient value of these two grains and it would be used sometimes for fuel, chicken or duck feed, or only occasionally, a food additive for the household diet. There is so much status attached to eating only white, polished rice and so much negative status associated with brown rice that only a very few households have the strength to fight such traditions and eat the more nutritious brown rice or the husks.

The extended family role, the need for so many individuals to play a productive part, and the importance of smooth cooperation in this critical harvesting process is very much a part of traditional, agricultural China. And it is exactly this fabric that is being unraveled by mechanization, rural-to-urban migration, and ever less importance associated with farming. Now you see it. Now it's gone.

STOP THE BUS!

One of the most interesting couples that we met in our China Tour years was Bill and Margaret F. They both were special for many reasons and they added a lot of energy to all of our discussions. Both were in their upper fifties when they took this China trip. However, the event that will never leave my mind about Bill is this one. We were in Chongqing, the old WWII wartime capital of the Chinese Nationalists. We were on a bus with our group of some twenty people. Bill was notable because he always worn high neck hiking boots with lots of laces. He wore pants that suggested he was ready for the full trek to Anywhere, just in case the opportunity came up. We were struggling through the city early one morning, fighting the heavy truck, bus, bicycle, and pedestrian traffic, working out way toward some spectacular temple on the outskirts of this large city. I noticed, as I looked around toward the back of the bus from my position at the helm, checking on things to point out as we drove, that Bill was making his way to the front of the bus.

"Kit," he said with some urgency, "you've got to stop the bus!"

"Stop the bus, Bill? We're just underway. What did you forget?"

"I didn't forget anything. Something has gotten on board that I need to send away." He looked to be in high discomfort.

"Is this really urgent, Bill?" Having done many of these trips, I suddenly realized I was seeing the agony of a person in need of a toilet in a world of uncertainty.

"Absolutely and completely. Stop the bus!"

We were just then in front of one of a major government buildings, built on designs that had come from the Classical world, through Washington, D.C. and right into the heart of the Kuomintang—Chang Kai-shek China that was trying to replicate American style. I asked the driver to pull over for an unexpected five-minute stop. I told the group that we were going to stop here to ponder the power of architectural transfer from one culture to a very different one. The driver begrudgingly pulled over and as the door was opened, Bill and his major boots were the first out the door. I tried to get the travelers' attention by talking about the power of white stone and monumental staircases leading to governmental decision-making. This large building reminded me of the Supreme Court building, but it may have been any one of five or six other major offices.

As the group asked whether they had to get out or not, their attention turned quietly and then laughingly to the figure walking up the hundred or so steps. Bill had stopped at the bottom of the steps, his head arched up to contemplate what stood before him. Instantly, he began the climb. What is so memorable is the image of this large man with maximum boots taking very little steps as he lifted his body from one level to the next to the next. In every movement it was clear that he was holding his cheeks together with a combination of will power and intense compression. Up and up and up, hoping all the while that his system would not suddenly lose control.

I made a little more effort to catch the group's attention with some focus on architectural style across the street, but it was clear that all of us were riveted on whether or not Bill would reach the top step and be able to make it to the imperial doorway and find a public bathroom in time to salvage his spirit, face, and clothes. When he reached the top step—

having done more than one hundred of his tiny steps to gain that new level—a roar flowed through the bus with something like, "Aww right, Bill....go, go, go. You'll make it!!!"

When Bill came back down the steps about eight minutes later, he was marching with the confidence and pride of a general who has just completed a difficult campaign strategy with total victory. As he stepped up on the bottom step of the bus and raised his head above the seat in front he said, "I've always wanted to see the inside of a really fine public building in China. I'm so glad I got the chance. It was a great relief to see what I saw. We're all fortunate that I had this little tour."

The few outsiders got back on the bus and we started, again, for another day of wonder and touring.

TOM IN TUNGHAI

Not long ago, I was sitting in an Eye Clinic waiting room. My eyes had been given drops to dilate. I had a thirty-minute wait for the next procedure. In my customary waiting room dynamics, I chatted with some of the nurses and with some of the other eye patients. There was a Chinese couple seated across from me. They were probably in their early sixties and seemed, curiously, concerned with me. Maybe, I thought, the concept of making casual conversation in such a situation was impolite or impolitic in Chinese tradition. I did not know and it did not matter very much. It was an easy time. Suddenly, the man stood up and walked over to me.

"Is your name Tom?" he asked, in soft voice.

"No, my name is Kit. Why do you ask?"

"Were you at Tunghai University in the early 1960s? Did you have a wife named Linda? " My jaw must have dropped three inches. I gave my answer in Chinese.

"Yes, to the Tunghai question. Yes, to having had a wife named Linda but we are no longer married. How in the world could you know this?" I was still surprised.

"I was a student at Tunghai. I graduated in 1967. You and Linda were there in my first year of college. I remember you had a bicycle built for two people."

At this point, my doctor stepped out of one of the examining rooms and called, "Dr. Salter...come on in." I put my hand up and spoke another sentence to the Chinese man. He told me he was on the MU faculty in BioTechnology and recognized me by my face and my voice. I shook his hand and was summoned into the eye exam room.

When I came out fifteen minutes later, they were gone. As I squinted my way out to my car with my funny plastic dark glasses on that are customary gifts as you leave an eye-dilation examination, I found myself just spinning with the thought that someone from forty years earlier would recognize a professor (I must have been about four years older than he) from a university experience halfway across the world.

My China experiences have been ones that have provided surprise after surprise after surprise. What a nation. What a landscape. What a people.

◆

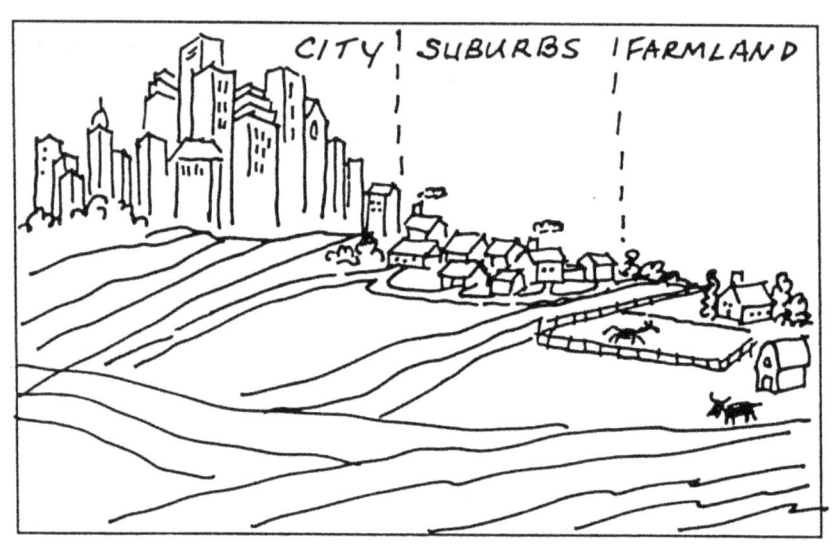

CHAPTER FIVE

HITCHHIKING, FREIGHTS, AND SPECULATION

MY ROAD TO HITCHHIKING

Everyone knows, broadly, the concept of family, travel and mobility, and many have images of China and Taiwan, but hitchhiking is more often outside the realm of genuine road experience in sustained travel.

I came to this uncertain but fascinating mode of movement not because of Richard Halliburton or more likely, Jack Kerouac influences, but because of a wish to return to a place once lived, but totally lacking money even for a Greyhound trip. I had become old enough to begin to feel the frustration of frequently changing schools, sometimes even several times a year. I was about thirteen when I first tried hitchhiking.

I got a Wisconsin map from a local gas station in Madison, spread it out on the floor in the place Mother and I were living at the time, and fell into that almost primitive fascination people have with maps on the floor or on large open tabletops. The scale phenomenon makes the distant places seem so very close! The road to Ripon was a major two-lane highway as far as I could see. I had not yet begun to drive but I had been on some road trips with sister Pat (who lived in Ripon) and my brother Joel who was back from the Navy and now a student at the University of Wisconsin. I could not ask either of them to drive me back to Ripon—Pat lived there, and Joel's life was full.

The map had the answer—Madison as A point. Ripon as the B point. Why not hitchhike from A to B? It wouldn't cost anything. It appeared that real highways linked A and B. And I was in a college town and there must be college kids who must have thumbed sometimes. Why not hit the road?

I do recall when I told Mother that I was going back to Ripon for a few days to visit friends she asked me, "How will you get there?"

"I'm going to hitchhike. It's only about eighty miles away so it won't take long. When I get there, I'll find a friend's house to stay at. I'm just going for a couple of days."

Mother was still absorbing the word hitchhike. "You mean you're just going to the highway and try to get someone to stop and give you a ride?"

"Yeah—that's how hitching works, Mother. People sometimes like company if they are driving alone and I'm pretty comfortable talking with people, even ones I don't know."

"Yes, yes...I know that." She paused. "But what about the danger? How do you know who will stop, who will pick you up?" I was glad to see that she blended the danger concept with logistics. That weakened the danger theme.

"There's not much danger, Mom. The scare about hitchhiking is what the hitchhiker does to the driver—not what the driver does to the guy being picked up. And, besides, I look so young, couples might even pick me up, or grandmothers reminded of their own grandkids who might get caught with a road problem."

Mother studied me, and the aspects of this new mode of travel making its way into our lives. "How will people know where you're going?"

"They won't. If they stop that will probably be the first question they ask. Since they'll probably be Wisconsin folk, they'll know of Ripon, or I might say Fond du Lac 'cause that's bigger town but in the same direction." I stood as tall as I could so that Mother would think of me as independent and capable of adventure.

"What will I tell Dockie if he asks where you are?"

"Has he ever asked where I am?"

"Not that I can remember, but he might if he shows up this week."

"Tell him I'm trying to find a job to help buy groceries."

Mother's response was, "I'm sure he won't ask. When are you leaving?"

"I think I'll go in the morning. I'll take a city bus out to Highway 14 and then start my adventure of the thumb! I'll call when I get to Pat's house."

And that began what grew to become a primary source of my education for ten years. The Ripon trip went well, up and back, and then we moved in Madison to another school district and the fullness of that new life kept me from the road until I went to college in Oberlin, Ohio. My life was shaped in part by getting to and from Oberlin. At that time I had a high school romance in Madison that seemed worth making the thousand mile round trip by thumb three or four times a year.

But the real introduction to hitchhiking came in learning how to make the rides work. Initially, I just stood by the side of the highway, put out my young thumb and arm, and tried to look non-threatening, even potentially interesting. In this first trip, I learned the value of a sign with a destination. Coming back from Ripon (I cannot remember how many rides it took to cover the eighty miles), I realized the potential value of a large piece of cardboard with my destination written in black marker in Big Letters. I wrote *U. W. Madison* and when a driver stopped and asked me, "How come you're going to UW when you're still a kid?" I would reply, "I don't go there, but I live in Madison." Then if pressed about the UW sign, I'd offer up, "My dad's a prof there and I know that everyone knows about the Badgers in Wisconsin." That would clinch the ride interview and I think I got back to my home base in just two or three rides.

In that first thumbing trip, I also learned something about intersections. It didn't take long to realize that if I stood on the near corner of an intersection on a highway going the direction I was seeking, it was awkward as hell when the light was red. Drivers would give a quick look, then pick their right ear or start looking in the rear view mirror, or searching for something on the floor of the car. I found the most comfortable spot was the far side of the same intersection, allowing the first several drivers to make an evaluation of 'the hitchhiker going his or (sometimes) her same direction.' As you'll see in the first episode that follows, even hitchhiking rules (of thumb?) are not constantly observed by even experienced thumbers.

The other verity I consider crucial to comfortable hitchhiking is travelling not with even a small suitcase, but a knapsack that you carry on one shoulder easily. This is great because the standard entry to a driver's car—and this I learned when I was doing so much college age hitching—was to greet the driver who had said, "Get in...I'm heading that direction." I put the knapsack between the driver and me in the shotgun seat. Even if the driver would say, "It's okay just to put the bag in back seat," I'd respond with the placement of the bag to my left, saying, "Nah, I like to have it with me in case you suddenly decide to change directions and you tell me to get out early because your plans have changed."

The placement of the bag was both my source of a candy bar for a long ride, or an impediment for driver-passenger friendship that I did not welcome. The strongest variant to the knapsack was something brother Joel taught me after I had begun hitching actively around the U.S. Joel told me he'd met a guy in the Navy who did a lot of thumbing stateside. His travel routine was to talk along the highway toting a red five-gallon gas can. He had cut the bottom open and—saving the bottom out of it—and made the can into a funky suitcase. He then reattached the bottom with a couple of easily workable clasps. He'd walk on the highway, carrying the red gas can in his right hand and put his left hand out with his thumb out. Joel said that the Navy buddy told him that trucks often stopped and told him he could put the gas can in the truck bed—and then usually—but not always, the driver would agree to take him on up the road as far as their destinations were in parallel direction.

The episodes that follow are just some of the events that hang in my mind as I recount some of the hitchhiking I did between my eighth grade virgin voyage to Ripon, Wisconsin and my last major trek to Indianapolis from mid-Missouri some forty-five years later.

◆

BLESSED AT PELL CREEK

In one of my early hitchhiking trips from Oberlin to Madison, I made the mistake of not staying at a well-lit intersection at about eleven on a weekend night. I had had a hell of a time getting through Chicago and when I did finally get to Wisconsin, I was dropped off at a poor thumbing intersection. A light rain was coming down and I was slipping into a classic road funk when nothing seems to go right. As I walked ahead up a dark two-lane highway, I looked at my scene: no car, no rides, no hope and I didn't even know this highway. Whine. Whine. Whine. Self-pity.

At one point I looked into the rainy mist and saw some light ahead. I could not tell what it was but I thought that I would play it smart and use that illumination to reflect on my situation and probably stay by that midnight light until a ride stopped. As I got closer, I saw that it was a neon cross on the side of a simple church steeple. Almost nothing else could be seen, but as I approached, the cross alone began to stand out in the elements. Hey, I thought…what the hell am I whining for? Here is the sign of a man who was born into one of the toughest chores of history and he never whined. I had a really nice ten minutes of getting my own troubles in scale with those of Jesus. I stood in front of the church and was blessed with a night-time ride and got to Madison by about one-thirty in the morning. I have recalled that cross and neon sign for more than sixty years.

◆

As I grew more confident with my road travel by thumb, I began to see that I could turn this uncertain, but almost always interesting, mode of travel into a college rite of passage. It was a doorway to low cost journeys that could have a real dimension of adventure and learning. This next episode is a strong example of this learning.

STICK SHIFT

When I was hitchhiking in southern Texas once, a couple stopped for me in a four-door sedan. The man was driving with his wife next to him. As I opened the back door with my backpack in my hand, the man said hurriedly, "Wait a minute, kid…Where ya goin' ?" I had one foot in the car and one foot on the pavement. I was holding my pack outside the car, just about to swing it into the far side of the back seat.

"I'm heading toward Austin."

"Who do ya know in Austin?" asked the somewhat uneasy driver, the motor still running but the car not moving. Everything was poised in a pause mode.

"No one… I just wanted to see the campus before I go back up to Ohio where I go to school." Such questions were not unusual, although getting picked up by a couple was rare because women usually put the kibosh on her husband stopping for a guy by the side of the road. "I've heard a lot about the University of Texas, and this will be my first chance to see it. Are you heading toward Austin?" I had learned in my long miles of thumb work that establishing some sort of connection with state universities was often useful in getting people to welcome me into the car. For that reason, I had a cardboard sign about a foot wide and two feet tall. It said, "UNIVERSITY OF TEXAS, AUSTIN." In bold, black letters. I almost always took the time to make a cardboard sign with the name of a university within one to two hundred miles of where I was thumbing.

At this point I saw that the car had a clothes rack that extended from one side of the back seat to the other. There were lots of hangers with clothes suspended on the rack. Hoping to nudge this indecisive stop toward acceptance, I was carefully sliding some of the hangered clothes toward the far side of the car, using my left hand to slide the hangers.

At this point, the wife—who had not said a word—turned her head and looked at my hand on the half inch aluminum pipe that was the clothes rack.

"Elmer," she screamed, "He's got a gun! Drive! Drive, Elmer, *Drive!*"

I threw my buns onto the seat while the road sailed away from under my still-outside-the-car right foot. I tossed my pack to the far side of the seat to act as a sort of ballast to keep me from falling out of the car. I hollered with alarm, "Hey... no, *No*...this is no gun. It's your blessed clothes rack," one foot bumping along on the pavement trying to shift my balance toward inside more than outside as the car was moving back into traffic on the two lane highway. "*I do not have a gun.* I'm a college kid trying to get to Austin—what you see in my hand is your own clothes rack! Can I shut the damn door? Are you giving me a ride or not? If not, pull over and I'll get my pack out of your car."

The lady had stopped screaming. Elmer looked over his shoulder with a further twist of his neck. He yelled out, "He doesn't have a gun, Myra...he's right. You saw the clothes rack. Maybe he'll help keep me awake. Whaddya say, Myra?" She was silent. Elmer had these words pour out of his mouth, "It's okay, kid....Get your stuff organized. We'll stop for a coffee in a few minutes and Myra will relax. Can you drive? She has never been able to drive a stick shift and this old car is a stick." He slowed way down so that I could get my right leg into the car and slam the door closed.

I told him that I was fine with a stick shift, but mostly I wanted Myra to know that I was a good passenger for them to have since I could drive while Elmer got some rest. I encouraged her not to worry about me. Myra stayed quiet until we stopped at a café for some coffee. I was asked to drive a leg north toward Austin after our coffee and pie. I'm not sure Myra ever did relax, but that was not unusual in the few times that couples—especially middle-aged couples—stopped and picked me up.

Signs of Lost Opportunity

The social dynamics of hitching are so curious. American highways are filled with cars steaming by, maybe 75 percent with only a single person. The single driver is usually male. The cars with a lone women driver are so unlikely to stop that I look at them with a lonely smile but am plenty surprised when one those options actually stops. I remember once in Colorado I was heading toward Madison, Wisconsin. I did not have a sign ready yet for UW Madison because I had been napping in some tall grass off to the side of the highway. I saw a convertible with the top down coming my direction and as it got closer, I could make out Wisconsin license plates. I stood looking as interesting as I could possibly look to a driver coming at sixty miles an hour, hoping that she might think, *I need some conversation*, but she looked with little interest at my undirected efforts to get further east...and she sped on by.

Giving her a wave, I went across the highway to a general store to find a piece of cardboard. I had a bold black marker. As I got my marker ready, and walked into the store, the lady at the counter looked at me with a condescending smile. "I see you missed your good ride if you're heading east."

"My good ride?" I asked.

"The girl in the convertible. I could see she barely gave you half a second as that yellow car sailed on down the road with an empty shotgun seat. You know why you missed that ride?"

I was fascinated by her observations, so I played along with genuine interest. "No, I thought I looked like a great free driver. I couldn't believe her not even slowing down."

"It's simple. You were taking a nap in the grass on the yonder side of the two-lane when you should have been in here getting your cardboard for a sign." She paused, seemingly proud of the attention I was giving her for her explanation as to why I did not get picked up. Then she added, "If you had a simple sign with some college town east of here—Lawrence, Kansas or even University of Iowa, you'd look like a better bet. Nice lookin' kid, headed back to college—but instead you're catchin' zees in the grass."

I suddenly saw this as one of those moments when you feel out of body. I was looking at her—a plain sixty-year-old lady running a small convenience store on a two-lane highway in eastern Colorado. If I'd told her how many times I'd encouraged other thumbers to "make a sign; use a college city" she would be sure I was just trying to flatter her. But—she was exactly right in her total observations. I had lost a good road opportunity by napping in the grasses; the convert and the gal with Wisconsin plates would have been a cherry ride; and I learned again, as I had before, that there is no clock in hitchhiking. The only chronometer is *Now is the time to get on the road!*

◆

There is a curious calendar with hitchhiking. In most cases a ride is a finite event. The car stops. You get in. You travel. You get dropped off, and the sequence begins again. But those trips fade into the memory. Toward the end of my years of hitching from Oberlin back to Madison, and then on to places all over the country and into Mexico, I totaled up the mileage I had spent in other people's cars on my travels. I came up with about 75,000 miles of thumbing and if I knock off a quarter just because it is so easy to exaggerate, that still means that I have used my thumb to travel around the world nearly three times!

I've said that my best education occurred not in my college days and nights, but in my lessons learned out on the road. I did not become a road scholar, but I did gain a lot of perspective on the nature of people and places by flowing with impulses and staying longer in some rides because they were fun but aborting other rides because they were going—in many ways—in the wrong direction. This episode below is built around a thumbing trip I was making back from Madison to Oberlin in the fall of 1956.

◆

FROM HERE TO ETERNITY

It is about five hundred miles from Madison, Wisconsin to Oberlin, Ohio. Coming east, the end of the ten- to fifteen-hour thumbing trip was always dicey because I would get stranded as I tried to get from the Ohio Turnpike approaching

Episodes in a Life   179

Cleveland down into Oberlin—the trip's final twenty-five miles. It could take hours. The fact that Wade M. stopped for me and we had the following conversation changed my view of the last leg of the Madison-Oberlin journey for years. I recall that it was a Sunday night about dinner time.

An old Pontiac pulled over when I was fifteen miles east of Cleveland and the lone driver reached across the passenger seat and rolled down his window before I even got the door open. "Where ya going?"

I spoke into the open window. "I'm trying to get to a small college town some twenty-five miles south of Cleveland. It's..." He interrupted me before I could add any detail.

"I know Oberlin. What kind a' hurry are you in?"

"I gotta class that meets Monday morning at eight and I have to turn in a paper by *no later than* eight a.m."

"Yeah—I don't feature us being on the road all night, but I do need to know whether or not you've got an extra hour or two right now."

I had become used to delicate interviewing conversations before a driver let me know that it was okay to get in the car. This was a little different, but I was in no position to turn down any ride who at least had heard of Oberlin, Ohio. I replied, "Okay—I'm good for a couple of hours of whatever chores you've got to do before you find Oberlin. Can I get in?"

"Sure—let me move some stuff on the seat. "He grabbed some sheet music and a Bible and put them in the empty back seat. But I saw that the seat was not really empty but had a guitar case on it. "Get in—we'll get back in traffic and I'll get us off the Turnpike in about six miles. "He popped up the lock button on the passenger door and I pulled it open, put my pack in the middle of the bench seat, got in and pulled the door shut with a slam that brought me relief and probably made the man I came to know as Wade wince just a little.

He got us back into the flow of traffic heading east and then did that customary half-drive and half-instruct me in the conditions of passage in his car heading toward Oberlin and other points. "It's Sunday night and I got some responsibilities for our church. You might have noticed the guitar in the back seat. I do a Sunday evening Bible and Music Circuit for my church. We have our La Grange Baptist service on Sunday mornings, but there are some families that cannot easily get to church. So, on Sunday nights I take my guitar, some music—but mostly just for show—and go to about five different families and play some hymns, give a three-minute message that sort of comes from this morning's service, and we sing a song or two together."

This was clearly the longest Wade had talked in a while and I let him catch his breath as I thought about the wondrous nature of thumbing and the serendipity of who you meet on the road. I'd been a desultory church-goer for years and years. In Oberlin, I'd go to the big First Congregational Church a few times a year, but nothing ever pulled me back in any pattern of real church attendance. The idea of spending an hour or two that first evening was just fine and I told Wade I'd be glad to ride shotgun on his circuit that Sunday evening.

We drove to four households that night. One was in a small town and three were in the countryside of northern Ohio—all within about thirty miles of Elyria and Oberlin. While the encounters with the families, and watching Wade bring them the joy of some hymns and prayers, was a joy that night (the last ride in a five hundred miles trip that takes you right to your dorm is always a great ride). But the real impact of meeting

Wade and seeing and hearing what he did was that it got me into a church world. I could not very easily go to the Sunday morning services because of kitchen work I had at Dascomb Hall at Oberlin—although Wade did come and take me a few times to the formal Baptist church in La Grange, Ohio.

What I recall about it now was that there was an energy in the Baptist sense of church that I had never really experienced. There was always a nice welcome to an outsider ("Oh, a college boy. How'd you meet Wade?"), and the preacher knew his parish well and spoke to them in ringing promises of hell on Earth but grand rewards in Rapture and beyond. I probably logged some twenty-five Sunday night circuits with Wade and grew very comfortable in the warmth of that glow of music and church life.

I abandoned that pattern in my second semester because I found that all of the church-talk was about the promised rewards of the Next Life. There was very little attention given to ways in which the church and its population might help modify the reality that was the backdrop for church assessment of the plight of the world we were living in. This whole perspective seemed way too mythical for me to give real attention to it as a serious belief system.

It did, however, make the mark of the longest friendship ever to come from a ride gained in hitchhiking. Ultimately, I failed to keep in touch with Wade M. and now it just plays the role of an episode in the fascinating world of thumbing and learning about the world and myself.

Asking for Directions

The value of questions to individuals—most often youngish men—'guarding their territory' was a source of road info, but also a deflection of potential conflict. As I got into more regular hitching between Oberlin and Madison (my first two years at Oberlin) I learned that that Chicago streetscapes and neighborhoods were foreign territory to handle with attention. I often got rides to Chicago, but most critical was learning how to get beyond the Windy City and find access to Highway 20 heading toward southern Wisconsin. When I got dropped off at a major Chicago intersection, my map on the back of my cardboard University sign would be my guide. But when I was dropped off in the middle of an unknown neighborhood, this kid with a backpack and a cardboard sign under his arm and walking with uncertainty could look like a mark for gangs or guys hanging around a corner or bar. It became clear to me that I had to have a plan for transit in such situations. Questions about locations were often ways to gain safe passage through hostile settings.

I fell back on a belief that I have had all of my academic life that everyone loves being a teacher. No one wants to grade papers or take students to task for not doing their work. However, many find pleasure in appearing like a local homeboy when asked about where some place is in or at thee margin of their turf. As the kid who might seem like an intruder, I could mask whatever anxiety I possessed walking through their turf by saying something like, "Hi—I'm trying to get to (and have some city in mind that would be known by most of the group) and it looks like Highway 20 is the best way to find a ride there. Can you tell me how I'd get to Route 20? Is there a city bus that heads out to the highway? What's the best road out that way?"

That all seems so innocent, but I found that even guys ready to sneer at any outsider walking right through home territory would open their minds and mouths and give me useful directions. The plan did not always work, but most of the times the two or three guys acting as guardians of the 'hood would switch from potential belligerents to a little curious. "You really don't have a car?" *or* " Where ya' trying to go?"

And, themes welcomed response, "You need to get through town and out to Route 20 and," interrupted quickly by another guy, "Naa...that's too crowded. Take Commercial Street here all the way to the end and you'll bump into Route 30. That's a faster road."

"Whadddya mean a faster road? Hell, the guy's not even got a car. If you got bus money, take the Johnson Avenue bus to the end of his route and ask the driver to point you toward that big-assed truck stop about a mile from where the bus turns around."

Those three or four comments peppered with classic irritation at not knowing where the hell you are and where you're going changes the micro-environment at that corner. And, if karma is really on your side, one of the guys will say, "I gotta go ta work—my job is near Route 20 North. Grab your pack and I'll take you right to the intersection." Then looking at the other guys, "Tell Jimmy I'm doin' my good deed for the day and I'll be back about three for that stuff he wants done."

Questions—with no papers to grade and no student conferences to hold—that's what brings unknowns from potential trouble to surprising friends of people on the road.

The Perfect Ride

After a year at Oberlin I'd become fascinated with doing more work in the Spanish language. There was an opportunity to go to Mexico City in 1957 and take eight weeks of Spanish classes for a very small fee. The Oberlin professor who talked up this summer session assured anyone interested that it had to be a great institute because the head of the program was named Jose Cervantes. I thought anyone with that classic name had to be worth studying with. I decided to hitch down to Mexico City alone for the excursion. I had been promised a room in the household of Director Cervantes.

I set out with knapsack and my usual cardboard panel with a map on one side and planned to pen in various universities on the other side as I moved south by southwest.

I had encountered nothing of moment (at least that I recall) in my thousand miles into south Texas. Then, in one moment, the dream ride in most hitchhikers' minds showed up. A 1956 Ford Thunderbird convertible was coming down the pike toward my sign that said UTEP in El Paso (University of Texas at El Paso). I had thumbed to Denver from Oberlin in a bunch of short rides and as I turned south toward Mexico, I was getting nervous about my progress. It was north of El Paso that I saw this vision of the perfect ride, just as I became eager to make tracks toward Mexico City.

The car's top was down and the driver pulled over, alone in this very cherry car. The driver asked, "Where are you heading? How far south are you trying to go?"

"Mexico City. I'm going to study Spanish for the summer."

Episodes in a Life

"All the way to Mexico City?" he asked with surprise in his voice.

"Yeah." I was still big eyed as I answered the questions.

"Can you drive a stick shift?"

"That's all I've ever had," I replied, getting a little nervous about the potential of this next question.

"Look—here's the deal. I've bunged up my leg in Colorado in a climbing accident but I've got to get me and my T-Bird to Mexico City in three days. Do you think you'd be able to help me with the driving—in fact, if you handle the car with any smoothness, I'd like to get a chance to stretch out as much as I can in this car and glide all the way to the heart of the Distrito Federal."

I was silent for a second. I looked at this car. I plotted the miles that lay between south Texas and the Mexican capital. I listened again in my mind to the driver's question: can you drive a stick shift? Can you handle this car smoothly? Could you drive most of the way from here to Mexico City? Then I answered, "I figure it's gotta be some twelve-thirteen hundred miles to Mexico City from El Paso. That means if I do most of the driving—and I'd love to—it will still take us the better part of two days to get the 'Bird to the capital. That means an overnight and if you'd be okay with me bunking on the floor of a motel or outside, guarding the 'Bird, I think we've got an arrangement that could work."

"Do you hitch a lot?" he asked as though he was trying to put his own equation together.

"I've done a lot of thumbing in the past two years and last summer I rode the freights and rails. I'm pretty comfortable with movement and can deal with just about any sort of meal. I've got a little money but mostly I eat light and nourish myself on experience."

"Money's not the problem. My damn leg is the problem. And this car has to be in primo shape when we get to Mexico City—no dings, no scratches, not even a tire change if possible. Can you manage that?"

I laughed as I explained, "My first car was a very fine 1938 Buick sedan that I got for fifty-five dollars in my junior year in high school. I drove it with a lot of travel and buddies in transit and I still sold it when I graduated for a hundred dollars. I'll sure as hell handle your wheels with kid gloves if you really want me to drive."

One more shared viewing of the other person, one at the wheel, one at the side of the Ford Thunderbird. The driver spoke. "Okay—let's give it a try. I'm going to drive the next miles to get us across the border and beyond Cuidad Juarez for a few miles. Toss your pack on the small space they call a back seat in Ford Motors design labs. I don't know how anyone does any shopping in a 'Bird. They must have a car that follows and picks up the stuff from the market and stores."

"I bet they figure anyone who can buy a T-bird convertible can afford to have a local kid follow the T-bird and bring home the shopping bags."

"Yeah...maybe, but mostly it makes shopping off limits. Get in. We've got miles to go to get across the border and into the training and the trip." I snugged my pack in the space behind the driver's seat, got in, belted up, and swung the door closed. I felt like I was in the cockpit of a small plane, but it felt damn good to hear the engine take over, the wind flow across the car interior, and think about the fact that I might actually have a ride for the next twelve hundred miles or so.

After getting through the border and beyond Cuidad Juarez we cruised ten miles while the driver showed me some of the features of the T-bird. He was clearly eager to trade seats and let himself stretch out as much as possible and give his leg some comfort.

The border crossing went well. I learned that the driver's name was Matt and that he was going to Mexico City on business. When we got past the border crossing, he stopped at a *cambio* kiosk and changed a hundred dollars for pesos and told me that we'd cruise twenty miles and then stop for lunch and he'd give me the keys. He said he was planning on a long nap. This surprised me but it all sounded pretty perfect. Get picked up by a guy with a fine car, a little cash that might buy some lunch, and an eagerness to give over the driving to a guy he'd known a little less than an hour.

Matt was true to his word and we stopped at a cantina along the road, had some lunch, which he paid for—telling me that drivers ordinarily cost way more than just cheap Mexican *comida*. We walked out to the Ford and as he handed me the keys he said, "Ease into the driving mode. Get comfortable with the power and the macho wish to test the machine. Trust me—it has a lot of go, but I'm not ready to have any driver training for the fast track. I want to sleep, and I want to wake up with us at least a hundred miles closer to Mexico City."

"Got it." As I was adjusting the seat, I explained to Matt that the closest thing I've had to a convertible was a beat up 1948 Pontiac two-door sedan that I'd customized in high school. I'd sawed out the roof above the sedan's front seat. I fashioned a tin border to cover the raw metal edge just above the front seats; at the top of the windshield, I rigged up a trough to stow the rolled-up canvas awning—literally a "rag top" I made for bad weather. This colorful canvas was secured in the front by metal screws above the windshield. It was hell in bad weather, but at least I got a real feeling for the elements.

But as we got comfortable I promised him that I'd treat the

'Bird like the jewel it was.

Matt looked at me with a mixture of curiosity and minor uneasiness but I grinned and belted in, put the keys into the ignition, and looking very carefully into the side rear view and interior mirrors, I eased into the long highway toward Distrito Federal in Mexico's capital city and began my charter driving experience with a nearly new Ford Thunderbird.

We traveled some six hours. Matt slept nervously at first and then seemed to feel as though he was, in fact, being chauffeured and just dozed, woke and watched the landscape and small town glide by, and finally—about three hours into our Mexico miles—sat himself upright, stretched out his jeans with his hands and turned to me and asked his first real questions not focused on his car and my experience with driving. "Why study Spanish? Why hitchhiking? And why college in a small school in Ohio?"

These questions were the first thing I felt about this trip that was ordinary and it opened the doorway to my own "trip talk." This dialogue was interesting and relaxed and fit right into the thousands of miles of my thumbing between Oberlin and points west, east, and now south.

Curiously, the trip was like a shadow across my travel path. We covered some four hundred fifty miles from his stopping for me until Matt decided we ought to stop for the night. The only curious thing that has stayed in my mind is that at the end of the first day, he asked me for a reaction to a motel room with just one bed. I told him that I was fine just bunking on the floor but that I was not ready to share a bed. As he looked at me, I could see his internal calculator entering these elements into an equation: *A T-bird, kid being asked to drive, already given lunch and small dinner, and now a motel bed made available.*

Matt spoke. "What the hell, Kit, I've given you a Grand Slam ride for nada—and you don't want to share a bed with me? All I was hoping for was that you might rub my bad leg a little so that I could sleep better." He made the last comment with a feigned innocent grin on his face.

"No…I admit that this is a hitchhiker's dream ride, Matt. And your leg does seem to be on your mind a lot—it's the whole reason that you've given me the wheel…"

He interrupted me and said, "I'm not a gay trolling the highways for companionship, Kit. I'm heading for Mexico City and I'm glad as hell that you've agreed to share the road with me. But I need of a little extra support with this damn leg problem. Can't you cut me some slack and help me?"

I kept my eyes on him and the road as I explained a "rule of the road" for anyone who thumbs. "Matt, there is a universe—a small universe, but one that exists—of men who seek quick, or short term, or all night benefits from picking up young guys hitchhiking. That's why I always place my backpack between me and the driver. In the 'Bird, I don't have that option, but you didn't seem to me to be trolling for gay encounters."

He interrupted again, but with a little more compassion. "Right—I am a lone driver going a long-assed way and plenty glad to have met a college student who seems to drive okay, stays awake on the road, and sometimes is even interesting." He shot me a quick grin with his comment, but I kept on with my own rule of the road narrative. "Right—I've played my helpful role with nice efficiency. Now you suddenly suggest that we share a bed for the night in the middle of Mexico and that ups the stakes of this ride a whole lot, even if the gesture is simply a way to get a leg massage. I'd rather have you just dump me here and let me figure out how to get in motion again rather than get myself, get us, into a stupid bind that I sure don't want and probably you didn't expect either."

"The leg, Kit, that's all this is…"

"Bullshit, Matt. The leg is real. The bed is real. The night is real. And five or six hundred miles tomorrow might be real. But the combination seems to set the stage for a big change in our travel arrangements." I paused, realizing that I was on the edge of losing this ride that had so many great aspects to it, and added. "Let me offer this. You get the bed and I'll bunk on a chair or on the floor. Before we turn out the lights, I'll be glad to rub some Ben Gay or whatever you have on your leg and give it a massage. Then lights out, rest your leg, and I'll be real glad you stopped for me and I got this much closer to Mexico City. How would that work for you?"

Matt studied me and then looked at his leg and then said, "Okay—or I can see if they have a twin beds room. I don't need a full sized or queen bed. Would you feel better with that?"

"Hell, Matt, it looks like you're picking up the room cost and if you can cover two beds of any size, that'd be my choice. But, in any room deal, I'll do the massage and then we bunk off on our own. Okay?"

"Okay—no more awkwardness. Let's go in and see what our options are."

The night played out by my script. In the morning, we both showered, put our same clothes back on, and stepped outside the doorway to see if there were any nearby breakfast choices. There was a diner-like café across the road. It looked just fine and we finished out check out, put the little gear we had unloaded back into the 'Bird and drove across the highway to where we could see it as we ate by a window.

The rest of the trip to Mexico City unfolded in fine fashion. Matt did about an hour of driving and then asked me to take over again. He assumed the shot gun seat, stretched back as far as the T-bird allowed and began to explain to me the skiing accident in Colorado that had bunged up his leg the prior spring.

We pulled into Mexico City about nine o'clock that second night, and he offered to have me share his room again so that I could begin my search for a place to stay the next morning after a good sleep, et cetera. I thanked him a lot for the whole trip and allowing me the T-bird driving experience. I said that I had one phone number that a teacher had given me for my first night when I got to the city and then he'd give me the info I needed to locate the place I would stay. Both Matt and I knew that a clean break at this arrival point made more sense than any other sort of an overnight accommodation. We shook hands, I secured my pack up on my shoulder and walked toward the heart of Mexico City.

◆

In my hitchhiking junkets I was often conscious of railway freight yards as I waited on the outskirts of cities hoping for rides. I had never ridden a freight, but in a college charity auction in the spring of 1957 I offered up a challenge that would award an unusual prize to the highest bidder.

The Trip to "Mountiful" or Climbing Mount Oberlin

I had a fun "career" working in the kitchen of Dascomb Hall at Oberlin all through my college time. When I was elevated from pot washer in my first semester to head waiter after two months, I had the chore of keeping order within the ranks of twenty waitresses and no waiters...and working with the rest of the kitchen crew. It was great work...I loved almost all of it, though I was glad to leave pot washing for head waiting. In about the third semester of this job, an after-dinner charity auction was held. Students offered stuff from their rooms and some services for the bid cost. I had nothing that would be of any interest to anyone but I did think up one service I could auction to the highest bidder.

My offer was to go to Mount Oberlin in Glacier National Park and climb to the mountain's 8,184 foot peak and carve the name of the highest bidder on a piece of rock, leave it there, and return with a photo of same for the bidder. I selected Mount Oberlin as my promised goal because the mountain had been named by Dr. Lyman Sperry in 1895 as part of a regional geology survey. Sperry selected Mount Oberlin as the name for this highest peak in this part of the Lewis Range in northwest Montana to honor his employer for this project, Oberlin College.

To heighten audience interest in my challenge, I said that I would do the entire round trip for no more than five U.S. dollars. My recollection is that the winning bid was fifty-three dollars, but I can hardly believe that anyone would have paid that much for something as ephemeral as the prize I had conjured up. However, a generous bid closed the auctioning and I left at the end of the spring semester in 1957 with five dollars in my pocket and a map of highways to Minneapolis and a railroad route map from the Twin Cities to Glacier National Park. I planned to get a park map there in the park so I could find Mount Oberlin.

STEAK AND RAIL

After the Oberlin Charity Auction, I charted my route to Glacier National Park to honor the fifty-three dollar pledge gained in the earlier campus auction. I planned to hitch to Minneapolis and then pick up a freight on the Great Northern rail line. It ran clear across to the west coast and it cut right through Glacier National Park. I figured if I got that close, I could find Mount Oberlin and do my promised climb.

This episode is about my last ride into the Twin Cities. I was traveling alone, as I almost always did in thumbing. It was late afternoon when I got picked up by a man in what appeared to be a nearly new brown Cadillac. I recall fins and the long body and thought, *Whoa, neat deal. Caddies don't often stop.* I had about fifty miles to go to Minneapolis and fortunately, the driver asked what my trip was about and where was I heading. As I recounted the bid and the challenge of the Auction, he got caught up in the effort I was making to complete this trip for under five dollars. I had spent very little up to that point because people often bought meals, or my mealtimes just slipped by unnoticed. I slept in building lobbies (things were more open then) or by the side of the highway in tall grasses.

The Minnesota guy made this offer. "How about if we do this? I'll take you out for a good steak dinner and then drive you to the to the rail yards of the Great Northern? I bet that no kid has ever been brought to his first freight riding experience in such style!"

"Wow...that's great. What's the catch?"

He continued, "All you have to do is promise that someday

you'll find a way to do the same sort of thing for someone on the road. Okay?"

I quickly agreed and he took us to a roadhouse where I had probably the biggest steak dinner I'd ever had in my life. After the meal, we got back into the Caddy and he drove me to the Twin Cities Great Northern freight yards. He even noticed a place where the surrounding chain-link fence had been pulled up enough for me to crawl under. As I push my pack ahead of me, he called out his window with this same line again. "This sure as hell is the first time any guy has been brought to a freight yard in a new Caddy to begin his first freight hopping!" I grinned and told him I was sure he was damn right and I walked off toward the great hulks clothed in the darkness of early night.

The first night of freights was a mixture of excitement and anxiety. I found a box car with an open door and threw my pack in and then did my first figuring out about how you get your body into a box car—and this car was not even moving. As I sort of wallowed in and tried to look confident in my moves—I had not seen anyone else in the car—I stood up, grabbed my knapsack and looked into darkness at each end. In that moment of decision-making, a voice came out of the darkness asking, "Which way are you trying to go, Kid?"

Surprised, I said, "I'm trying to get to Montana."

"West...you do know that don't you?"

I laughed nervously. "Yeah—but I wasn't expecting a travel guide to ask me where the hell I was going."

"I'm no travel guide, but I could tell from the way you bumped around getting your ass into the car that this might be your virgin voyage on the Great Northern Railway boxes."

"You're on the money. In fact, these last two hours have been a first for me in lots of things."

"Whaddya mean?"

I realized that this freight experience was already playing like a hitching trip. I slipped into that more comfortable mode and told the still unseen guy that I had been picked up by a Caddy, taken to a great steak house, given the biggest steak dinner I'd ever eaten." I paused because I was still dumbfounded at what had happened in the last two hours. "... and then, the driver actually drove me to a break in the chain link fence at the edge of the freight yards. As I got out of the car and moved with my pack toward the crawl space leading to this whole new world, he wished me well with this proclamation, "You sure as hell are the first hitchhiker ever to get fed a steak dinner and dropped off at the local train yards to begin his first trip on the rails—and driving to the yards in a Caddy, too! What a deal!" The driver then raised his window and drove off.

"Whaddya have to do to get a deal like that?" said the voice in the dark. He then stepped out of the dark of the boxcar and stood near me in the early evening light. He was somewhere north of forty and wore simple jeans and a denim shirt and scuffed boots. He had a beard of inconvenience and his hair was capped by a farm implement company logo hat.

"What did I have to do? Nothing. I think the guy just got caught up in the stupid deal I am working on to get to Glacier National Park in northwest Montana for five dollars or less."

"You've got no money?" I listened carefully to that question, just the way I'd learned to on the road generally. This did not feel like a set-up for some sort of shake down.

"I've got about five dollars now. I'm playing out on a college dare that says I can get to Glacier National Park, climb Mount Oberlin, and get back to Cleveland—all for five bucks total."

"So, this is some sort of prank? Some college boy's idea of a good joke on the system? Are Mom and Dad waiting for a phone call to send you some emergency money on the sly?" I could feel the testing going on full tilt as the guy searched for a better sense of who and what situation had invaded his private car.

"No—there's no Mom and Dad backup for this gig. I took it on myself as part of a charity auction near Cleveland, Ohio trying to get bucks for some sort of a place needing money to keep its doors open for people on hard times. Some college kid won my auction bid by offering to give fifty-three dollars to the charity. That was the highest bid." I added quickly, "but I didn't get a cent of the money raised."

My car mate paused a moment, looking over my pack and my jeans and flannel shirt and my canvas tennis shoes. Then he changed his posture a little and...as is so often the way with hitchhiking, became "the teacher."

"Here's the deal, kid. Riding freights has a much better press than it oughta. You get chased by railroad dicks. You gotta watch your bag of gear every minute. And you gotta learn some rules of the railroad so that you don't get whacked by the train even if you can dodge the fellow travelers who will see you a mark that they can maybe gain from."

He then slipped more completely into a new role and set the stage for the arrival of the teacher. "I'm a teacher—not in a boxcar, but in a Midwest community college. The pressure in that crazy system plays hard on my body. Every now and again I slip into the bottle to hide. I only do it during vacation breaks, but I've learned that by hitting the rails I free myself completely from the suffocating school walls—and I don't drink on the road." He could not help but see that my wide eyes—even in the slim light of the boxcar—were telling him he had found a good audience for this revelation.

The maybe-a-prof guy went on. "I'm going to figure that

you've been sent to me by some cosmic Dean of Men or something to remind me that teaching is a good life, and that I oughta have the discipline to play the role of teacher all the time, and not just when I'm on campus." The guy stood directly in front of me by the open door as though the window on the dark railyard was his blackboard for his lesson.

"We're gonna think of this boxcar as our classroom for an hour—this freight will roll in about that time—and you can decide whether or not you're ready to carry out your crazy-assed promise to go another thousand miles for about the cost of a carton of cigs. Or are you going to grab your pack, slip into the darkness before the Great Northern rolls west, and take to the highway, or spend your last five dollars on phone calls to some buddy who can get you out of this curious bind you've dreamed up for yourself."

As I write these paragraphs some sixty years after the episode's occurrence, I am as stunned now as I was in that Twin City nighttime as I had nervously made my first awkward climb into a boxcar with an open door, thinking it was empty in the darkness. And then, to find that the one guy sharing the maiden boxcar of my new travel world was willing to tutor me for a bit on the things that I really needed to know as I scrambled into the world of boxcar and freight riding. But I recall all of this with frightening clarity.

I looked at the guy differently at this moment. "You're serious? You're willing to teach me some of the basics about riding freights even though I'm here for different reasons than you? If you're being straight with me and want to play 'teacher,' I'd be a good student for that hour you're talking about. I'm staying aboard as the Great Northern starts to roll west. Better yet, I'll listen just as though I was in a ship's crew being told what to do on a sinking ship."

My new teacher stood up a little bit taller and walked over to the doorway of the box car. The opposite door was closed. The door I had entered was about half open. From where we stood, all that could really be seen was line upon line of boxcars awaiting engines, direction, and purpose.

"Take a look at this world you've decided to explore. What do you see out there?"

I stepped in closer to the steel edge of the boxcar floor and looked into the early evening dark. "I see boxcars, gondolas, flat cars and more boxcars." As I paused a second to gather up my observations into a more useful scene, the teacher broke in.

"What you don't see—or mention at least, is the most important part of the entire world there—is the rails, the rail system that carves through space as though it were butter. The rails that we are separated by only about four feet stretch tens of thousands of miles from ocean to ocean to Gulf to international boundaries. They're the reason that any of the things you saw have any utility. A thirty ton, ten-by-fifty-foot steel boxcar with two doors would have almost no use if it were not for rails." He paused just for a second or two, and then looked directly at me as though he was going to share a really import code word and said, "And…if I jumped off into the gravel and very, very carefully reached under the edge of the box car and grasped the rail with my hand, I would be in direct contact with damn near every mile of rail laid since the middle of the nineteenth century! This bond is nearly unbroken… and it was laid in by immigrants who mostly knew almost no English, but knew they were hungry, ambitious for security, and bloody ready to show they could accomplish the task of laying rail lines."

By this moment, I was almost giddy with the evolution of our chance meeting turning into a stimulating prep course for moving myself west via the rails. I said, "I don't see any engines from our niche here. I don't see any men working the yard. I don't even see a tall building like an observation deck that would let some crew manager or operations person know where the moving parts are. There clearly has to be a nerve center to keep this yard productive, no?"

"If you had explored farther into the hundreds of boxes all around us, you would've seen crew, even a railroad dick, and someone would have yelled at you. They might have asked what you're doing here—or just told you to get the hell out of the train yard."

"So there really are railroad cops? That's what I always hear about if I talk with anyone about trying to ride freights."

"Yeah—and like most things, their images in common lore are too narrow, too harsh, actually. They're told to keep people out of the yards—not just because of trespassing—but because these places are dangerous as hell. You fall off the edge of a box car while flopping around trying to get on board, like you were forty minutes ago, and your life could change big time. You could fall to the gravel and somehow get one leg under the train—and if the train were moving, you'd be having a helluva different next fifty years." He paused for that image to play across my mind.

"Like for example, wait till you try catching the ladder rungs of a moving boxcar as the train is building up steam on its scheduled trip. You'll be damn shocked at how much tougher it is to get a good grip, pull your legs up, keep your pack on your back, and then get secure on the ladder of the moving boxcar. And then what? Movie scenes make everyone think any stud can do all that freight hopping stuff. Fat chance, kid…it's all a lot tougher in a working yard with crew and railroad dicks all doing their best to hassle you out of their territory."

I started to comment but he put his hand up to silence my reaction.

"Get back up here in the doorway again and just listen for a few minutes. You gotta learn more stuff before you start asking more stuff. You been in too many classes with open discussion. If you're trying to learn how to save your ass on a virgin trip of freight riding, you gotta listen way more than talk. You gotta listen to the 'teach!'" I closed my mouth and he had the two of us stand at the edge of the box car. There was still no motion underfoot. Everything was fixed in space as well as time.

"This train that your buddy with the Caddy seemed to happen on is a 'hot-shot freight express' heading toward the Pacific Northwest. It is scheduled to take off in about half an hour. If you lean out—I'll back away so you can get some feeling for what your gripping places are on the door jambs of an open box—and look toward the engine on the left, you'll get a sense of how long a train this is. It's been adding cars for the last couple of hours. I got into this box earlier because I could see that it had just carried grain from the west. That means that even though the car is emptied, there is always enough grain left in the corners to be able to sweep up a pile that makes a pretty fine sleeping pad once the train is in steady motion." I looked around the car. My eyes had become adjusted to the weak light and I could see a small pile of wheat kernels pushed up again the back wall of the box. I stayed silent.

"Here's one of the most basic rules of freights. Never sit in the doorway of an open box while the train is moving. In this first trip, you might get a little cabin fever and think of hanging your legs out, even kicking them innocently a little, and *wham*, when you're not looking carefully, the train will cruise at some sixty miles per hour by a close metal sign. If you're kicking out at that instant, you'll have your leg whacked and maybe your whole body pulled out on to the gravel road base and who knows where your arms and head might land in that instant of stupidity. Never dangle your legs out of an open box car—even when the car's not moving!"

The teacher—funny, we had not even exchanged names yet even though I felt as though he fit right into the teacher model that I had grown comfortable with in some of my Oberlin classes—but I still didn't want to diminish his teacher role by chatting him up for a name. He walked back up to the open door and continued.

"You've probably got a flashlight in your lumpy pack. If you've got one, you'll get it out and look to see what the car is like…and then you'll come up to the door and use the light to look up toward the engine and then toward the caboose." He paused and then said in a bold voice, *"Don't!* Train crews use flashlights to communicate between the engine and the crews in the caboose. If you're doing a 'Lookie Lou' out of the box car door during motion, someone at either end of the train is going to wonder what the hell that flashlight message is. Keep the light to yourself. The most use it can have for you is if the train comes into a stopping place on the edge of a town. You can then look out at night to see if there are any vegetable gardens nearby. Neighborhood gardens at the edge of towns are like having a small vegetable market right around the corner in a city neighborhood."

I found my mind jumping this way and that. I wanted to learn everything he was saying, but I also wanted to slap myself on the face to remind myself of true serendipity in finding this guy, this car, this evening, and now—this trip. A maiden voyage on the Great Northern hot shot heading as far west as a train could go—how could I have planned it any better? Did I say 'planned?'

The lesson continued for more than the promised hour. As the freight engine did some final moves adding a few more loaded boxcars, we both allowed as how we were lucky as hell that they did not shunt this empty off to a sidetrack and give this space to some load of midwestern products bound for the Pacific Northwest. As I offered up gratitude for such a decision, the guy told me, "I don't know how any trains make any money. Ya look across that yard and see—literally—hundreds of box cars. Whose are they? How does any firm know where their empty boxes are? Hell—how do they even keep track of the full ones? At least they seal them up damn tight. Mostly there's no one getting into the sealed box cars and finding haven in a car interior."

The freight gave a great jolt—and we heard some powerful diesel whistles and felt the train began to pull west...west... west. This was great! I was actually on board; I knew enough not to hang my legs out and flashlight across the landscape in excitement that I had made the second part of my auction bid—go to Glacier Park for less than five dollars and turn that into a round trip. In the dim light I moved to the other end of the boxcar and began to push the scattered grains toward the raw black wall, keen to make my own bed to serve as a base for the thin sleeping bag I had in my backpack. Class was over but it had been absolutely vital and top notch!

◆

There are two universes on a freight. The in-boxcar world has its own protocols and it seemed to me that the universal rule was: Watch your stuff! Like I'd learned in my Twin City Tutorial, loose wheat or any grain was good news. But it was clearly, first found, first captured, and first slept upon. I heard a lot about things that had "fallen off" the truck or that had come out of large equipment cartons I sometimes saw, but I did not see any loose spoils of hopping freights. There seemed to be an unspoken agreement that all of us taking and making free passage ought to be at least modestly respectful of the freight system that flowed along this vast rail network. This honor system may be mythic and a function of the fact that I hopped only for the bulk of the summer of 1957, leaving a lot of calendar and landscape unseen.

The other freight car universe is the adjacent world along freight yards and rail lines. Sometimes I'd make a dumb (ignorant actually) choice of boxcar to flop into and the train that set them in motion was a local and we'd get shunted off onto side lines and dead ends so that we could clear the main tracks for the hot shot freights that were kept to a much tighter schedule. In situations like that, the train would come to a dead stop and sometimes a yard man would come along and check the boxes and might even respond to "How long a stop do ya think?" whispered in a friendly voice to the railroad crew member. An answer might come—or the more unsettling words, "There's a dick in this yard. He'll be coming around sometime in the next hour. You oughta be gone or be damn quiet."

It was in places like this that a quick and judicious exploration of local gardens could be productive. The rule was to talk to the garden folks—if the garden lady or man spots you thinning the row of carrots or beets—"I'm only taking a few for Pa. He's hungry as can be and he wants a few fresh vegetables and no more beans." That response line tended to play out well, especially in the Midwest.

The episode below shows another side of the culture in the shadows of the tracks.

MINOT, NORTH DAKOTA

Our train pulled into a siding outside Minot, North Dakota. Three guys who were riding freights had gotten out of their box car to make a small fire to warm up some hash or soup. They agreed to let me share their fire to warm my own can of soup. A little later a fifth guy came from the dark and stood at the outer ring of the fire's glow.

This setting was not cozy, but it was convenient. Everyone knew the same forces in life had led them to this sort of travel. Only very rarely did I run into a boxcar person who was out on a lark. Even the teacher I introduced in the earlier episode was in a kind of mobile therapy as he used boxcar riding to dry out.

The new guy outside the circle of this fire, this night, was working with the disadvantage of being alone, and not being a young-faced college kid trying to learn a new world as part of his road education. Although I did not really feel part of the trio, I did have the advantage of having asked about the fire earlier and with less threat.

The new traveler had emerged from the shadows with a small bindle and a can of soup in his hand. He spoke first.

"Would you guys care if I shared your fire a bit to warm my soup?" He asked in a firm, even toned voice.

One of the trio said, "Yeah, but can ya bring us another branch or some sticks over there?" The speaker pointed toward some brush behind the questioner. The new guy put his pack and can down and walked back twenty feet into the rough brush. In a minute or two he emerged with a branch that he was breaking up as he walked back toward the fire. No one was saying anything.

The new guy carefully dropped his wood on the fire and squatted down over near me. He pulled a can opener out of his pack. As he was working the spinner to get the top off the can, he asked, "Where you guys heading?"

The answer flew out into the night instantly. "West, we're goin west, probably Washington or somewhere near Seattle or somewhere with apple country." There was a look of expectation in all three faces in case this guy had some news that could be helpful. But the guy opening his soup can kept silent.

"Why'd ya ask?" asked a guy in a blue shirt. There was a touch of uneasiness in his voice as he was asking this question.

The can top came off. The guy put the soup can right into the edge of the fire. He nudged it with a stick so that it stood with good warmth on at least one side. He then looked up at the older guys and asked, "Do you have any contacts? Do you know anyone in Washington's apple country to set you up with picking?"

It seemed as though all three voices spoke at the same time. "No." and then Blue-shirt went on. "Shit, you don't need no introduction. You jest walk up and pick the apple and then pick another. You don't need no fuckin' introduction!" The questioner was silent.

Another one of the trio then asked him where the hell he was going. He, a little cautiously, told them that he was heading back east. "I've just spent six Goddamn weeks in 'apple country' trying to find any work at all. Hell, there's one guy there for every friggin' apple in the state already." As he gave this reply, he looked quickly around at the older faces. He finished his reply by saying, "I'm heading back east to starve with people I know. It's no Goddamn fun to do it with strangers on all sides of ya."

Then, with the quickest move I'd seen any one of the three

guys make in the day I'd shared their boxcar, Blue-shirt stood up, kicked over the can of just opened soup and yelled at the new guy, "What the hell are you tryin' to do? How do we know what the hell you really know? You're probably just screwing up our heads so that you'll have a better chance of finding work in the west!" Blue-shirt stood tall and watched carefully as the new guy got up, reached back for his pack, and backed a little way from the fire. He hung his pack in his left hand and stared at the four of us—but mostly at the initial trio. "Have you toadies ever heard about the myth of the marathon runner? Do you know anything at all about life beyond empty boxcars, rail yards, and life on the move?" The man speaking looked down and saw that his soup was gone anyway. "More than 2000 years ago an army from Persia did battle with Athens in Greece and the Greeks won. A day-runner in Athens was sent to Sparta—these are all places a helluva lot farther away than Seattle, you savvy road men—to tell about the Greek victory and seek help to keep order. The runner covered more than twenty-six miles to reach Sparta. When he got there, he cried out, 'We have won. We have conquered!' but he then fell dead from the pressure of bringing news those twenty-six miles in haste. It was the death of the runner but the birth of the Marathon.

"I've just given you three toadies and the kid great news—good and useful news, but you're pushing me out. You hear my truth as bad news and it makes me want to say, "don't kill the messenger," but my news will save you weeks and weeks of bad assed apple polishing, trying to get any kind of job." The outsider stared at them from his standing position.

Only Blue-shirt responded. He faced the news bringer directly. "How the hell can this be good news if what you're telling us is true? Shit, our whole plan is based on being able to pick up simple, easy jobs and maybe find something else along the Pacific coast. What you're telling us is crap—it's all bad news." The two other members of the first trio now stood up. There was a stalemate built around what the messenger had brought to the circle.

"I don't give a damn whether you believe me or not. I've already learned my ten-week lesson. I've ridden the Great Northern lounge boxcars resting in the small wheat piles from near Chicago to points north and south of Portland, and Seattle. I wished t'hell that someone had grabbed my attention before I began my trip west and given me any idea of the reality out there. The west coast is like the damn handbills in the 1930s in the *Grapes of Wrath*. Stories about 'help wanted' fly through the air like lightening bugs. You can hardly grab one, you only see a flash of light and somehow you're so damn hungry you 'take it as a sign' and head for the rails to get west."

There was a nervous silence. One of the originals scuffed his boots in the gravel and brush. I took a chance and offered a reaction to what was happening.

"Guys, what I've learned from hitchhiking for years and riding the rails for about a week is that road news is never reliable. You hear some towns throw hitchhikers in jail. Others have church parish houses where you can earn some meals for some yard work. Some people scare the hell out of you saying local railroad dicks are goddamn brutal to keep riders out a' the yards, but yesterday, I had a dick take me to the engineer of a massive Great Northern diesel, walk me up the iron steps and introduce me to the engineer. He told him, 'Johnny, — here's a kid new to the rails. He seems clean and eager. Why not give him a leg up here and that'll keep him outa the way of the stuff going on in the yard. Drop him off anywhere west of here. He's trying to get to Montana.' The engineer did a quick study of my face and gear and said, 'Okay, kid. Just don't fool with any of the dials.' And I got three hundred miles in the heart of the engine room."

Turning toward the guy just leaving, I added, "What my friends here do with your news is hard to tell. It's clear they're pissed to have their dreams of apple picking and easy cash hammered with your news. But, hell, not a one of the five of us really knows exactly what to expect out west. Even when ya drive your own Ford or Chevy, you always gotta be ready for radiator problems or a fuel pump going bad, or at least tires blowing out. All you've lost"—I said this focusing on the newsbearer—"is the can of soup. My buddies here who were feeling optimistic an hour ago, now gotta figure out 'what next?' My plans don't change a bit. I'm heading to Glacier National Park and as far as I know apple picking isn't an issue there."

By the time I'd finished my statement on my road realities, everyone had been lulled into a more thoughtful state. As the new guy headed back toward the brush and darkness, I caught up with him and slipped him a can of soup I was able to pull from my own pack. He refused it at first and then took it when I explained that he was smart to get away as quick as he could because the marathon man had died in the mythic delivery of the news to Sparta. "Get away while you can," I told him.

I returned to the fire where the three men were giving attention to their own cans of dinner. No one was forming a new plan. Then the man who had jumped up and yelled at the outsider spoke in a decisive voice. "Hell, if we'd never listened to that guy, or if we hadn't asked him anything, or if he'd not even been near us, we'd still be heading west. And, we'd still be hoping to find apple picking...but damn, the fact is, we don't know shit about what we're going toward. The kid is even a little bit right when he says 'news you get on the road is damn unreliable.' We all know that." He stopped there, thinking that someone else might have joined in with a supportive "Yeah—right," but no one did.

I felt that I'd said all I wanted to risk as the junior member of the road club. When I finished my soup, I was glad no one had knocked it over, and I felt as though I'd had about as much social work as I wanted for that day. I picked up my stuff and said, "I'm goin' back to the car and be damn sure I'm on board when it starts west again. If you guys are changing your directions, holler at me so that I can scarf up some of your grain and sleep on the wheat wonder foam bed tonight—okay?"

"Yeah, Kid. I bet you're not gonna get any of our bedding tonight. I think our heads are too, too west to think about any other direction tonight."

◆

In recalling this episode, I find myself moved by the flimsy information that is at the heart of travel decisions on the road, whether traveling by thumb or by rails. In both cases, there is a curious bend in time, because if hitchhiking, every break you take for a burger, or to find a bathroom, or even to get a coffee, your mind imagines dozens of lonely drivers heading toward the very city you seek, all wishing they had someone to talk to…but you're unknown and unseen to them. In the railyard, you search for a good empty boxcar and you find one that is filled with concrete dust or slivers of carried lumber now removed and yet you take the car, because at least it is uncontested.

But your mind takes over then with images of auto carrier cars just four lines over with one car without locked doors—

or you imagine a daring batch of Girl Scouts doing a scary "railroad boxcar trip" for ten miles and you could be there as the group counselor and traveling tutor. But, no, you've made your dibs on cement dust and solitude. You never, ever, know what the full scene is!

Let me say, however, that by hitching and working now and again in cafés and two days for a minister's wife, I was able to do the entire thirty-five hundred miles for under fifty dollars while becoming acquainted with freight hopping and the beauties of Glacier Park. Travel is really a head trip!

◆

I spent a lot of the summer of 1957 on the road, and on freights. When I got back to Oberlin in the fall, I fell into the full rush of sophomore year and suddenly, it was full time education, followed by three years in Taiwan, teaching for an Oberlin Program at Tunghai University in the middle of the island. That was followed by beginning graduate school in Geography at UC–Berkeley. The following episode occurred.

The Dixon, California Railroad Yard

When I had begun graduate school at Berkeley in 1965, my friend, Tom, asked me if I wanted to do some more freight riding. He had never ridden, and he wanted to get the experience. We took off on a weekend and went north on the Union Pacific line in the Sacramento River valley. I had asked around a little about freight riding in California since I had never tried any there, or at least not since the summer of about 1957 when I did my first freight hopping. I was told that the

Union Pacific north was a great ride because that was such a beautiful part of the state. "However," continued the counsel, "look out for Dixon! There's a railroad dick there who's like the ol' time railroad dicks and he wants no one cruising through his yard."

We decided to take that trip and we had a good time charting our success on the line. We had selected not an open boxcar, but rather a gondola car that was pretty well filled with lumber. The load came to about six inches below the edge of the car. As we followed our progress on the map and the railroad, we could see we were getting close to Dixon. We both lay down on our backs, face to the open sky, and noses just below the upper edge of the gondola car's side panels. We had taken our hats off. As the freight train came into Dixon, a town of maybe six thousand, we both closed our eyes. We thought that would really make us invisible. In the warmth of the California sun, this was not a bad deal... smoothly flowing air, intense light kept out by tightly scrunched eyelids and the slowing pace of the train's movement.

As the train stopped, but before we dared to open our eyes and give ourselves away by such over-confidence, we heard this raspy voice say, "Hello, boys... riding the rods, eh?" We looked up in disbelief. The rail platform in Dixon was a raised concrete surface and the Dixon railroad dick was standing alone, above us, with his shoes at just about our head level. We were separated from him by maybe three feet. He continued, "You boys maybe heard that Dixon has a helluva yard dick.... well, it does, and I'm it." Still no action on his part beyond speech and the only action on our part was to feel pretty stupid, lying on our backs and looking up like a kid who has been caught sneaking a pie from the bakers' shelf in some college kitchen.

"Yeah, I guess that's what we heard," I said. Tom kept silent. The train was still stopped. "Well," he went on, " I'm going to walk over to the yard window and when I come back, I want to be able to see all of the lumber that you're lying on. I want to see it and not you." He paused a second and then finished with "If you get out and cross over to the far side of the yard, you'll see a highway through the fence. That road can take you right back to Sacramento....and your thumbs will work just fine in Dixon."

He walked away. We hustled out of the car, grabbing our packs, and dodged our way across the other tracks and went for the fence. We climbed through a big break and began to walk south on the berm beside the two-lane highway. We considered going to the southern end of the yard and trying to catch a southbound freight but decided that it was a good day to try hitchhiking. What zeros we were to just walk away!

◆

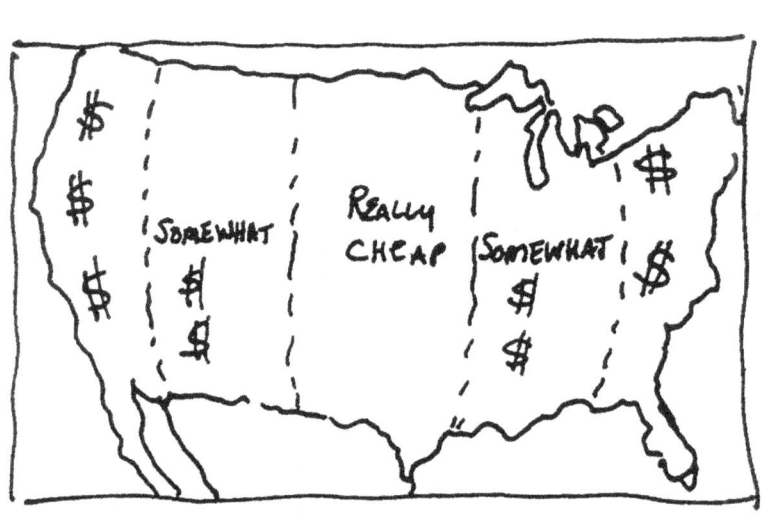

CHAPTER SIX
Teaching–The Essence of My Life

This chapter focuses on the many life lessons I have learned during my most exquisite teaching career. These are the best of many wonderful moments I experienced and teachings of others—from mentors, other instructors, and not so surprisingly, students!

Tossing the Rock

At Oberlin, I was greatly interested in geology and especially paleontology. The professor who was most important in this was Dr. Larry DeMott. He had done his graduate work at Harvard and he was a young professor when I got to Oberlin in 1956. One day in 1957, a few of us were in the rock lab and talking about stuff—some of it having to do with geology and some of it just stuff. At one point one of the students was talking and as he spoke, he took the sample rock that he had been looking at and began to toss it up and down, describing maybe a fifteen inch lift. He went on with his sentence but was keeping a kind of cadence with the floating piece of lab sample.

All of a sudden, from nowhere, out came Professor DeMott and caught the stone at the apex of one of the tosses giving a visual aspect to the student's comments.

"That's all, kids. Lab's over. Leave." He said this sharply, but not meanly. "I have learned that when students start tossing the lab specimens into the air while they talk about their dates or even the quiz on the horizon...It's clear that no more learning going on. Rock's up, so time's up. Leave."

STUART ALLEN AND RAVEN PRESS

I spent the Summer of 1969 teaching an East Asian geography class at the University of Oregon in Eugene. I had a class of some twenty students. One of the assignments was to do a paper that helped create the flavor and personality of a country or political unit in East Asia. Because the class was small, I was better able to work with students and have more student-faculty interaction than was often possible. I had one student named Stuart Allen. When I had finished reading the draft of his paper, I sought him out in class and returned the fifteen pages. "Stuart—this is a good paper. You've got a nice beginning on creating a sense of Mongolia. But," and I continued with a more exhortative voice, "you've left out a major geographic element."

"I'm not a geography student, Professor Salter. In fact, I don't know what I am going to be."

"Fine... you do not need to be a geographer to know that a *map* is necessary. In these pages, you are talking about, writing about, a world that no one in Oregon has ever been to or, in most cases, even heard of. Without a map, you do not anchor this place to the larger world. Where is it? What it is next to? Location, location, location!"

I continued, "It does not need to be a fancy map. I only require that it *not* be a Xerox photocopy of some map. A simple sketch map of Central Asia would work well to show how China and the USSR bother putting the squeeze on Mongolia."

Well...Stuart Allen handed in his final paper with a handsome map done in ink and colored pencils. He mentioned as he handed it in that he found making the map a lot of fun. "Just doing the research and the drawing made me feel as though I better understood the place."

I trotted out a common line from geography professors to students newly fascinated with maps. "Map love is the most common explanation people give for becoming geographers, Stuart. Maybe you're launched now!" I accepted the paper and was pleased to give him an A on the project. The map was a nice additional facet of his argument trying to illustrate what made up the world of Mongolia.

Why do I mention all of this? Stuart Allen went on to do work in geography and cartography and, after graduation, began a firm called Raven Maps. They are located in Medford, Oregon, and the firm produces some of the most beautiful maps and cartography in the United States. Raven maps are given as visual gifts nearly as often as they are bought as representations of map artistry and clarity.

In teaching you never really know what you have set in motion....Stuart, in subsequent correspondence with me remembered this event in just about the same way. He allowed as how he got more and more captured by the art and utility of really carefully done maps. How satisfying to the professor who opened that map door! Check out www.ravenmaps.com to see where Stuart and his firm have gone since that classroom talk in the summer of 1969 in Eugene, Oregon.

The Spirit of East Saint Louis

One of the most stunning lessons in the differential power of place I learned in Missouri is the function of East Saint Louis in comparison to the better-known Saint Louis. Both urban settlements are on or near the banks of Mississippi River, although Saint Louis has the extra dynamic of the Missouri River confluence with the Mississippi. Early railroad bridges linked both cities with markets and manufacturing in the east, and later on, in the west and the north. However, East Saint Louis is an enormously depressing black community with rows and streets of abandoned buildings strung along the main drags. There are some major chemical factories on the river and these places represent the majority of the viable working factory sites. They sit in the shadow of abandoned stockyards, factory sheds, and burned-out residential neighborhoods. The city is not totally without commerce or homes. Habitat for Humanity has put up many homes. There are churches and some fast-food places. Overall, however, you feel that East Saint Louis has been passed by and abandoned by nearly anyone who has a chance to go across the river or up the road.

There is a place in East Saint Louis where I staged group discussions because of the way in which geography seemed to have failed the city. It was a disused baseball field with the empty outfield on one side, bordered by some newish homes and some burnouts. On another side was an elevated railroad trestle carrying train engines and cars across the Mississippi and into the greater activity of Saint Louis proper. By standing around second base and doing a slow revolution, you could see the trestle, the neighboring homes, the hardware of the railroad system, and—in the distance—the sixty-three story high silver arch of the Thomas Jefferson Park at river's edge in downtown Saint Louis. The monumental arch stood tall and gleaming like The City on the Hill for all to see. The day I have in mind was a spring Saturday in the first year of the new millennium. I was leading an optional field trip of the Geography Club at the University of Missouri. There were eight or nine students in a van we had from the University Garage. We drove into and then around East Saint Louis as part of my circuit.

The van was pretty quiet. Lots of eyes were looking out the windows, and hands—in silence—had reached up to make certain that the van doors were locked. After fifteen minutes of visual exploration, I drove them to the ballfield that Chloe and I had found one day when we were scouting East Saint Louis for another field group. I parked at the curb and invited the student geographers out and we all walked toward the open diamond. There were no base bags on the field, but the chain link backstop was still there and base paths were minimally evident. There was little outfield grass and it looked as though the field had not been used for years. We clustered in the middle of the field. There was a crisp wind that seemed particularly strong because of the bleak appearance of the houses (some lived in, some burned out) that ran along one side of the field. A train was just beginning the modest pull up to the top of the elevated trestle as it labored toward its crossing of the Mississippi.

My words were simple. I outlined a number of the spatial and geographic verities that seem to underlie successful urban siting and development. The best mix is a conjunction of river, rail system, population center, proximity to markets, and a productive hinterland. All of these conditions seemed to be met. Looking across the maze of trestles and bridges and the distant factory on river's eastern bank, we could see the gleaming Gateway Arch of downtown Saint Louis. We talked a little about what has happened to East Saint Louis. How could Saint Louis—itself a city in steady decline—still looked so healthy, and here, just across the river and at the foot of a very prosperous state (East Saint Louis is in Illinois), was this shell of a city. Everywhere we looked there was stark evidence of failure, abandonment, and depression. We talked about demographic shifts and the ways in which 'natural laws' do not always work.

At one point, a student named Ellen Z. (we called her EZ) stepped into the center of the circle and said something like this. "None of you has said the black, or the colored, or the Negro word yet. You have all been thinking it: 'East Saint Louis is more than 90 percent African American,' but no one has said this openly." There were a few somewhat uneasy nods in the heads of the all-Anglo student group paying close attention to this seemingly spontaneous outburst. She went on.

"Most of us are from Saint Louis and we have grown up with parents warning us not to go to East Saint Louis, or even downtown at night because we are so scared of blacks. Now Salter brings us to this city and all of our prejudices are suddenly terribly confirmed by seeing how depressed this city looks—is this still a city?" She stopped a second as though to regroup the issues in her mind and then continued.

"I have a black roommate at MU. We have just spent a year together. I did not know her in high school. She is not some amazing honor student or National Merit Scholar. She is just a black girl who had a posted a 'call for a roommate' notice on a campus bulletin board a year ago. We met and talked and we decided to room together. We did it. It worked out fine. And in that process, I learned a lot about black people. I am not here to tell you all about that, but I am going to tell you that this city of East Saint Louis is not simply a black experience. Or, more accurately, this city is not the product only of black mismanagement. There must be another hundred things that are wrong with this side of the river to explain what we are seeing this morning."

She stopped, looking across the river again at the Saint Louis Arch and then concluded, "Leticia, my roomie, taught me that life is a whole lot tougher for her and her sisters than it ever has been for any one of us. And even though you might think that you understand what they have to deal with, you—not one of you—knows crap about the way life stacks up against them. Just keep that in mind as we—Anglos all—think about East Saint Louis. It's okay to think, "God...I'm so glad I don't have to live here!!!" but it is *not* okay to think this is just another example of black inability to manage anything."

The group stood quiet for a minute. The train had completed its crossing. There were no cars coursing through the streets by the abandoned ball field, although a couple had emerged from their home and was standing by their front door looking at us. The man—a fifty to fifty-five year old black—called out, "Is everything okay? Are you all right?"

I called back that we were fine, just talking about the spirit of East Saint Louis. He grinned a little and called back, "Yeah...we're coming back. We're going to get a casino and that will bring some businesses back again." For a second I thought we might go and talk with them, but EZ said, "Can we go now? I need to get dropped off in Saint Louis." She had told me of this special need earlier and it was already later than I had expected it to be. "Sure...we'll go." I waved to the black couple and we walked back toward the van.

As the students were organizing themselves, I ran across the street to the couple and thanked them for their concern. I said that more learning had just occurred on that baseball diamond than I seemed ever to be able to achieve in a classroom.

We drove back to Saint Louis, dropped off EZ, and headed back toward campus.

DIFFERING SIXTH GRADE PERSPECTIVES

When Heidi was in sixth grade at an elementary school not far from UCLA, she had a teacher who was one of those lifetime treasures. Mrs. Beverly Revness became one of the great teachers in our kids' educational experience. Both Heidi and Hayden loved her—although I do not think that Hayden had her at school—and the Revness family and our clan became good friends. As an outgrowth of that, I began to do occasional short walking field trips with Beverly's classes in the mid-1970s. One of those trips was a five-block walk up to the UCLA campus.

On this trip I told them as we trudged uphill toward our goal that I was going to show them a really special place at UCLA—the campus Sculpture Garden. In that acre of land (just adjacent to the building Geography was in), landscapers had mounded small hills and planted beautiful jacaranda trees and some fifteen world-renowned sculptures had large pieces of metal art work on display. The whole park environment was done with some delicacy with Geography and the Social Sciences, on one side, Theater Arts on another, the Business School on the third, and the University Research Library on the fourth. It was the jewel of the UCLA campus crown.

The reason I mention this tiny trip is this: For the walk up toward the Garden, I had been explaining to the mixed bag of sixth graders how special this place was to UCLA planners when they were transformed early orange orchards to the land for a brand-new University of California campus. As we were in the final approach and going between two buildings on a pathway that opened into the garden, I heard a small black student tell his buddy, "Why, hell...dis ain't so special. Dey ain't even leveled it out and put up a hoop."

It was a grand lesson to me on the concept of landscape enhancement. In my whitey eyes, the small hills grassy mounds that had been added to highlight featured sculpture in the evolving Sculpture Garden. These gave strong identity the naturally flat landscape that had been here in 1929 when UCLA was founded. But, to a child daily bussed in from some very different part of the city, the concept of making a landscape special meant—of course—leveling it, paving it, and putting up a hoop. It was a telling lesson and I was able to get a few minutes of discussion from some of the kids as we stood on a little mound in the center of the Sculpture Garden.

THE BAR IS THE PLACE

As a geographer, one is supposed to be continually sensitive to space and place. The short hand for that is sometimes boiled down to "location, location, location." I have been booked on as a lecturer for a number of cruises in my life. Each has been more wonderful than the prior one. In the last one (1995 from San Francisco to Australia in thirty days and then flown home) Chloe and I had tight accommodations but a grand, grand time. The bar was the lecture venue for the majority of talks I was asked to give. The talks were at ten in the morning during the week. As I would go early and work at the bar on some notes, I realized what an evocative setting a bar is for non-drinking. It was—not for all, but for many—a setting of relaxation, story telling, and careful listening to what is being said to you.

In a bar, conversations range more freely than they do in most any other settings. There is a stronger sense of distance from your working environment in a bar than in almost any other setting. You are more often likely to talk with people you hardly know in a bar than you are in most conversational niches. And, you tend to go more deeply into your reservoir of narratives than you might in a living room or on a car trip or certainly in a lecture. The bar setting is the portal to more ease in conversation than most all alternatives.

That is why on the lecture circuit on the cruise ship, the bar is the place where you can find more energy in your own teaching narratives. You are more willing to tease responses, even argument, out of the people who have come in (on their own) to hear the comments of this Wednesday or that Monday. The bar is a great place to lecture.

And, as a footnote, I offer up the church sanctuary as another location that is good as a classroom. It does not evoke or accommodate nearly as full a range of narrative as the ship's bar (any bar in the morning), but it is a strong setting for thoughtful discussion and student recognition of the importance of town or world issues. I have worked both settings and both make teaching a great profession.

SIMPLIFY... SIMPLIFY...

I was hired at UCLA in 1968. I had set up my new office with the art and graphics that I had slowly been learning to drape across the walls of my offices as I had in Berkeley as a grad student. On the top of a four-drawer file cabinet by my office door, I had put a small refrigerator. On the door, I had the one graphic that my late brother, Joel, had penned in calligraphy and given me. It was a Henry David Thoreau quote. My door was open, as it generally was, and a student walked in. I was on the phone halfway across the office and I used my arm to welcome him in. He stood and then moved around studying the art and posters on the walls. Surprisingly, he pulled a pencil from his pocket and walked over to the small refrigerator. Very lightly he drew two diagonal lines through two words on my brother's quote. I hurriedly hung up the phone and walked over in some alarm. "Hey....why did you deface that quote? That's my brother's work."

He looked concerned but not alarmed. "Don't you see—all I did was do what the quote told me to do?"

The quote says, "Life is frittered away with details. Simply... simplify... simplify!" He had drawn a very neat and thin editor's pencil line through the second and the third "simplify." I looked at the change and grinned...he had me... he was right. A full half century after his editorial coup, I still have Joel's calligraphy with the two thin pencil lines through the final two words.

DESTROYED BY THE DEADLINE

One of the most continual struggles in teaching is getting students to meet deadlines of required papers. Even with a bold-faced note on the syllabus that **Late Papers Will NOT be Accepted** there are always papers dribbling in later in the day or week. I decided one term to have a little theater with this issue.

I had, of course, printed my deadline policy on my syllabus. That same note said that the papers were due at the beginning of class so as not to have a whole cohort of students coming in over the seventy-five minutes of the class with embarrassed grins on their faces as they put their *late* papers on my desk as I was lecturing. On the day of this event, I had my regular lecture notes and a box into which I was going to be putting the incoming papers. I got to class a little early so that I was ready to receive and laud the timely students in our class. The class was nearly full as the nine o'clock hour arrived. I pulled the box of papers close to my edge of the desk and thanked the class for their observation of the rules on the syllabus. I began the day's lecture. About five minutes into class two guys came in, grinned embarrassedly and scurried by the front desk, dropping their papers in the cardboard paper box that was filled with the other students' assignments. I slid the box over by my notes and stopped lecturing.

"When were these papers due, guys?"

"Today," one of them replied, just getting into his seat.

"When today?" I followed up.

"Just today, I think," he answered.

"Get out your syllabus—each of you two. Read the note about the paper and about this date." The class was fascinated at this drama, for there are few things so interesting as having someone in class get caught up in some little sin that the prof has noticed and responded to. "Read out the note about today, either one of you."

The guy who had not spoken read "Papers are due November 7. They are due at the beginning of class. No late papers will be accepted."

"What do you take as the meaning of those instructions? Either one of you...."

The first student spoke up. "I meant to get here on time, but I couldn't find a parking place. I was only five minutes late. Come on...cut us a little slack."

"Did you get a copy of this syllabus on the shopping day and the first day of this class?"

"Yeah...." He spoke a little more softly this time.

"And did I talk about this paper assignment and the due date and the due time?"

"I don't remember, but you probably did."

"What about that class? Did I discuss these items? Did I go over the entire syllabus with you all? Did I act like it was all only an approximation of requirements and deadlines and topics?" I widened my gaze to look at the forty or so students in the classroom.

"You mentioned all of this stuff," said a girl in the front row. "You even talked a little extra about the due time for the papers because you were trying to not have a whole bunch of us dribble in all through the lecture hour." If I had written a script for a by-standing student I could not have had a better testimonial.

I nodded agreement and looked again over the class. It was silent. The two guys had their notebooks open now and were trying to disappear into the anonymous class face. I reached over and picked up the two papers on the top of the stack, held them in front of me and the class, and tore them in half and then tore those halves in half again. I put the stack of paper off to the side of the box with the remaining papers and turned back to my lecture notes. I continued with the topic of the day.

This narrative should end there, but, *wait—there's more.* I stopped the two guys as they were leaving class at the end of the hour. They looked mad as hell, but I was armed with the syllabus language. "Guys, were your papers late?"

"Yes" they replied with reluctance, one looking at me, one looking at the floor. I reached into the box with the rest of the class's papers and pulled out the two on top. I showed them to the guys. "Are these your papers?"

With some amazement, they each took one, looked at the cover page, and then looked over to me. "Yeah…"

I took each one and marked, 'Five points off for being late.' I threw them back into the paper box and looked at them closely. "Live by the syllabus. Learn deadlines. They are major in the structure of life." I grabbed the box, my lecture notes, and the piles of torn faux assignment pages that were at the side of the desk. "I'll see you on time Thursday, right?"

They both nodded, still trying to figure out what they had just witnessed. I left.

What none of the class knew was that while I was quizzing the guys about when the paper was due as they were trying to get into their seats and blend into the class, I had taken two long-dead student papers out of the stack of my lecture notes and had put them on the top of their two late papers. This enabled me to have the theater of taking the top two papers out of the box and tearing them up in dramatic fashion.

I do not know whether or not the drama had any impact on either of those two students or the rest of the class that witnessed this minor drama I staged for intensifying deadline importance. I do know that I had three or four students mention the event to me over the next class meetings. One student had told me, "You're lucky they didn't write longer papers or use thicker paper. It would have been tough to tear them up."

"Naw," I replied. "I had the benefit of a lot of adrenalin flowing in my system just then. I could have torn up the phone book."

When I told daughter Heidi and Sugie about this caper,

they came back to me with a split decision on whether or not it was fair. The feeling was that I might have embarrassed the boys too much, building a wall between me and the rest of the class— except the front row—for the rest of the term. My only defense was that I see teaching as primarily motivation and that meant you had to catch the attention of the class. I felt that there had been an intensity, an electricity in the learning scene for those ninety seconds. That was enough pay-off for me...though I still cannot walk away from the event without some little bit of ambivalence.

Lessons in Cultural Classroom Geography

In 1967, I taught a summer session class at Berkeley in cultural geography. It was early in my geography teaching career. I had done some teaching at Cal State Hayward, south of Berkeley, and I had taught three years of English and some informal geography and Spanish at Tunghai University in Taiwan before this summer session stint. The room was mid-sized with eight rows, about seven or eight chairs wide. The class had maybe thirty-five or forty students. I had already learned the importance of *Ask the class questions* to keep interest higher. So, the students had learned to get ready for questions that related in some way to the assignment for that day, or the lecture that I was giving. I put forward a question about some aspect of plant domestication. After a short pause, an answer came from the back row. And it was not only from the back row which ordinarily does not contain kids who volunteer to answer questions unless the question is, "Who wants to end class early?" The answer to my plant question came from a black, and from his looks, he was a beefy black athlete. I paused just about three seconds while I processed the information that I had: *A good solid, correct answer had come from the back row.* This volunteered answer was hanging in the air between us.

As I processed this, the student said, "I've fooled you, haven't I? I got the right answer. I'm in the back row. And I'm black!" Some of the other students turned around to see who this new player was in our class interaction. I looked at him directly.

"Yeah....yeah....you're three for three. I hate to say it but you *are* exactly three for three." I figured that I ought to use this opportunity to talk about "back row geography." I explained that although I had not been teaching too long, I had learned that when classes took their own seats, the students who ended up in the back row were generally there because they wanted to be as far as possible from the prof *or* they got to class late and wanted to be as invisible as possible *or* they perceived the class as being the "lite class" on their schedule and were not doing any or much reading so they wanted to be out of discussion range. And, I continued, the jocks who took classes in Geography tended to hide in the back row where they were a small team of distant and generally quiet non-participants.

And, finally, I observed that the blacks who took Geography classes tended to not offer answers in the class dialogues. "So, you're right. You're batting a thousand."

The guy was quiet, but he looked satisfied—not smug, but satisfied. Then he said, "Yeah, I'm an athlete. I'm a wrestler but that doesn't mean anything. I like the back row because I get more independence that way. And being black is not a big deal, but I get damn tired of profs being surprised because I often both volunteer *and* answer a question correctly."

Well...that was that. The class went on and the guy played an interesting role for the rest of the session. He was a good student and he—and I told him this after the final—had modified my perception of back row geography in a productive way. I continue to see the back row as my least engaging students, and blacks generally continue to provide less in class interaction, but I look at the back row and the blacks differently now in every class, waiting to see if someone else is going to further nudge me toward a still newer perspective.

ROLLING DOWN THE COYOTE HILLS AND THE SAINT LOUIS ARCH

During a class I was teaching at Cal State Hayward, south of Berkeley, I went with a few students to see a local landscape they were proud of. They had talked about the Coyote Hills when I had made some reference to the Berkeley Hills. They claimed that their hills were every bit as spiffy and wondrous as the more famous hills to the north. At their invitation we drove over to these golden hills near campus. The four of us parked at the bottom of the hill and walked up a pathway to the crest. The hills were maybe two hundred feet above the settled plain below. They were covered with the soft golden grasses that creep across the landscape of the Bay Area in the fall. From the peak where we stood you could see the soft curve of hill flank that ran all the way down to an open field at the base of the incline.

I looked at it and figured well, this is an optional deal. This is not a really professorial outing. So, I put my wallet in my side pocket, turned to the students and said "I'll race you to the bottom...but no running, only rolling." With that, *I* dove into the golden grasses and began an erratic but wonderfully enjoyable roll from the top to the bottom. It took us all a bunch of stops and starts and reorganizing directions but we finally all got there, laughing and feeling all very silly. "Not a word about this, okay?" We all grinned.

Some twenty-five years later I had a formal field class on a two-day trip to Saint Louis. One part of our trip was a walk down Market Street to the park that is on the edge of the Mississippi River at the base of the stunning stainless-steel Arch that stands as the Gateway to the West. At the western edge of the Arch, there is a sloping hill that runs from the bold base of the Arch some one hundred feet to the lip of a small half-acre pond. It is part of the park landscape that makes this whole setting so handsome.

As we were talking about the attention given to ceremonial landscapes in large cities, the student who was most often unpredictable in class—Alexia—suddenly ran forward, hit the ground, tucked her arms close to her sides, and began a fast roll toward the edge of the pond. Seeing that there was really not much of a flat area at the end of the incline and before the pond's lip, I ran after her fearing that she would not know when to stop. I may or may not have recalled my Coyote Hills roll as I tried to catch her, but if I did, it did no good. She got up a good head of steam, did not wander much in her course, and rolled right over the small lip of the pond and sailed into the water. I got there just as she went under and was a nanosecond short of jumping in to make sure she was okay when she stood up. The water was about two feet deep. She was wringing wet and looked like a cat caught in a sudden rain shower. She grinned at us all. "I thought sure I would know when to stop. I guess I didn't. Oh, well..."

She climbed out and our group gave her a hand. This was a fall trip and it was already a little cool so a couple of the coeds (is that still an acceptable term?) pulled off thick sweatshirts and gave Colleen a rub down over her wet blouse and then had her wear one. Since the hotel we were staying in was only about a quarter-mile from this pond, I had two of them walk back to the hotel so Alexia could change into something dry. We agreed to meet at the old Saint Louis Courthouse in thirty minutes. It was about a ten-minute walk from this spot.

There is something wonderful about a roll. These are the two teaching rolls I recall most keenly.

THE PASS/NO PASS STUDENT ENCOUNTER

In the early 1970s, UCLA teaching adopted a Pass/No Pass option for classes. A student could not get explicit credit for classes required for a specific major, but they could earn class and academic credit toward the one hundred eighty class hours required for graduation. In evaluating how my class of one hundred fifty students had done in the first midterm, I noticed that one of the highest grades in the exam had been gained by a student who was taking the class as a Pass/No Pass option.

I called him in after the class when I returned the Midterms and encouraged him to switch to the grading option since he had done so well. There was still that option, although it would close within a week. He thanked me for making him consider this switch but said that he liked taking the class without the grade pressures that traveled with the rest of his Pre-Med curriculum. He said that he was doing a geography course just for the fun of it. I told him that I would sign the request to change form the minute he gave it to me, and encouraged him to get the more formal reward for the good work he was doing. "No...but thanks."

As the class unfolded, this student was more vocal than Japanese-American students usually were. He answered questions that I tossed out into the classroom and he offered some questions of his own when I was able to get the class out of the straight lecture mode and encourage students to raise some of the issues that the reading and lectures might have stimulated.

At the end of the term, Nakamoto got the third highest grade in the class, but he was still Pass/No Pass. Since I had his phone number, I called him just before I was set to fill out the class grade sheet and take it over to the registrar's office. He said that he was coming to campus to pick up a paper and he would stop by for a minute. When he showed up, we had this conversation.

"So...I was third highest? Hey...that's okay, isn't it, for a Pass/No Pass student?"

"No, it's stupid. If I write a letter to the registrar, there is a good chance that we can change your status even at this point. You would have three hours of A grade on your record instead of three hours of Pass."

"Yeah...but I knew what I was doing. I got the benefit of a less pressure situation and I liked the class. I'm okay with the Pass. This won't count toward my major anyway." He seemed peaceful with the decision.

"What are your plans? Are you really going for medicine? Do you think you'll stay in the L.A. area?" He was only a sophomore so there was a lot of time for plans to wander all over the place.

"This is my home. My parents came to the States before I was born. They live in the Sawtelle area and my Dad has a small shop in Little Tokyo downtown. Medicine is what they want me to do; a doctor is what they want me to be. They have done everything to help me focus completely on school. I owe them a lot." He did not say this with the customary grimace.

"Do you have any special ambitions yourself?"

He paused. I have long wondered (as I relive this short conversation) whether or not he was trying to decide if it was cool to crank out what might have been a family or an ethnic joke, or if he was just thinking about the question. In either case, the answer gave me has has stuck with me for decades.

"Yes. I do have one ambition—I mean one ambition beyond getting into Med School and doing well and setting up a practice in L.A." He looked at me and smiled. "But my real ambition is for my parents, too. I would like to get rich enough to be able to hire a Jewish gardener!"

There was no back slapping, no over-wide grin that would have signaled that this was a common Japanese-American joke. He just looked like a guy who had answered a question honestly and now had to move on to his other tasks.

"Thanks again for the class. It was great and it was even greater to not have to sweat the tests and the grades. I've told some other students about the class." He extended his hand and we shook and he walked toward the office door.

"I'll remember this conversation and your role in class, Nakamoto. You've been good news and a fine education for me. Good luck in Med School."

Let me exit this teaching episode by mentioning that Los Angeles has some of the most beautiful yards and gardens in the world—and the majority of these are in Beverly Hills, Belair, and other landscapes that are often Jewish in their populations. The trucks that are parked weekly at the edges of these works of landscape art almost always represent Mexican or, to a lesser degree, Japanese firms. These are the two populations that have become specialists in the creation and maintenance of this landscape symbol of wealth in Southern California. I have never, ever seen a landscape truck with a Goldstein or Liebowitz name. It was this image, however, that seemed to be central in this Japanese-America student's mind.

An Unusual Road Measurement Approach

There is a segment of old Highway 40 about fifteen miles from the MU campus in Columbia, Misouri. It is a wavy line of broken blacktop, slowly being encroached on both sides by volunteer grasses moving in to disappear the road. On the east of the old road are farm fields and farmsteads with some new homes and some old farmsteads. To the west of the road is a narrow band of grasses flanked by a broad highway easement, then a leg of recently surfaced new Highway 40 that weaves through mid-Missouri. I use this abandoned segment of Old 40 for a field class because I can drive a van up the gravel driveway that crosses it, turn my wheels around and leave it off to the side of the gravel. I always park with my car or van's nose out just in case it is essential to get away quickly from some field site. We then walk fifty feet over to a good teaching segment. One day when I was teaching at the University of Missouri, I took a bright senior out to see this segment because she had been unable to go to one of our field class outings. I used the driveway again, did the turnaround, and then we walked over to see this relic of our country's early infatuation with the automobile and cross country mobility.

I explained a little about the importance of the initial Highway 40 and its role as the first true trans-America blacktop highway. She looked disbelieving, saying, "This *couldn't* have been the major highway. It is way too small." I told her that it was at least sixteen feet wide, saying, "Look...with my hat I am nearly six feet and if I lie down on one lane, you can see that each lane is at least eight feet wide." Saying that, I lay down on my back and stretched out across the crumbling surface. I extended my arms to reach the faded yellow line in the middle of the road and had my feet in the encroaching grasses to show the dimensions.

At that instant, a heating and cooling truck was passing by on the adjacent new Highway 40. The old road segment is only about forty-five feet from the new highway, and the segment we were on could be clearly seen from passing trucks and cars. The truck driver hit his brakes, slithered across the gravel and came to a stop just next to where I had left my car.

The driver leapt out, yelling "What happened? Is the old guy okay?" running over to stare at me while asking the student this question. The student was clearly trying to look away as though she was no part of this road study.

I hopped up (actually, I have not hopped up in a long time) telling the driver, "It's okay...I'm okay. I was just trying to show her how wide the old road is."

"Is she blind? She can't see how wide it is unless you lie down?" The driver seemed to have switched gears quickly from his "good samaritan" role to the "suspicious of all college professors" role.

Danielle—the student—said, "No...I am not blind. I could see the road, but the prof was just trying to convince me that each lane was at least eight feet wide."

The driver stared at me, and then turned toward his company truck. We both said thanks to him for his willingness to stop and be concerned about the ol' guy lying across the road. He grinned weakly and got back in his van. I could just imagine the spin he would give this incident when he was reviewing the flow of stuff in his day as he stopped for a beer late in the afternoon.

He turned the truck around, and went on his way. I planned on bringing a tape measure for the next showing of this piece of old Highway 40.

THE TOOTHBRUSH CAPER

One day I went to the men's restroom in Stewart Hall, the home of geography for my fourteen years as chair of this small department at the University of Missouri. The floor plan of the Men's Room is two stalls, three urinals, and two sinks. There was someone in one stall. There was no one else in the room. I saw a 'buttered' toothbrush on the small counter by the sinks. And, coincidentally, I had in my hand my own buttered toothbrush. So I thought, *This is too sweet an opportunity to miss!* I turned on the water and rubbed all the toothpaste off the unidentified toothbrush. At the same time, I brushed my teeth with my brush—making all of the sounds that one can possibly make while brushing teeth. There is no ambiguity about what is going on, even if one cannot see the event taking place. As I did this, I heard a hurried flushing and standing up and buckling up in the one occupied stall. I did a final loud and mouthy rinse into the sink and, leaving the wet (and now unbuttered) toothbrush on the counter, I darted out of the men's room and down the hall into my office.

Just as the bathroom door closed behind me, I heard the stall metal door slam shut. My face hurt from the grinning that had rippled across my face as I thought of the guy coming out of the stall, seeing his wet and empty toothbrush, saying "What???? No!!! How can this be? How could anyone come into a public bathroom and brush his teeth with an unknown toothbrush??? Who in the world could do this?" I have no idea who was there but I have taken deep pleasure in this recollection for years.

◆

A footnote to this story. Elder brother Joel and I used to go to thrift stores together to get clothes and things in the 1950s. Once he told me, "Kit, never buy underwear or toothbrushes in the thrift shops!" Years later on one of the last visits we had together we went again, to a thrift shop just to see what was available. Joel, at one point turned to me in the men's shirts aisle and said, "Kit, remember that I told you once about not buying toothbrushes and underwear in thrift shops?"

"Yeah....it was years ago."

"Well, whenever it was, you ought to know that I have eased up on underwear. But I still hold the line on toothbrushes."

Fall Field Gig

One of the innovations that I was most proud of at the University of Missouri was something that was called The Fall Field Gig that I introduced in the 1990s. It was a simple thing. I convened all of the grads and all of the faculty for a Thursday afternoon through Saturday afternoon field exercise. We selected some field site that was within a two-hour drive

Episodes in a Life

from campus. The faculty would know in advance where we were going and they would each make some decisions about a day of field work with a group of three to five graduate students. The major task for Thursday evening was our "Introductory One-Slide Slide Show." I asked each faculty member and each graduate student to select a single slide, a slide that they would use to introduce themselves and explain why he or she had come into the field of geography. I would take the slides and put them into a carousel in random order and then begin to show them after our first camp dinner on Thursday night. Each person—and this included faculty, current graduates, as well as new arrivals to the MU Geography program— would have three to five minutes to introduce themselves and explain the image and its connection to their life in geography.

The uncertainty of the order, the enormous range of photo images selected by all, and the narratives that explained the slides made for a usually pretty fun ice-breaking session for new grads, and for faculty and old grads, too. Beer was available and the evening evolved into conversations.

Friday was a field research day. A current MU faculty member in geography would be teamed with three or four grads. The pod would meet early Friday, workout a field project with faculty member, write out any guidelines for the day and then, in the professor's car generally, drive off to begin a field day.

At the end of that Friday, the field groups would come back to our campsite and spend some time on report preparation. We would then cook and eat a camp dinner. That evening, from seven to nine-thirty, each field group would have twenty-five to thirty minutes to report on what they had learned that day. Then at the conclusion of the talks, we would adjourn into easy conversational groups.

Saturday morning was given over to a bodacious camp breakfast and some time for me to talk about the plans and events of the year forthcoming. It was also the time to elect the Graduate Student Representative to the faculty meetings. And, it was our first open forum to talk about things on the minds of the new and expanding graduate population. The field gig concluded with groups driving back to campus. We were usually home by mid-afternoon.

The general reaction of the faculty was "Oh, bother" when I would bring it up again for the following fall, but as the event took place and we debriefed after the three days, there was generally a pretty good feeling about what had been accomplished. Each prof had a primo chance to show his or her interests in the field exercises they selected and enacted for the full Friday field day.

One year I was on leave in the fall. The replacement chair replaced the field gig with a driving van trip of Columbia and a potluck dinner. At one of the first faculty meetings after I returned, I asked the faculty and grad rep how come the fall field gig had been dumped. The replacement chair said, "It was not dumped, we just replaced it. We just cancelled. We had a good drive and a nice dinner. I think the grads liked it fine. Right, Dan?" she said, turning to the grad rep who had also been at the recent field afternoon.

Dan's reply was "No, not right. I felt as though I was being cheated out of one of the things I had heard most about in deciding to come to the MU Grad program. It was tough to miss the camping, miss the easy getting together, and miss working on field issues as a team."

I must admit that that was one of the most satisfying ninety seconds I had in my entire fourteen years as MU Chair of Geography.

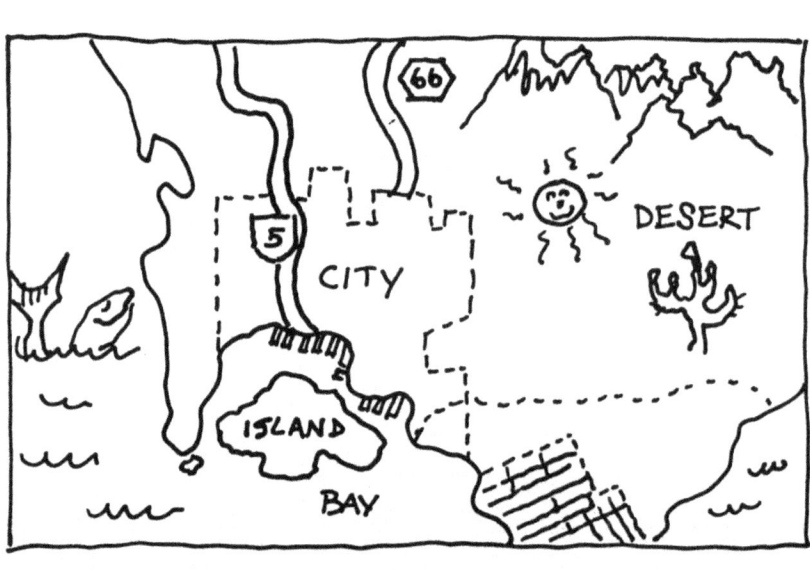

CHAPTER 7
PROFESSIONAL GEOGRAPHY

Having lived with the idea of geography at the center of my life for more than sixty years, it is good to remind the reader about the power of landscape in geographic thinking. All history, and in fact, all of everything tangible has its origin in the earth around us. Whether you are interested in nineteenth century railroad patterns or contemporary migration patterns of health care workers, there is a need to set the issue in the landscape, or at least on a map.

My doctoral mentor, and most wonderful professor I ever worked with, Dr. James Parsons of Berkeley, used to remind his classes that "All thinking has to begin with observation—whether the issue is a geographic one or anything else. And in terms of geography, the best place for such observation is in the field. Whenever possible go to see the landscape that is at the heart of the geographic phenomenon that has caught your attention." It is Dr. Parsons' exhortation that sets in motion the episodes that follow.

◆

"Just Do It!"

One summer Lucia P., my niece and daughter of sister Jean, came to California for some Summer School work at Berkeley. I was already at UCLA and she and I planned some California day trips to field sites that would help her see the vitality and reality of field geography. This event began with some exploration in the Central Valley looking at irrigation schemes feeding the agriculture of the region. Late in the afternoon, we found a café and went in for dinner.

Lu looked like the pretty college girl that she was, and I had the casual attire of a young professor who likes going into the field. We were traveling in my convertible VW bug. About seven-thirty, we finished our meal and coffees and came out to the parking lot. Next to the VW was a bunch of people getting ready to get into a truck. They were having an intense conversation about whether or not to do something they felt was unusual for them.

I listened offhandedly as I got my keys out and put the field notebook I had taken into the café into the back of the car. The top was down. As I pulled my door closed and was getting my key into the ignition, I said—in response to a tiny lull in their discussion: "Just do it. Go ahead. Just do it." I said it in good spirit and not in any provocative or daring manner. I offered the phrase just as an encouragement to take some action and resolve the tensions of the discussion.

At that instant, a guy reached over and grabbed me by the neck and pulled me partly up from the seat yelling, "What the hell you talking about? You don't know shit about what we're talkin' about. You're just some fuckin' college guy who goes around pushing people into doing goddamn stupid things like they do at Berkeley."

I was astonished. I pulled his arm off while Lucia said, "Come on, Kit...let's go, let's go *now!*" This guy was clearly ready to have me get out of the car and face him off, but I saw no merit in that. I started my car and backed out while he hung near the edge of the convertible ready to bash me. I looked at him more with curiosity than animosity and drove to the edge of the lot, and out onto the two lane highway. My niece and I were silent for a moment but both shocked as we built up highway speed. As we drove farther, we laughed a little bit about the danger of field work in some parts of California.

DOUBLE ADVENTURE IN ACAPULCO BAY

In the summer of 1957, I hitchhiked down to Mexico City in order to study Spanish. I had had two years in high school and had done a year at Oberlin. However, I knew—as we all know—that the only real way to learn to speak a tongue is to thrust yourself right into the cultural zone that will demand the use of that language every day, every night. I arranged an exchange with—I am not making this up—with Jose Cervantes, the owner and primary faculty member of a Mexico City language institute. He agreed to provide me with language instruction if I would make tapes for him in American English for his students. It was a great deal.

As part of that summer's adventures I thumbed over to Acapulco Bay to watch the wave-divers (young men who dove off of cliffs into cresting waves on the beach of Acapulco Bay). I overnighted on the beach, awakened by the fishing crews that launched their small crafts into the bay at dawn for a day of fishing. I talked one fisherman into letting me go with him and his two brothers on their day's mission. After an hour of bobbing up and down, up and down, up and down, up and down with them, I asked them to bring the boat a few hundred yards back toward the beach and said I would just slip into the water and swim back to where we had left at dawn. He, the 'captain' was disinclined to just drop me off, but his brothers—who had argued against the whole passenger deal anyway—yelled him down and with my providing a little cash, the small boat took me to about five hundred yards from the beach and I slipped into the water.

I was much relieved. I loved swimming and it was so good to get out of the boat going up and down, up and down (you recall the pattern?) that the swim in the morning light seemed just fine. As I slowly closed in on the mouth of the inlet that marked the beach where I had slept and where the young daredevils dived for coin-tossing tourists, I spotted a triangle of rock sticking out of the water some seventy-five yards from the sandy beach. The rock was dark and I thought that would be a fine place to stretch out flat on the rock, absorb the sun, and think about the rest of the day. I swam my way toward the dark rock.

As I was moving in that direction, I noticed the wave force had picked up and I was trying to figure out how I could intelligently get carried almost to the rock in a wave and then lift off and land on it without getting smashed into that dark surface. Working on that triangulation and not really sure of my ability to give my body much focused direction as I approached the wedge of stone, I suddenly realized that the darkness of the rock was not from a mineral, but from a carpet of dense, black fauna. The rock was crawling with black, spiny sea urchins. They, too, had decided this was the place to hang out in the sun with the occasional wash of big waves. By the time I realized what I was headed for, I was about one wave away from being delivered onto the rock and sea urchin surface. I rolled to my left with all the energy that good old-fashioned fear gives you and just scraped by the rough edge of the wedge and was carried on toward the beach. I made it to the sand and crawled (real crawling this time) up to the margin between dry sand and firm, moist sand, and laid my frightened body out.

A footnote to this caper is so unusual that I fear this will make the sea urchins seem like regular stuff. As I had been swimming in from the fishing boat—and before I had decided to launch myself toward the dark sunning rock, I had noticed a small but long set of stone steps carved from the rock that surrounded this bay and its beach. It was from the high parts of the arc of rock that the divers did their daring dives, but that was on the north side of the bay. I was coming in from the south side. The steps looked as though they came from out of the water, winding up the irregular stone face of the escarpment to a wooden door right near the top of the cliff. After catching my breath and recovering my confidence from just about impaling myself on the sea urchins, I swam back into the bay and went over to the bottom of the carved steps. They looked to be totally unmaintained and old enough to be some sort of historic approach to the heights of the stone bluff. I lifted myself out of the water and slowly worked my way up the steps, nervous both about slipping on the rock shards that were the surface of the steps, and worried also about what I would do if the door some hundred and fifty feet above the water level was locked. The anxiety about slipping absorbed much more thought and energy than did the locked door potential.

When I finally got to the top step, I turned and looked back and could barely imagine the labor that had been spent in etching out these scores of smooth, flat stones from the mother rock of this wall. This was no casual project.

But this is the part that makes even me feel as though this is all fantasy. There was a large brass handle and hinges on the wooden door that opened out from above the top step. I very carefully pulled the door outward. Slowly, the door swung open just enough for me to see that there were another fifteen steps and then the green edge of someone's garden or at least yard. I entered the small access space and pulled the door closed behind me. I crept up the relatively dry final steps, bringing my eyes, then my torso, and then my whole being up and stepped into a stunning garden. Surrounding it was not only the wall with the door I had just entered, but now the sight of a very impressive home nestled within the walled enclosure of some sort of private estate. I was wearing only my swimming suit, but I was very careful to have my traveler's smile on as well. As I was getting my head adjusted to the secret garden world that I had just climbed my way into, a fifty-year-old Mexican with a small trowel came into view and walked toward me. Fortunately, he was only a little suspicious and more completely surprised. We had a conversation in Spanish that went something like this.

"*¿De donde viene usted?* (How did you get here?)"

"I fell off a fishing boat out beyond the mouth of the bay and as I was trying to get back to shore, I saw the steps and thought I might be safe up here." I had decided to modify my traveler's reality just this little bit, hoping that a predicament might make me a more attractive visitor than the reality of just being a college kid exploring the bay and beach.

"Did you really come up the steps?" he asked in some amazement.

"Yeah...they seemed more likely to lead to some place to catch my breath than the open beach. And besides I was too tired to swim much farther so I got to the bottom step and rested a bit and by the time I felt better, I could not make myself ignore what might be at the top of the stone steps."

"You're not allowed here. No one is allowed here, especially anyone who has come up those steps. They have not been used for years, maybe many years." This surprised me because I do not see how college kids or even teenagers could see these steps and *not* come over to explore them.

"Please do not think of me as a visitor. I am just a stupid college kid who fell out of a fishing boat and needed to get out of the water before he washed away."

The gardener stood silent a moment and then spoke. "If I let you leave by the front gate, would you go wherever it is you have your whatever you have and not come back? And if I did that, would you promise *never* to tell anyone about the steps?"

As unlikely as being able to hold to this word, I quickly said "Sure. Let's go. I'll be gone before you know it." I stepped forward and he led me through amazing gardens and by a patio and porch that allowed me just a few images of a world that I was curious as hell about, but I was by now ready to wrap up this morning of unexpected encounter.

"Do you know whose villa this is? Do you know what you have come to?" The gardener seemed as though he was now just a tiny bit interested in taking advantage of this arrival of his unexpected visitor. He wanted to play tour guide for at least a minute.

"No....I had no idea what was at the top of the steps. Whose place is this?"

"This is the old home of the muralist and artist Diego Rivera. He has just died, and it is not certain yet what will become of his home. You are fortunate to see it." He gave me his first smile as he told me this.

"Can I see the house? Can I see any of his art?" I asked even as the outside door was being unlocked and opened. He looked back at the house for just a second and then turned to me again.

"No...I am already doing much more than I ought to do. Know that you have been luckier than most to even see this much. Go back to the beach by walking down this road to the left. Just keep walking and you'll finally get to where the boys dive."

I looked over his shoulder one last time, thinking to myself that I will wish for a long time that I had somehow talked my way into the interior of the house, but I did feel lucky to not be hanging out on the rocks anymore.

"A thousand thanks for your kindness. I will try to tell no one of this experience and of this place."

"It is better that way, son." I left and walked the twenty minutes down the road to the headland where tourist stands were already opening up and taking over the dramatic and majestic look of this area.

NEARLY MUGGED IN PHILLY

At the AAG National Meetings of 1976 I was invited by a publisher's representative to dinner at Bookbinders on the Wharf. Lynne R., the representative working for Fred Praeger was sharing dinner with me. She had been told to get together with me to see if I wanted to sell *The China Geographer*. This was a small quarterly journal that my grads and I produced in Geography at UCLA. I had begun it with my students focused on China a few years earlier to provide a modest forum for students who wanted to focus on the geography and landscape of China. The Bookbinders dinner was fine and we walked back about eleven that evening from the wharf. It must have been about one mile away from the Convention Hotel we were staying at that this event happened.

About a block from the convention hotel, three young blacks pulled in behind us and then ran around in front of us and one of them pulled a knife and said "Gimme your wallet!" I said "No" and told Lynne to run to the hotel lobby. I grabbed the guy's arm that held the knife. He looked to be about eighteen, and he was very nervous. This must have been early in his mugging experiences. He started hitting me, as did one of his buddies, while the other chased Lynne, but she got away before he could get her. The idiots were punching me in the chest and stomach and not my groin. As I worked at fighting off the guy with the knife, I found myself thinking, *Geeze...how dumb can they be? If they hit me in the groin, I would sure let go of the arm with the knife...but it is not hard to tolerate stomach and chest hits with adrenalin flowing like this.*

More powerfully, the real thought that came to mind was *What do I do with this knife now?* I had control of the guy's rather weak arm and was turning the knife toward his chest, toward his face. *Should I carry through with this? Should I drive the knife into his body?* I wondered as I felt myself gaining control of the situation. At that point, one of the three bashed my nose and a lot of blood began to flow. They turned and began to run but only after the guy with the knife took my white panama hat. (They never did get my wallet). As they fled, I ran after the guy with the hat and grabbed it back. They kept running. I went back to the hotel and Lynne and I went to her room and I washed my face and put a cold washrag on the nose. We laughed a lot but mostly I felt damn lucky that it had played out the way it did. I was sorry to see that no geographers had raced out to help a fellow conventioneer in trouble, but I was proud to have my hat, my wallet, and no knife wounds. And my nose had already been busted twice in wrestling. It was like an encore injury. No big deal. And, I did sell the *The China Geographer* for a dollar to Fred Praeger, who published a few more editions before it vanished.

Skid Row Garden in L.A.

In the early 1970s, I took a small group of USC students to downtown Los Angeles late on a spring afternoon. We were headed for the Bus Station—always a locus of interest for any bunch of students who had never felt the power of urban uncertainty in downtown L.A. We parked and began walking like a pod of nervous tourists, each walker careful not to drift away from the pod leader. Over on 5th Street, this urban stretch (south of Broadway especially) felt most like a Skid Row showcase. We were in the initial heart of The City of Angels.

In the middle of one block, we saw a black guy of maybe sixty-five years of age in the doorway of his personal niche, which was a retail store that looked as though it had been closed up a long time. The shop windows were covered with scrap plywood. I did not see any relict sign that told what the store had once been.

The guy had a wizened beard and cheap clothes, but he had a hose in his hand. The hose ran from his kitchen sink (I learned in conversation) and he was watering a garden about one foot wide and five feet long that he had made from old concrete blocks, bricks, and rocks. Into the one-by-five-foot rectangular structure he had put soil and had planted flowers—pansies and petunias. All around him were the signatures of urban loss, abandonment, and despair. But he was tending his homemade garden. It was a wonderful sign of human optimism in a setting that otherwise radiated pessimism and failure. The guy was willing to talk a bit, but was not as expressive about what he had done as I had hoped he might be, but the pod of geographers that afternoon all felt he and his garden at the front of this abandoned shop were a grand visual; a great way to see the mix of landscape and cultural signatures in a central city—and a wonderful symbol of the variety of personas in a "Skid Row" neighborhood.

"This is no Goddamn Experiment!"

On a short trip to Eastern Oregon in the late 1960s to explore signs of the many failed settlement efforts that had characterized the tough settlement conditions of the eastern part of this state, I got into this situation. Two of us had been exploring a bunch of relic foundations, abandoned barns and farmhouses, and landscape evidences of general decline and many aborted settlement efforts. The landscape was tragically desolate. The area was a sign that many nineteenth century migrants crossing the Plains in quest of rumored lushness of Oregon greenery had stopped too soon, too far east, too far from the well-watered western flanks of the Cascade Mountains that separate two powerfully distinct regional geographies in western and eastern Oregon.

We went, late in the afternoon, to a tavern in Bend and stood at the bar, each drinking a beer. We chatted about the things we had seen. There were maybe six or seven people along counter and a few at tables. At one point I said—just talking in a normal voice to the guy I had been in the field with, "This whole eastern Oregon thing has been one helluva experiment…" Before I could carry that sentence any further, a guy down a stool or two came over and grabbed me in a choke hold from behind. With considerable intensity, he yelled in my ear, "This is no goddamn experiment, asshole. *This is our lives!*"

He raged on, "You shithead outsiders come in and drive around and then come and have a fuckin' beer and talk about 'our experiment.' What kinda asshole are you?" I pulled myself out of his grip and faced him, yelling something about how every goddamn effort at settlement in coming west had been an experiment. I told him he oughta back off and feel good about the fact that Bend was still working. He was not interested in any geographic discussion, so my field buddy and I put some money on the counter and got out of the place as cleanly as we could.

It was a great punctuation mark for lessons about how to interpret and how to talk about the reading of marginal landscapes.

The Lawn Issue

One of the themes that so often became part of the field work in any field class was the lawn issue. We would so often see people working on their front lawns and, in conversation, hear how they were bothered by the continual demands of lawn on their weekend time. They would say this while they were on their knees clipping, cultivating, trimming, sculpting, trimming more, and clipping more. Yet, as we talked about their sense of place in that house, the look of the house as linked with the garden was often cited as one of the pleasures of that place. Again and again we would see people fertilizing, irrigating or watering, or mowing...and then often talk about the way in which their leisure was increasingly defined by their lawns and associated continual, even relentless demands.

The resultant discussions we would have in the field class about how we make our own decisions about lawn care, and then we often slip into a pattern of complaint about how such care cost us in terms of lawn goods and time. Sometimes a student would ask, "Why not just leave it? Why, at least, decide not to fertilize or water it? Why not use that time for something else?" The homeowner would look surprised at such a suggestion and say, "What? And see my property values plummet? And hear my neighbors complain to me, or to other neighbors, that I was ruining property values for the whole neighborhood by not maintaining my lawn and garden?"

It was a sweet equation for it had all the elements of a landscape paradox and both the students and lawn owners talked it up in just that fashion.

◆

One unlikely aspect of field work in geography is illustrated in this episode below. In the professional life of college teaching, you need to have some visibility of your creative research or educational outreach that helps expand the world of geography—and very specifically—the public awareness of geographic utility in contemporary society. This leads occasionally to textbook writing and publication.

THE VON HOFFMAN PRESS COINCIDENCE

In late 1999 Joe Hobbs of MU Geography and I had completed a new edition of *The Essentials of World Regional Geography*. It was a major project and we wanted a sneak-preview of the outcome of our fifteen months of labors. The editing and writing was directed toward the book written by geographer Jesse Wheeler, long active in Missouri geography. Since the publishing firm, the von Hoffman Press, is just thirty-seven miles from the University Missouri campus, we put together a visit for the two of us to see the press run of the new edition. There was considerable security to go through to gain admittance to the actual printing plant, but once we got into the interior of this very plain looking industrial building in Jefferson City, we were taken to a very nice conference room. The walls were books on three sides and a wide bay of windows overlooking the factory floor with its massive web presses all racing through a stunning number of copies of our book per hour.

After Joe and I had seated ourselves at a handsome dark wood conference table, a vice-president came into the room, apologized for leaving us alone for a few minutes while he had completed a conference call. He then slipped into what was clearly an oft-given lecture on the process of turning manuscript pages and art into state-of-the-art five color college text books.

He walked over to a shelf that was just partially filled and picked up a bundle of book segments not yet bound together into a full book, referred to as signatures. These were baby books awaiting the final collating, cover and binding. He opened a signature in front of us. "This is what we are doing here. We have the most modern presses in the Midwest and feel proud of the graphic clarity, the color registration, and the text crispness that von Hoffman achieves with its web presses." He turned a few pages, giving us a chance to ooh and aah at what we saw before us. I was amazed.

"Why have you selected these particular pages, this particular book, to demonstrate von Hoffman's work?" I asked.

"Why? Well, we are particularly proud of this text series. We did it for Houghton Mifflin and we have sold a whole lot of this book...in fact, this series of books," he said with a modest but evident pride.

"Did you not choose this particular book for any other reason?" He was curious about my question and Joe and I both felt that he wanted to get on with his spiel so that the three of us could go down to the printing floor.

"No...I selected this text because it is the one I generally use when I am trying to illustrate the sort of work von Hoffman does. Why do you ask?"

I picked up the signature that he had opened, and I asked if he had the lead signature for that particular volume. He walked back to the shelf and shuffled through the loose segments and came back with the opening signature. "Here. Is this the one you want?" He laid it out before Joe and me.

"Look at this...what are the odds that you would select this one, for this tour?" Before he could answer—since he had just told us he used this often—I went on. "This is my book." I am one of the four authors of this text. It is a Social Studies series done by Ligature of Chicago and published by Houghton Mifflin of Boston. You better believe you have printed a lot of these because—at least Houghton told us—this is the largest selling school social studies text set ever printed in America!"

Joe and the VP looked at the title page, looked at me, and looked at the title page again.

"Wow...so you'll be a double von Hoffman author. That's great...you have written us great business already. I hope that your college text does just as well as this grade and high school series did."

"It won't," I responded. "I did the Ligature and HM series for a fee. I am doing the text you're going to show us for a royalty. With my karma, the royalty book won't sell many, but the fee book has knocked the top off the publishing trade. Just my luck."

He finished his talk and the three of us put in ear plugs and went down some metal stairs and spent an hour amidst the presses, watching pages of our new text just stream out of these massive purveyors of knowledge and automated (including robot arms) technical publishing. Even these years beyond that coincidence, I still feel a pride at having the Ligature/Houghton Mifflin signature featuring my authorship selected for showcasing.

THE WATER LECTURE

In 1998 I set up a field trip with a small MU field class—a trip to the Lake of the Ozarks. We spent part of the morning exploring the interior of a major dam—the 1929 dam that was the civil engineering project that allowed the Lake of the Ozarks to be created. The plant manager was, like so many people in resources work, glad to get the chance to talk to interested students and a professor about water issues. He explained that his job had begun, some thirty years earlier, with the primary focus being concern for the pace of water flow through the dam's penstocks for the efficient generation of power for the city of Saint Louis and environs. He said that more recently his task had become much more closely linked with marina managers both upstream and downstream. If he let out too much water, the upstream Lake marinas screamed because water levels were sinking and that was critical to wharf and berthing levels. If he held back too much water, the downstream marinas screamed because it played havoc with the fishing areas and water levels for their dock piers.

That day I had counseled the students to bring enough money so that we could all have lunch at one of the really fancy resorts on the Lake. We went to the Lodge of the Four Seasons and ate in the café there. It was quite nice. It was a frustrating meal because the students whined so very much about having to spend three bucks for a burger and kept asking the waitress of they could split orders or just have more water. I left the meal when I finished so that I would not be there when they had the waitress split the order up so that no one would be forced into paying twenty cents too much because they were contributing to a classmate's fries or something.

Outside the café setting there was a swimming pool, a decorative pool with a small fountain, and a vista that overlooked the drama of the Lake of the Ozarks and its wooded and settled margins...replete with a world of docked and anchored boats. I had noticed the way a decorative outside pond spilled into a fabricated stream system that descended through two floors of the lodge. The waterfall flowed into a smaller pond and was then lifted back up to a stream that fed the decorative pond on the margin of the large outside swimming pool. I was leaning on a railing looking at the intricacy of the engineering and landscape architecture for this system when the class came out. I called them over and positioned them at a spot where they could see the lake in its handsome setting, the decorative pond, the swimming pool, and still be by (and within earshot of) the flowing water of the interior stream as it went down through two floors of café, conversation court, and plantings, and windows.

I used this setting and prospect to talk about how human history was, in good part, defined by the skills developed in managing water. To control water is to control the earth, I pointed out...and then I illustrated the various scales we use in such management. From the evocative mountain stream in the interior of the lodge to the decorative pool, the swimming pool, the Lake of the Ozarks, and—not visible then but still in our minds—the massive 1929 dam itself. Without the control of water, and the acquisition of a settlement site that had a predictable and reliable source of water, human settlement was hardly ever possible. I spent about fifteen minutes on this whole pitch and then headed us out to the cars and toward the next stop.

Two months later, one of the grads in the class came into my office with some questions. As he was departing, he said the talk I had done on water at the Lodge of the Four Seasons was the best cultural geography he had heard in his entire education. That guy is now doing a doctorate in geography (fully supported) at Penn State and has won two awards for his writing. I have looked back many times on the fun of spontaneous field presentations and this one in particular. You never know at the moment whether anything is working or not...but sometimes it is.

Lurking in L.A.

In downtown L.A., I was traveling with a small field class of about seven or eight students in the early 1970s. This was our first day in the CBD (the central business district of any city) and there was a lot of interest in walking through the central city. I took them to the Greyhound Bus Station for an early stop because of the power of that setting. It was great for UCLA students to get a sense of how many other L.A.s there are than the one they have become accustomed to. At one point, I had them off to the side of the station and I was talking about the ways in which a geographer (or any field person) could read a scene.

I talked about participant observation as the classic mode for really coming close to understanding a locale. But that process demanded a more serious time commitment than did the process called called "lurking." I explained that lurking was the process of being close to a scene, but *not* becoming directly involved in the flow of people and activity that you were trying to witness and understand.

As I was making my point, a black guy of maybe thirty-five came up and nearly in my face, belted out. "Lurking? Whas dis lurking shit? You teach yo white kids dat it's okay if dey come to the city to lurk? Why dontcha tell 'em that if I lurk—me, Leonard—if I lurk, de Man come and ask me what d' hell I'm doin' hangin round dat place? Why dontcha tell 'em dat if I lurk by lying down on the bench, de Man come and hit my shoes wid his stick and tell me ta move ma ass? Why dontcha tell 'em dat stuff?"

It was electric. What had minutes earlier been a reasonable mini-lecture on field techniques had now become a field lesson of real moment! I talked with Leonard and he seemed surprised by the fact that I—and a couple of the students—asked him about living in the central city, and about any work, or about the territory he covered. He stayed with us about an hour as we walked and observed the bus station area and the blocks around it.

The Logging Road Scare

In the summer of 1965, I had a few short field trips with Professor Jim Parsons of Berkeley. He later became my dissertation mentor and ultimately one of the best friends I ever had. On this Yolla Bolly trip, we were three new grads traveling in a pickup truck. It was late in the afternoon and we had somehow gotten ourselves lost in this weave of mountain logging roads that draped along the flanks of a small mountain system north of San Francisco. The only thing scary about this situation was that logging trucks were bringing massive tree trunks down slope. These rigs moved with a lot more speed than seemed to make sense. At one point we had tucked our pickup truck into a seemingly safe niche and had gotten out some topographic sheets of the area in search of a road or a landmark that might give us a plan for getting back to a paved highway.

Mr. Parsons (we always called him Mr. Parsons just the way he had spoken of Dr. Carl Sauer—his mentor—as Mr. Sauer) was standing out in the logging road, trying to get enough sun to read the map clearly. At that moment, we could feel and hear a logging rig pounding down the road toward us, probably eager to complete one more run before the daylight was gone. We felt the rush of the truck before we could see it on the curvy roads.

Mr. Parsons—with his wonderful confidence in field situations—stood in the middle of the road and waved the driver to a stop. The three of us grads gathered around Parsons as he held his map in the air and asked the driver for help. The driver looked like a stunt double for some Pa Kettle character in a B movie. His hair was all over. He had about a five-day beard. His remaining teeth were brown; just as many were

Episodes in a Life

not there at all. He spoke with some awkwardness, probably because he never expected to see anyone on this route, and especially anyone looking as misplaced as our quartet.

"Hey…thanks for stopping," opened Mr. Parsons with the quad map held between the driver and us. "I've gotten us lost as can be up here and I wonder if you might help us find our way outa here?"

The driver twisted a smile together and said, "I don't read those maps so good. My eyes have gotten real tired. I drive more by feel." He paused while we looked at the eight or nine logs chained on to the trailer behind his cab, thirty-feet long, two- and three-feet in diameter. "I probably cain't get you to where ya wanna go, but I can get ya off the mountain. Why don't ya turn your truck around and folla me down to the blacktop?"

There were two good things about this idea. First, it meant that we would *not* be in front of his rig. Second, we all had complete faith in his capacity to get us back to civilization. We climbed in our truck and backed in and out until we were set to pull in behind him. He gave us a big smile and began some of the endless gear work as he plummeted down to road level and a highway we could name and follow. We gave him a big wave as he headed off with some urgency. Once at the main Highway, we stopped at the first roadhouse we found and all had a beer, feeling very fortunate about the karma of Mr. Parsons, and our soon to begin graduate career in geography at Berkeley.

"What About Miss Jones?"

One of the tasks that cost me so much concern in my professional life was my role as the national co-chair of the Geography Standards Program for twenty-seven months from 1992-1994.

This Miss Jones event was one of the most delightful aspects of a role that was otherwise mostly hellish. Dr. Norman Bettis of Illinois State was the national co-chair. He was a professor of Geography and Curriculum Instruction at Illinois State University in Normal, Illinois. He was the son of a dairy farmer and he carried himself with considerable grace. He had a fine little mustache and he almost always wore a suit. If the committee of seven to eight geographers who worked for months and months in weekend meetings in hotel basements in Washington, D.C. needed to send someone out to meet the media, we would often select Norman because he was always well-dressed and gracious.

However, he was often maddening because of the frequency with which he would interrupt our wide-ranging discussions about things geographic that school children in America ought to know and be able to do. That was exactly our task: Define such tasks and design and write curriculum guidelines to achieve them for grades four, eight, and twelve. When we thought we had defined the perfect blend of task and language, Norman would often say "Wait...wait...what about Miss Jones, the fifth grade teacher?" He would look at us like a pastor in a rural church, wondering how it could be that we had not thought of such a simple constraint on the language and the geographic item we were creating.

This give and take went on for those twenty-seven months. At our final committee dinner near Union Station in D.C. we were all together celebrating the completion and the impending publication of *Geography For Life: National Geography Standards 1994*. The spirits of the group were awash in relief and some pride at having worked so tenaciously for this moment.

At one point in the evening Norman got up in his dark suit, having finished his traditional vodka neat. As he searched for the head, I looked around the restaurant space and saw a nearby table of about four lovely young women. I ran over to the table and interrupted them.

"Hey…here's a deal. I've got a twenty dollar bill for the one of you who will give our table a little drama. But I need a quick decision." The group turned silent. "When a nice-looking guy comes back to our table—he is in a dark suit and has a mustache—I want one of you to walk up to our table and put your hands on his shoulders from behind and say, 'I have heard that you are Dr. Bettis. Oh, I have heard *so much* about you. I am Miss Jones; a fifth-grade teacher, and I hear that you have made a tremendous difference in having the geography standards be written just *for me!*'"

"Is there a taker?"

The most striking one of the group—a blonde with a sparkling smile—said, "I'm a teacher and I'm in drama, too. You bet I'll do it." I put a twenty in front of her and said, saying, "Great, go for it, and don't let Dr. Bettis know this has been set up."

I ran back to our table and got seated just in time to feign conversation as Norman headed back to our group. The others asked, as he was approaching, what I had been doing. I mumbled, "Hush," and we went on about our conversation.

After two or three minutes this great looking gal walked over to our table, did a slow circle around the seven of us, appearing to study each of our faces. She then came to Norman and walked behind his seat. "You must be Dr. Bettis. Oh, I have heard so much about you...so much." She paused just the right amount of time as Norman wondered who she was and what those hands were up to. Then she continued, "I am Miss Jones, a fifth-grade teacher. I have been told that you have virtually rewritten the Geography Program just so I could teach it. I want to thank you so very much." She tweaked his cheek and squeezed his shoulders and then slinked (well, not quite slinked, but she did walk with attitude) back to her table and group.

Norman, just a little bit red-faced, looked at us, looked at the waiter, looked at the receding image of Ms. Jones and then turned and said, "I have said so many times that we ought to think of Miss Jones. I'm certain now that I will think of her for a long time, indeed." We laughed and went on with our meal. Norman never raised the issue again and no one spoke of its orchestration. It was an amazing and dramatic geographic treat!

Amazement at Change

In the early 1980s, a few of us in Southern California began something that came to be called the California Geographic Alliance. It was a coalition of university and college geography instructors and classroom teachers from grades seven to twelve initially. We assigned ourselves the task of going to state and regional meetings to talk about the Geographic Alliance concept in an effort to get more teachers to join us. This was before the National Geographic Society adopted us as a favored organization and gave us a national base.

Gail H. and I drove up together to San Jose, California for the California State Social Studies Association annual meeting in 1984. The first morning, I was slated to give a ten o'clock paper, and Gail was giving a paper in some other session at the same time. About nine-fifty, I went to the hotel meeting room and saw it was filled. I quickly backed out and sat down on a bench in the hallway, planning to wait for the earlier speaker to finish his or her presentation and empty the room. Ten o'clock came and went and no one came out of the room. Others were still going in. I checked my watch and figured it was wrong.

But, by five minutes after ten, I was losing precious minutes, so I got up and walked into the back of the room. The place was booked solid. I asked aloud "What session is this?"

Someone replied, "It's yours, Salter...where have you been? We've been waiting for ten minutes." I was dumbfounded! Never in the general flow of Social Studies meetings had geography drawn very big houses...and here was prime time in the morning and our discipline had a full house. I mention this as an episode because the house stayed full for the full presentation, and had an active question and answer session—uncommon in many meetings.

This emergent geographic interest of California teachers led to more than a decade of travel and presentations all around the country in the promotion of geography education. That San Jose morning was my first evidence that we had come upon a really exciting innovation with the creation of the California Geographic Alliance. The National Geographic Society would later make it the model for a national effort bringing geographic education to the K-12 world and curriculum. Big changes can spring from innocent small-scale innovations.

The Other Side of Discovery and the Art Caper

In 1991, I wrote a twenty-page play called *"The Other Side of Discovery."* It was intended to be a thought piece for discussions of what the consequences had been of the Columbus arrival to the Caribbean in 1492. I used it in multiple classes a number of times and it was published in *The Journal of Geography* in 1992. A few of us were invited to the international meeting of the National Council for Geography Education (NCGE) that year. The meetings were to be held in Santo Domingo, Dominican Republic and Chloe and I and a third person planned to do a reading of the play. We asked Charlie F. of our first Summer Institute at the National Geographic in 1987 to be "the Timekeeper," the third character. It was all quite exciting to take this play (actually "Readers Theater") on the road and be able to present it in a place very near to where Columbus actually landed that October five-hundred years earlier.

The presentation went well. We had a house of some four hundred geographers, and we found themes drawn from the play bubbling up in conversations for the next several days. But the really fun part of that trip was the art caper! Cathy and I have long had the custom of bringing home a piece of art from foreign travel. To select such art, we live by our "five minute rule." What this means is that if, in the first five minutes of seeing a new piece of art, a piece of furniture, or meeting a new friend we are not both uniformly delighted in that object, we do not even *think* of getting it. This keeps us from making art acquisitions or bringing a new friend into the home unless the initial impression has passed the five minute test.

In the 1992 Santa Domingo NCGE Conference, Cathy had a lot of meetings. I had made my presentations and had a little more free time. I went to an art market searching for an unusual piece of Caribbean art that I could bring Chloe to and we could decide on whether we wanted it or not. As it was in a gallery, I did find a marketplace painting that was simply brilliant in its color and composition. It was stunning. I asked the man about bringing my wife down to see it. He explained to me that he was leaving in an hour and would be closed the next three days. I knew that we were leaving the next morning at dawn for Saint Louis. I felt I could not buy it solo because the presence of both of us was a solid requirement to test out our five minute rule.

I made a deal with the purveyor. He agreed to take me to the convention hotel with the piece of art and wait while I showed it to Cathy for a decision. He had a Vespa and he raced us through Santa Domingo traffic, he driving and I on the back of the seat with the artwork under my arm. We got to the hotel and together we went through the lobby in search of the meeting room where Cathy was making major decisions on something to do with the Geography Bee or something.

I found out the hotel meeting room where she and her committee were gathered. The driver cum gallery owner and I took off through the lobby with the art in my hand. The Vespa man was quickly taken with all the possible other customers draped around this convention lobby. We went into the meeting room, hurrying because everything was behind in his own calendar. Cathy looked up, saw our hurried duet, the piece of work in question (face hidden) under my arm. She looked at the committee and said, "Oh, boy…I think I'm in trouble now!"

I went to the front of the room and apologized to the committee and explained that I would need no more than ninety seconds of their time. I asked Cathy, "Would you please close your eyes for a second?" She agreed. I then put the oil on a chair in good light and said, "Okay...open up and tell me what you think." She slowly opened her eyes, taking in the brilliant colors of the work, and slowly her face was covered with a smile. "Wow...it's wonderful! I love it!"

With great relief, I introduced the artist and gallery man to Cathy and the crowd, thanked them all, and said that he and I would do the rest.

We went back to the lobby and I squared for the painting (he had run a Visa slip and I had not signed it yet—he carried it with him) and he went out to his Vespa with the voucher and a look of clear relief. I had the fun of organizing a place in our hotel room that showed off the colors of the work and had it resident in that niche when Cathy finished up her meeting. We showed that oil in one of our most favored niches on the walls of Breakfast Creek (1992) and then it was displayed in Boomerang Creek (2020), and now resides on a wall of Crystal Wells, our new residence in California.

Serendipity and an East Asian Editorship

In the national Association of American Geographers Meetings in Kansas City, Missouri in 1972, I shared a room with a colleague of mine at UCLA named Norman T. He was an internationally known cartographer and historical geographer. He was a Brit and since we were UCLA colleagues, we roomed together while he was trying to teach me the best patterns for making national meetings productive.

At one point Norman was at a session and I was in the room getting my own presentation organized or trying to muster spirit strong enough to go out and do battle with the psychological and geographical forces that give character and personality to all the lobbies of professional meetings. Norman and I were staying in a non-conference hotel in order to save money. We were a few blocks away from the Convention Hotel.

The phone rang. I said an unadorned, "Hello."

The voice said, "Oh, hi…I am glad you are there. How would you like a drink?"

It was late afternoon and that sounded just fine. "Sure. Who is this?"

"This is Bob Pearson. I'm with Prentice Hall." Now, in retrospect, I know how dumb I was not to explain to him that he was talking to Kit Salter and *not* Norman Thrower. But, in the exuberance of youth, I thought that maybe he actually wanted to talk with me. Wrong.

Pearson went on, "I'll be at the bar in the place just next to your hotel. It's called The Philips Pub. Can you come down now?

"Give me a couple of minutes and I'll be there." I had heard that book people were able to produce drinks, dinners, free examination copies, and even reviewer jobs for geographers who were willing to work with them. I closed up the stuff I was doing, got my AAG notebook, and went to The Philips Pub, which was only three doors away. I walked into the dark, pretty low-grade tavern, which was populated by only a few people at tables, in a booth or two, and a few guys at the bar. One fellow who reminded me of the sort of character I had been told not to take rides with when I had been in the midst of my hitchhiking years looked up when I came in and saw my AAG notebook.

"Hi, come on over…what would you like?" I came over, but thought, *This is so much like a movie pick-up scene that it seems funny to be playing this role as a young faculty member at a national meeting.*

"I'll have a beer," I said and sat down. My eyes were getting used to the low light. He had a name badge but I had forgotten to put mine back on.

"Well," Pearson said after ordering me a Bud, "I am glad to finally meet you. I have heard so much about you and I know your work. But I gotta say, you are a lot younger than I thought you would be." He smiled at this reference and touched my beer glass with his drink glass. "Here's to a possibly productive future together." He raised his glass. I did the same, wondering where in the world this was coming from...and with just as much curiosity, where it was going.

Pearson continued, "I'll cut right to the chase because I know that you have lots of things you have to do. My publisher wants to know if you would be willing to serve as an Editorial Consultant for Western Europe. You would not have to do much in this job, but you would get your name on every atlas we print, and you would get a small check each summer."

Slowly, ever so slowly my tiny mind now saw what had happened. I grinned and looked at him and said, "Who do you think I am?"

"What do you mean who do I think you are? You are Dr. Norman T. of UCLA, right?"

"This is really curious....my name is Kit Salter. I am rooming with Norman, but he is over at the Marriott convention hotel at a session right now. "

There was an awkward silence and then, "You are *not* Norman Thrower? *Who* are you?"

"My name is Christopher L. 'Kit' Salter. I joined UCLA four years ago and have been friends with Norman because his office is right next to mine on campus. He is a great Western

Europe scholar and the best cartographer we have at UCLA. I am a cultural geographer and East Asia specialist." I still had a smile on my face because I felt like I was getting a free beer under false pretenses, but not pretenses I had orchestrated.

Pearson paused and then went on. "Do you have tenure?"

"Yes."

"And you do China?"

"Yes, I spent three years teaching at a Chinese university in Taiwan."

"Have you published anything on China or Taiwan or anything?"

"Yes," I replied with young pride, "I wouldn't have been tenured by UCLA if I had not made some professional mark." I added, "My family and I live in Los Angeles but not in as fine a neighborhood as Norman." The book man was regaining his composure now.

"Well," after a short pause, "what about the same question? How would you like to be the East Asian Editorial Consultant for Prentice Hall? You would not have to do much, and your name would appear on every atlas we print, and we would send you a small check each summer. What do you think?"

"This seems unlikely," I responded. "You came here thinking you would meet Norman Thrower. I am sure that he will be interested in your offer, but now you're tossing a plum to me just because I happened to pick up the phone and respond to your offer for a free drink." I felt good clarifying exactly what had happened.

"Yeah," Pearson responded, "Yeah, I know all of that. It's kinda strange, isn't it...*But* I was told to get as many Editorial Consultants at these meetings as I could. I did not come with anyone in mind for East Asia. I thought I would ask Dr. T. for some recommendations after he said Yes to our offer. Do you think he would support your name for the East Asia spot?"

I thought a second and said, "I think he probably would because we talk a lot of geography and I think I have been able to answer his questions pretty well. But I cannot speak for him."

"Well, in fact in my mind you *did* speak for him. You said 'Hello' and that gives me a lead on my East Asian Editorial Consultant. Would you take the job? The check is pretty small, but we print a lot of atlases and your name...."

"Yes, I know...my name would be on every one," I concluded. "Sure, I'd be proud to do it. Do I have to do a lot of editorial work?"

"No, we do all of that...if you ever see an error, you call us up and we'll feel good about having hired you. I'll even get a nice nod from my boss." After a second he added, "But please don't tell Dr. Thrower what's happened. Let me give you two of my cards and you give him one and say that you and I have talked and that I want to talk with him about an Editorial Consultant role for Prentice Hall. Okay?"

I took the two cards, gave him one of mine, and finished my beer, for I could see he wanted to get back to the Convention Hotel and organize a more productive encounter. As he was paying and leaving, he said, "I'll send you the contract and a free copy of our most recent atlas. Don't forget, if you see an error, call me and I'll get you in touch with our editor." He left, and I stayed for a second to study the pair of cards, turn down the barman's offer for another beer, and then laughed and walked back into the late afternoon sun.

◆

www.ingramcontent.com/pod-product-compliance
Lightning Source LLC
Chambersburg PA
CBHW031430160426
43195CB00010BB/679